About th

Nigel Pennick is a writer and le_____ __ mysteries, an authority on Northern European geomancy, runemaster, practising geomant and traditional symbolic craftsman. Trained as a scientist, he researched marine micro-organisms for fifteen years. In 1975, he helped found and run the *Institute of Geomantic Research*. He has edited the journals *Arcana*, *Walrus*, *The Oracle of Albion*, *Journal of Geomancy*, *Templar* and *Practical Geomancy*. He is author of many books and papers on subjects ranging from Church architecture and symbolism to Tube railways in London. His practical work includes geomantic design on an architectural competition entry for the La Villette Park project in Paris and in 1986, the laying-out and supervision of the first stone labyrinth in North America. He has lectured on geomancy, labyrinths, runes and underground tunnels before many organizations and colleges in Britain and abroad.

GAMES OF THE GODS

The origin of board games in magic and divination

Nigel Pennick

RIDER

LONDON MELBOURNE AUCKLAND JOHANNESBURG

A Rider Book published in 1988 by
Century Hutchinson Ltd, Brookmount House, 62–65 Chandos Place,
Covent Garden, London WC2N 4NW

Century Hutchinson Australia (Pty) Ltd
PO Box 496, 16–22 Church Street, Hawthorn, Melbourne, Victoria 3122

Century Hutchinson New Zealand Ltd
32–34 View Road, PO Box 40–086, Glenfield, Auckland 10

Century Hutchinson South Africa (Pty) Ltd
PO Box 337, Bergvlei 2012, South Africa

Set by Avocet Ltd

Printed and bound in Great Britain by
The Guernsey Press Co. Ltd., Guernsey, Channel Islands.

British Library Cataloguing in Publication Data
Pennick, Nigel, *1946* –
Games of the gods : the origin of board
games in magic and divination.
1. Board games. Occult aspects
I. Title
133

ISBN 0-7126-1972-0

CONTENTS

ILLUSTRATIONS

INTRODUCTION

Human beings have always felt there is more to life than the immediately apparent material world, and that it is possible to go beyond the confines of body and time. Because of this, various methods have been developed over the years to attempt to transcend the obvious limits of human knowledge. Science is one of these, the study of the material world based upon observation and experiment. Divination is another. It includes all of those methods by which human beings have striven to discover hidden knowledge, most especially the knowledge of future things to come.

Divination is primarily a non-scientific method of acquiring knowledge unavailable by other means. The underlying principle of divination is one which transcends or bypasses the materialist picture of the world which is the prevailing view today. The scientific world-view is analytical in the reductionist sense. It attempts – and succeeds brilliantly in most cases – to explain the myriad phenomena of existence in terms of physics, by breaking down every object and each interaction into its basic components. Unfortunately, the innate belief-system of the scientific world-view automatically discounts any other – it is exclusive, claiming to be the only objective reality. When it bothers with divination at all, materialist science sees it as nothing more than a belief-system to be studied by social anthropology.

According to the modern interpretation of divination, the numbers coming up on dice, the figures formed in divinatory geomancy, the hexagrams appearing in the *I Ching* and the casting of the runes are not just a matter of chance and nothing more. Although they conform to the mathematical principles of randomness, the concept of randomness has nothing to say about *meaning*. While it applies perfectly to numerical events taken in isolation, in reality it is not in any way separate from the state of the universe at the time it is applying, operating according to its own mathematical laws. Randomness is thus, paradoxically, a form of well-defined structure inherent in the universe.

The only constant factor of the physical universe is change. However, like randomness, change operates in a sequential and progressive manner, manifested as patterns recognizable to the human consciousness. These patterns take shape as the forms inherent in the nature of the instant of time when they are observed. In divination, these patterns are actively sought. They are manifestations of the present state of cosmic being, and have much to tell us of the nature and potential development of that state. This is apparent in the concept of synchronicity. The synchronous interpretation of the universe, that all things, by their very existence in space and time, are linked to each other, has produced a bridge between scientific materialism and the older, magical, view of the universe. The major elements of the situation extant in the universe at that instant are revealed by these patterns.

The structure of events and the position in which we find ourselves is accessed by divination, which produces relevant interpretable patterns. The questions we ask of these systems are our response to the progressed positions of the various sequential patterns which are part of the way the universe works. Because the universe has processes and structures which conform to certain patterns, the divinatory methods which also conform to these patterns, being part of the material universe, likewise reproduce the patterns apposite to the time that they are conducted. Cracks in dried-up mud, the rustling of the wind in the willows, birds flying in formation, patterns of beans cast on the ground, and spontaneous ripples in a holy well, are just some of the patterns upon which people in a state of heightened awareness can focus their consciousness. In this state of focused consciousness, parallel perceptions of reality can arise. From whence these perceptions come is a matter of argument, and perhaps personal belief.

As living beings, we are subject to a bewildering multiplicity of forces and energies. These range from physical forces like gravitational, magnetic and electric fields to more subtle ones, such as human behaviour, belief-systems and the innate structure of processes. As a means of gaining useful information to deal with this seemingly chaotic array of influences, divination has proved beneficial. There are whole areas of the physical universe which are unfelt by the human senses. Other members of the animal kingdom can sense things which to us are unapparent. For example, many insects can see ultraviolet light invisible to humans; dogs can hear sounds inaudible to the human ear. It would be folly indeed to assert that there is no reality in forces and powers of which we have no direct experience. All human investigations seek to expand our knowledge of the universe, because it is obviously easier for us to handle situations if we have some knowledge of their origins, the complex relationships within them and their underlying processes. Over millennia, scientific knowledge has increased until we now understand the inner workings of matter, can create new materials, predict the behaviour of electrical, mechanical and mathematical systems, and avert many of the ills which plagued our forebears. This increase in scientific awareness has tended to diminish the awareness that although we understand a great deal, there are forces operating in the universe which are of such awesome complexity that they cannot be monitored by the essentially digital or step-by-step methodology of scientific analysis.

The main aim of divination is the obtaining of information from these areas which can be acted upon to bring humans into harmony with the environment. Although the relative effectiveness and mechanisms of divination are contentious, the principles underlying a belief in the efficacy of divination are identical the world over. Being performed by a specific person at a specific place and time, each divinatory act is an unique event, and contains within it the uniqueness of the whole of space and time at that instant. The same applies to any act, of course, or work of art, but the specific intent of divination is to manifest the conditions of the universe at that instant in a manner which will be intelligible to the person conducting the divination or to the questioner.

Many traditional systems of belief hold that time, history and the passage of events are not linear, but proceed in ever-returning cycles. Many divinatory systems have this belief at their core. The sacred order which people have recognized in the form of nature has been seen as the law or norm ordering

human society as well. Whilst cyclic, the law of nature is an
eternal norm to which all human laws must conform and from
which they derive their ultimate moral sanction. The person
who infringes a sacred restriction or interferes with a sacred
rite releases forces of destruction which may prove fatal at
least to the individual, and perhaps to the entire community.
The most harmonious of ancient and traditional societies were
characterized by the perfection of the unbroken continuity of
the sacred order. This order was present equally in the order
of nature, the order of ritual and the social order. It was
present also in the co-ordination between the life and actions
of the individual and the life of society, both of which were
subordinate to the laws that rule the universe. Harmony was
attained by the perfect co-ordination of the heavenly, human
and earthly orders in a cycle of ritual activities. These took the
form of the ordering of the year and seasons; ensuring the
fertility of the earth; the propitiation of non-human entities;
and the obtaining of divine guidance. All of these necessities of
life were obtained by the correct performance of the annual
cycle of sacred rites, and by the conduct of daily life in a manner
related to the exoteric and esoteric nature of the times. This
way of life is now broken, but although many humans no
longer recognize the sacred order, it exists still.

Divination, auspice and augury are still means for individuals and communities to come to terms with difficult and
unpredictable situations. Divinatory methods have also
proved of value when all so-called rational solutions are seen to
be ineffective, or under conditions grossly and dangerously
deviant from the normal. Here, means are sought to bring
seemingly irrational and impersonal forces of fate and destiny
under the control of humans, or at least to gain insights into
methods of circumventing or mitigating the inevitable. Divination derives its strength from the security and hope that it
gives against indecision, feelings of powerlessness and fear.
Divination exercises a stabilizing influence in times of crisis,
giving a means of resolution of a problem when rational
analysis can no longer be used, or as a 'wild card' to give
insights into unforseen hindrances.

The systems of divination and play presented here are
techniques in their own right, as valid today as they ever were.
Some are of great antiquity, whilst others are modern versions

of ancient techniques. Just as each age has its own versions of philosophy, religion and aesthetics, so it has its own mantic arts. In the words of Josef Heinsch, the German researcher into 'sacred geography':

> Sacred and cultural structures can be understood only by adopting the viewpoint of the ancients. For them, everything mundane was bound up with the divine. All human thoughts and actions were subordinated to the energizing influences of the all-powerful divine forces. Their philosophy and wisdom culminated in the knowledge that 'as above, so below', and in the attempt to bring all their activities and ambitions into harmony with higher nature, the Divine Will.

ACKNOWLEDGEMENTS

I would like to thank the following for assistance over the years in which this book has been in gestation: Paul Devereux, Prudence Jones and Patrick McFadzean, for permission to quote from their works; Jeff Saward, for some illustrations and information; Chris Ashton, Michael Behrend, Marco Bischof, K. Frank Jensen, Rupert Pennick, Professor Peter Schmid, Helen Woodley and Mark Valentine for numerous pieces of useful information and other practical assistance. Also the staff of the University Library, Cambridge and the Cambridgeshire Collection in the Cambridge City Library.

1

SHAPES OF THINGS TO COME

God also created man after his own image; for as the world is
the image of God, so man is the image of the world.

> H. C. Agrippa, *Occult Philosophy*

Since the appearance of human consciousness, perhaps a
million years ago, people have attempted to glimpse the
hidden worlds of the past and future. In dreams, people have
been afforded visions of alternative landscapes peopled by alien
beings; have walked and talked with the dead; and experienced
premonitions of events which occurred later in reality. In the
deliria of illness, ordeals on the edge of death, self-induced
trances, and through the medium of naturally-occurring
hallucinogenic substances, humans have unwittingly or
deliberately contacted an area of experience seemingly totally
separate from the everyday world. It is within this area that
diviners operate, by means of whatever technical devices with
which they have chosen to work. Some may use sophisticated
alphabetic disciplines, whilst others manipulate geometric or
numerical patterns, but whatever the medium used, the final
interpretation of meaning is within the consciousness of the
operative. It is through an alteration of consciousness that the
most basic form of divination occurs – that in which the
shaman is expert.

Shamanism

The term *shaman* is derived from the Siberian Tungus word
saman, which means 'exalted' or 'excited'. It is used only to

describe the person who combines the functions of diviner, medicine-man and mediator between the worlds of humans and transcendental powers – spirits, demons or gods – in an ecstatic manner. The shaman is the archetypal magician/priest of the human race, existing or having existed in northern Europe, all over Asia, among various native tribes of north and south America and in various parts of Africa. The shaman was an important character in ancient tribal societies before the creation of established priesthoods and colleges of magical technicians like astrologers, geomants and augurs. Like most ancient traditional offices, the office of shaman was largely hereditary. Local variations determined in part by ethnic or cultural differences are far outweighed by the common features of the craft the world over, and remnants of ancient northern European shamanism exist to this day in our own culture.

The features recorded from Siberian shamanism are found throughout the world in various forms. They involve a separation from normal society and the acquisition of powers that enable the shaman to see beings and events beyond the boundaries of normal space and time. This separation from the normal world usually involves going to some isolated or sacred place of power where the boundaries between the everyday world and the unseen realm seem to be ill-defined. The features of the initiation in which the shaman is separated from mundane society are recognizable from other contexts, for example the acts of Biblical prophets and Tibetan holy men. For his initiation, the would-be Yakut shaman was led up the local holy mountain or into some desolate spot by the elder shaman responsible for his magical education. At the appropriate place and time, the initiand was given the clothing of his office, a shaman's drum and stick, and then swore an oath of allegiance to the spirit which had adopted him. The elder shaman then revealed to the new intitiate the locations and character of the different classes of spirits, the harm they wreak and how they may be propitiated or thwarted.

After this initiation, the new shaman was sprinkled with blood from a sacrificial beast to indicate his dedication to his new life. In some traditions, the new shaman was actually dressed in the skin of the sacrificed beast. The red coat with fur at cuffs and collar traditionally worn by Santa Claus at

Christmas time is a memory of the shaman's appearance in the freshly-flayed skin of the ritually-slaughtered animal, worn with the fur inwards. The catskin gloves which were part of the paraphernalia of the Norse *vólva* (female shaman) were worn with fur inwards, and wearing certain items of clothing 'inside out' has long been the mark of magicians, symbolizing their separation from the normal world, and a blurring of the accepted boundaries between past, present and future, male and female, animal and human, living and dead.

In addition to being a gift for the spirits, parts of the sacrificed animal were used in divination and for the fabrication of some of the shaman's tools, so they were forever after with the shaman. These parts are recognizable in the various items of the shaman's costume and paraphernalia, both in surviving shamanistic practices and those known from historic records. The Norse *Saga of Erik the Red*, recording a period a thousand years ago, describes the items which made up the vólva's traditional costume and equipment. She wore a blue cloak covered in magic stones and straps or hangings, a hood, catskin gloves lined with white fur, calfskin boots with the fur outmost, and glass beads. She carried a skin tied with

1. *A Lappish shaman of the eighteenth century – the ancient trappings of shamanism have continued in many aspects of folk custom, including traditional dance.*

drawstrings, in which she kept her magic charms, and a staff bound in brass with a knob at the end. Every part of her clothing had a ritual purpose and symbolic design, qualities which underlay every action in ancient societies, but which have since become ignored or forgotten.

Not all shamanic traditions had specific initiations. The Ostyaks of northern central Asia, for example, had an hereditary shamanism, handed on from father to son, with instruction in the craft being almost from birth. Here, initiation was of secondary importance to the fact of birth itself. The Altai shamans received their initiation spontaneously, without ceremony. A person (male or female) who suffered convulsions, serious injury or near-death illness, and who subsequently recovered, was deemed to have received the power of the ancestors to be a shaman. In Britain, too, the *vatis (ovate)* or shaman-diviner was not an initiate. According to *The Privileges of Bardism*, both Bards and Druids were initiates. The Bard was the recipient of transmitted discipleship, and the Druid, transmitted priesthood. The vatis, however, was something outside the normal order of things:

> having his degree under the privilege of genius and commendable sciences: discipleship shall not be required in respect to him ... and this is for the purpose of protecting sciences, lest there should not be found customary teachers, and, consequently, that the science and art of record and wisdom should pass into oblivion, from a deficiency of systematic teachers and disciples. And, likewise, for the purpose of improving and increasing the sciences of art, by adding everything new to them.

Far from being a traditionalist or fundamentalist, the ancient British shaman was open to everything new that was worthwhile, and thus acted as a useful adjunct to inherited traditional knowledge.

Under whatever system the shaman is professed, he (or occasionally she) undergoes various out-of-the-body experiences and undertakes seer's journeys (the *Vision Quests* of north American holy men) and comes into contact with the transcendental powers that underlie existence. These journeys, both physical and astral, bring the shaman into contact with all of the various landscape types of his area and each of the regions of the heavens and the underworld. According to traditional interpretation, the shaman gains his insights, knowledge and power from the familar spirit with which he is associated. This spirit is his guide and protector in the dangerous terrain of the non-material planes of inner space. Often, the spirit is shown in the form of a bird, and the shaman-gods invariably have birds in attendance. In mythology, the hero-king Bran of Britain and the Nordic god Odin both had ravens which brought them knowledge and acted as protectors to their followers. The bird also symbolizes the out-of-the-body experiences which shamans undergo, and the trance-inducing dances which are based upon the mating 'dances' of cranes and other large birds. Odin's ravens had a direct connection with consciousness, being called Hugin and Munin – specifically thought and memory – in the state of abstraction from the body. When in these self-induced states of bodily or psychic extreme, shamans converse with the denizens of the non-material world to gain knowledge valuable to themselves and humans at large.

Divination

The visionary experiences and states of ecstasy bordering on possession that shamans undergo are identical with the frenzies endured by the seers and seeresses at the great oracles of antiquity. The oracles stand at the meeting-point between the individualistic, unpredictable, and sometimes anti-social behaviour of the shaman and the responsible social functions of the priest. Similarly, divination stands in a precarious relationship with established religion, for it accesses the uncertain terrain of the unconscious, ecstatic and supernatural worlds with which established religion tends to keep a low profile. Divination has rarely been integrated into the hieratic ritual order, because its elements of uncertainty, of the possibility of a bad result, cannot be tolerated by a religion which has at its core the concept of Divine Providence and stability. The delicate balance between will and randomness that characterizes divination can play only a subsidiary role in established religions.

In many formalized religions, this divinatory aspect was

2. *Many divine beings are represented as carrying or embodying the sacred grid. This image from an ancient Indian manuscript shows the goddess as a chequerboard, with an encircled navel prominent.*

transferred from the sphere of the human to that of the divine, and oracle-gods were worshipped in place of the original shamans. The symbol of this divine diviner was the grid, which is found in association with ancient representations of many gods and saints. The stag-gods of Mesopotamia, central Asia and Europe, derived from earlier shamanry, are associated with the grid pattern, which displays their dominion over space and time. A representation of the Celtic god Cernunnos from the shrine at Roqueperteuse in France has the grid, as do several of the saints in the Irish Christian illuminated manuscript known as the *Book of Durrow*. It is a common attribute of Babylonian and Hittite deities.

Divination of all kinds has the underlying implicit belief that transcendental powers control everything of importance, and that nothing happens by chance. This viewpoint, not unknown today, has always had as many critics as adherents. Seneca, a sceptic wrote:

> The difference between us and the Etruscans is the following: whereas we believe lightning to be released as the result of the collision of clouds, they believe that clouds collide to release lightning: for as they attribute all to the deity, they are led to believe not that things have meaning in so far as they occur, but rather that they occur because they must have a meaning.

According to this belief, everything that happens has a significance that relates directly to the powers supposed to underly the event. Because these transcendental powers are endowed with conscious will, they can express their will in various ways: through bolts of lightning, storms, earthquakes, strange celestial phenomena, the flight of birds, or through human beings in dreams and through oracular utterances at places of power. But even if we dismiss all of this as a misinterpretation of the nature of reality, the information encoded in many things can still be of value, and we may even be obtaining correct information when our ideas of the nature of what we are finding are completely wrong. As in all essential human activities, often the determination of the meaning of the observed phenomena, seen as the will of the transcendental powers, has been organized by a college of experts or a priesthood, and become a formalized system of augury. In traditionally-organized states from ancient Rome to Imperial

China and the Tibet of the Lamas, state augury has been an integral part of government.

For an effective use of augury to take place, however, a correct relationship had to exist between humans and the sacred order. In this view of things, all of the transcendental powers to whom humans look for protection and guidance are potentially dangerous, and a correct relationship between them and humans has to exist for augury, or indeed any form of external prayer or magic to be effective. In less developed societies, this necessary propitiation of the spirits has been done through the medium of the shaman, but in more settled, organized communities, it is the concern of the priesthood. The correct relationship is attained when the prescriptions of ritual and taboos are observed at the appropriate places and times. According to traditional belief, every place has its own spirit, the *genius loci*, which may be manifested in a number of ways. If treated with respect, according to the correct prescriptions, the *genius loci* would aid human activities, and, conversely, human beings would expect this aid to be shown by spontaneous signs, interpreted as omens and portents. Likewise, on an urban or national level, the tutelary deities of cities and states were expected to show their approval or disapproval of things by supernatural signs either produced spontaneously or as the result of formal requests made by priests.

Shape and form

The notion that nothing occurs by mindless, random chance, but has meaning, is reinforced every time we see a pattern which is recognizable to us. Since the earliest times, people have seen human faces in rocks, humanoid forms in trees, animal shapes in the clouds and other seemingly non-random patterns which they have taken as evidence for the creative and communicative action of the gods. To the person with the ability to examine and understand, encoded within these patterns is valuable information concerning the present state of the world and its immediate future.

The patterns we see in nature are infinitely recurrent. The spirals visible in distant galaxies are identical to the spirals that the cream makes when it is stirred into our coffee, or when the water goes down the bath plughole. Dendritic formations of tree branches echo the shape of river deltas, whilst certain cloud formations resemble the pattern of sand dunes, snow-drifts or the colouring on the side of a fish. These patterns have been recognized ever since humans gained consciousness, and our language attests to this. The Mackerel Sky resembles the fish patterning, Kidney Stone resembles the organ, starlings' colouring resembles the night sky studded with stars, etc.

Those who can 'read' these patterns are in the position of Shakespeare's Duke in *As You Like It*, who in the Forest of Arden, one of the ancient centres of England,

> Finds tongues in trees, books in the running brooks,
> Sermons in stones and good in everything.

3. There is a recognizable order underlying everything in the universe. This crystallized seawater, magnified a thousandfold, shows the interaction between rigid geometries and other forms of non-linear order. Despite its complexity, it is not chaotic, its features depending on regular physical laws.

These patterns exist because of the underlying physical laws of the universe. If these laws were slightly different, then physical matter as we know it would not exist, and life would be impossible. Because of this, our very physical being is related directly to these laws of the behaviour of matter, and hence the patterns are manifestations of the underlying causes of life. Over the last 100 years, scientific researchers and mathematical theorists have probed this great mystery, and produced fascinating results. Scientists working with the patterns created by sound vibrations, such as Chladni and Jenny, have shown that the geometric forms in nature and art are expressions of the inherent patterns of sound waves. These patterns are a concrete manifestation of the ancient religious belief that *In the Beginning was the Word*, the primal vibration of Sanskrit and Runic, the *Om* of the Buddhists.

The patterns which are manifested in structure reflect the driving energy of the natural order. The dynamic relationships between matter and energy naturally take certain forms, which can be expressed in mathematical formulae or geometric patterns. The patterns caused by physical effects are the same regardless of material, and are scarcely affected by scale, ranging from the galactic to the molecular. They may even occur in dynamic systems, such as the patterns formed by concentrations of swimming micro-organisms. Dynamic, self-organizing systems can be viewed as the underlying driving force of physical and even spiritual evolution, a tendency to approximate as closely as possible to the natural patterns inherent in the universal order.

Scrutiny of patterns in divination to extract information from the natural world is not greatly different from any examination of an object or system by an expert. The expert has an intimate knowledge of the correct pattern which is required, and compares the pattern under observation with his conceptual model of the correct one. If the two patterns concur, then the expert has precise knowledge of the status of the examined object. If they do not concur, then by close comparison, the differences can be determined, and, through experience, evaluated. To the outsider, the expert's intimate knowledge of a subject may appear to border on the miraculous. In untutored societies, certain technologies and abilities were indistinguishable from magic to the average person.

The islanders of the Pacific were always noted for their epic voyages between islands, perhaps hundreds of miles apart. These voyages were undertaken regularly in small sailing craft, without the aid of anything which modern navigators would deem essential. The islanders had no charts, no compass, and no navigational instruments whatsoever. Yet despite this, which to a modern sailor would mean disaster, they were able to plot accurate courses between islands. One of the reasons for this was an intimate understanding of wave patterns. Even though wave patterns are formed in accordance with certain well-defined laws of behaviour, to those without knowledge of such things the examination of wave patterns by navigators would be interpreted as some form of magical divination. Western oceanographers did not start to investigate wave patterns until the early twentieth century, but the inhabitants of the Pacific islands had done so for centuries, and were able to use them for navigation. In any part of the world, the patterns of waves in the ocean depend upon various interlinked factors – the prevailing winds, the state of the tide, and the shape of islands and land masses – which have precise effects upon the shape and pattern of waves at any place. The intimate knowledge of their own environment possessed by the navigators of Oceania enables them to tell, by looking at the wave patterns, where they are.

Wave and swell pattern observation is known throughout the Pacific islands, but it is in the Marshall Islands that teaching was formalized with the use of a geometrical aid. These instructional diagrams were made of sticks, forming intricate geometrical shapes, sometimes in the form of grids containing subtle distortions. When encountered in museums, they are often described as 'maps', and have been taken wrongly as primitive representations of the relative physical positions of islands in the ocean. They are maps of a sort, but rather the equivalent of a Western scientific graph, for they show the various forms of waves and interference patterns which are encountered at specific places under various conditions. The *Mattang* and *Meddo* illustrated on p. 17 demonstrated to trainee navigators the patterns which they would need to know to find their way around the islands. This sophisticated knowledge is an example of the sort of skills it is possible to acquire and preserve in a society without a written language and without the formalized scientific method of the modern age.

On some islands, stone structures, known as 'stone canoes', are used as simulators of the real thing. To the uninitiated, the structure would appear to be a lozenge-shaped arrangement of stones, in the centre of which is a rectangular stone for a seat. In fact, the stone canoe is a representation of several things. It is oriented to the cardinal directions, and at night is

CHLADNI'S FIGURES.

4. *The nineteenth-century researcher Chladni found that when a metal plate covered with a thin layer of sand is vibrated by drawing a violin bow across its edge, the vibrations cause the sand to form various geometrical patterns.*

used to teach the student the courses of the stars important in navigation. When wave patterns are being taught, it has the same function as an instructional diagram of sticks, representing an island. By their size, shape and orientation, the triangular stones at the apices represent the characteristic wave swell at each place. In their geometry, stellar orientations and location close to the sea, there is a parallel with the stone circles of ancient megalithic Europe. Might the connection of the Pacific stones with navigation have had some parallel in ancient Europe? The irregular grids found on several ancient artefacts, including the Portpatrick Slates illustrated on p. 20, may be part of a lost system of knowledge at the border between navigation and divination.

In addition to the patterns of the waves, the Pacific navigators look out for other signs. Luminescence in the sea at night, caused by phosphorescent marine organisms, occurs as flashes about a fathom deep, indicating a distance of about 25–30 miles from land. Rather like the Roman augurs of old, the navigators observe the birds, which indicate the nearness of land. Frigate birds fly as much as 50 miles from land; boobies, called locally *kakarau* or 'signal birds', venture no further than 35 miles from land, whilst noddies are encountered 25 miles away from islands. Banks of cloud, and star-rise positions add to the repertoire of reading the natural environment to gain useful information.

In pre-scientific societies, there was no distinction between the magical and the practical. Arts which are now seen as separate, even antagonistic to one another, like astrology and astronomy, were parts of the same discipline. The navigators of Oceania would see no difference between their magical and divinatory practices and the recognition of wave patterns. In such a world-view, the various techniques available for people to gain information are equally valid. The only difference is the nature of the information, and its application. An ancient concept connected to this world-view is that of the pre-existence of everything encoded in the structure of nature. All we have to do to get information is to tap this limitless storehouse of knowledge in the correct way.

Aberrant natural phenomena have always been interpreted as the physical manifestation of spiritual powers. Often, the behaviour of springs or holy wells has been monitored closely by soothsayers. Marvel Sike Spring in Northamptonshire was said to run erratically before a catastrophe, and St Helen's Well at Rushton Spencer in Staffordshire would dry up, no matter how wet the weather, in similar circumstances. The famous Durmming Well at Oundle, Leicestershire, has been known for centuries as a place of prophecy, generating a drumming sound when national disaster is imminent. Baxter, in his 1691 book *The Certainty of the World of Spirits*, records that the well at Oundle drummed before the invasion of the Scottish army during the Civil War, and again to herald the death of King Charles II. Chad Valley Spring, now in the city of Birmingham, once foreboded bad events including forthcoming battles and the arrival of plagues, whilst at Atherstone, also in Warwickshire, Corn Spring predicted the price of corn!

In Cornwall, girls used to go to the holy well of St Maddern to find out by divination when they would marry. They would tie two straws together in the shape of a cross, and drop it into the water of the sacred spring. By the number of bubbles which rose from the water, they knew how many years would pass before their wedding. Divination such as this, and by the sounds, flow of springs, and perhaps the psychic effects their electrostatic fields may have on the human body is known as *pegomancy*. Closely related to the divinations undertaken at holy wells is the ancient art of *hydromancy*, otherwise known as *hydroscopy*. This term covers everything from the observation of spontaneous patterns in water to ones created specially for the purpose of divination. The former includes surface ripples and waves on the sea, known from ancient Europe as well as in their sophisticated form from the Pacific, whilst the latter is part of a more occult method. The recommended method was to go to a still pool and throw in three stones. The first of these was to be spherical, the second pyramidal and the third a cube. The wave patterns caused by the three was noted, and the diviner referred to a pattern book which interpreted the meanings. Another use of water in divination is *lecanomancy*, in which the diviner pours water into oil or oil onto water. The size and number of droplets formed have specific meanings. *Aleuromancy* involves shaking flour onto water to see what

shapes are formed. In ancient Bablyon, the compass orientation of these shapes was important.

Divination by shapes

Divination by wax, known variously as *cereoscopy* or *ceromancy*
uses a refined wax which is melted in a brass bowl and stirred
carefully with a ceremonial spatula until fully liquified. Once
liquid, it is poured slowly and deliberately into a bowl filled to
the brim with cold water. The wax will spread into thin layers
on the surface of the water, solidifying into shapes which are
then interpreted. Similar to cereoscopy is divination by lead,
plumbomancy, a dangerous version which is not recommended.
Lead is inherently very poisonous, and when molten lead is
poured into cold water it can spit hot globules of metal back at
the pourer. Here, molten lead is dropped into water, and the
shapes noted, with the interpretations being as for cereoscopy.
It is likely that the patterns described in modern readings of
tea-leaves or coffee grounds are derived from the older
cereomantic figures.

   Divination by dough of bread or cakes, *crithomancy*, applies to
two unrelated forms of divination. The shapes made when the
dough is kneaded may be examined and interpreted, or the
dough may be placed at a crossing of paths and watched to see
what sort of person is the first to step on it. The first form is
obviously related to cereomantic patterns, whilst the latter is
unrelated to material or shape. The various forms of *geomancy*
dealt with below, are concerned with the discernment of
patterns in the earth, either natural or created by human
agency.

   Looking at certain objects to find meaningful patterns has
always been an important aid to seership. Scrying with a lens,
or with the aid of a crystal ball (known as *crystallomancy*), is one
of the more common of the divinatory arts practised today.
Divination by light rays is another ancient method which may
originate in ancient astronomy and the orientation of buildings
to catch the rays of the morning sun. Prehistoric observatories
like the great Irish megalithic structure at Newgrange have
long passages lined with stones bearing symbols such as spirals

and zigzags, upon which rays of the sun shine at certain times of year. The ancient temples of Egypt likewise combined orientation with symbolism. In his masterly work, *Architecture, Mysticism and Myth*, published in 1891, W.R. Lethaby described the magical wonder of the rising sun, as witnessed by ancient devotees:

> It is the moment of sunrise, chill and expectant; all the gates are thrown open to the east. The worshippers are waiting, and the golden tips of the obelisks are already burning. The sun shows its red rim through the open ceremonial gate of the outer court. They prostrate themselves. There is a sudden awakening sense of heat and life and light, a passing vibration in the air. The little bells festooned from pillar to pillar shiver out silver notes; a deep strain vibrates from the sanctuary. They stand on their feet. The great gates of the temple close with a clangour that reverberates like thunder. Baal has entered into his temple.

Reflective ornaments and objects were part of the repertoire of ancient magical practice. Not only did they catch the light of the sun and moon, but also reflected away harmful spirits or energies. In traditional practice, it was customary to drive iron nails into trees and the main posts of timber-framed buildings. A famous tree, almost solid with nails, known as the *Stock im Eisen* is still preserved at Vienna, and ancient nails can be found in profusion in the corner and king posts of many old wooden buildings in northern Europe. These nails were used once by seers who caught glimpses of patterns created by sunlight reflecting from them. This *onychomancy* is an almost-forgotten art, though it is doubtless related to *crystallomancy* and seeing patterns in running water, one of the many variations of *hydromancy*.

Rhabdomancy or *rhabdoscopy* is divination by the wand. Nowadays, the word *dowsing* is used to describe the divination of underground water, oil, minerals or treasure, and more esoteric 'energies' in the earth. In the traditional practice of the art, at the time of full moon, and on a day and planetary hour assigned to Mercury, a wand was cut with a single stroke from a hazel tree. It was carried horizontally, with each end held in one hand, and slightly under pressure, bending it. When the sought-for minerals or water were beneath the feet of the rhabdomancer, a torsion of the wand was felt. Later, the

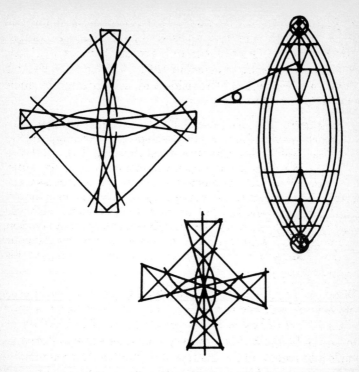

5. *Two cross-shaped* mattangs *and a* meddo. *Navigational 'stick charts' from the Marshall Islands in the Pacific Ocean. The geometric forms of these mnemonic graphs record the patterns of waves and ocean swell encountered between specific islands, enabling the sailors to navigate by the waves.*

familiar forked twig of dowsers became more popular, and finally plastic versions of this and the two separate metal 'angle rods' encountered today in dowsing circles.

Libanomancy is divination by smoke. Incense or wood shavings are placed on a fire, and the direction and form of the smoke is noted. This is related to directional magic, for if the divination is conducted out of doors, the smoke direction relates to the direction of the wind, and hence shows the quality of that wind. Conducted outdoors, it becomes a form of *austromancy*, divination by winds. *Capnomancy* is a related form, being the interpretation of the smoke from a burnt offering on a sacrificial altar, which itself would be orientated.

Augury

The interpretation of certain unusual phenomena as omens or portents is of interest here, for throughout the world they have been envisaged as being indications of divine wrath, and people have acted accordingly. In ancient Rome, for example, whenever a notable phenomenon was observed, it was reported to the *haruspices*, who decided whether a sacrifice was required to avert the impending disaster or rectify some omission in ritual which might have led to the gods' displeasure. The Roman tradition of state augury, which was essential to the conduct of public life, grew out of this practice. In Rome before the Imperial period, the chief official at state religious rites was the *Rex Sacrorum*, successor of the Divine King. He oversaw the correct conduct of those rites deemed essential to the continued well-being of the state. Originally, he was accompanied by three augurs, whose duty was to interpret the perceived will of the gods and determine any action to be taken with regard to the auspices. Later, the number of augurs increased to six, then to nine, stabilizing at fifteen, to which a final sixteenth was added by Julius Caesar. The number 16 occurs in many systems of divination and justice, and Caesar may have felt it necessary to bring the ceremonial number of augurs into line with it for numerological or symbolic reasons. This would be consistent with each of the augurs being considered equivalent to one of the figures in divinatory geomancy, the one added by Caesar being equivalent to the *reconciler* (see Chapter 3). Perhaps the increase in numbers paralleled the development of such a system of divination. The senior augur was automatically president of the College of Augurs, being responsible for the *inauguration* of the *Rex Sacrorum*, and the three high priests: the *flamines* of Jupiter, Mars and Quirinus, who were the chief clergy of Pagan Rome.

By Caesar's time, many educated people considered state augury to be an archaic survival. Its origins in Greek and Etruscan magic were seen by some as heroic or romantic, but by others as barbarous and backward. As in modern times, people in ancient Rome adhered to a spectrum of beliefs ranging from atheism and materialism, through state religion to the more fringe mystery cults and messianic sects. This mix is nowhere better demonstrated than in the person of Cicero. In 45–44 BCE, he wrote the books titled *On the Nature of the Gods* and *On Divination*. In the first work, he laments that 'through the negligence of the nobility, the craft of augury has been lost. Men no longer believe in the veracity of omens, which are now taken merely as outward formalities.' In the second book, he attacks all forms of divination, though he notes that all of the great philosophers, including Aristotle, Plato and Socrates, but with the exception of Epicurus and Xenophanes, had faith in the craft. This rejection was strange, because Cicero himself had held the office of state augur since 53 BCE. He justified this contradiction for reasons of state. or personal position, rather than belief and practice. Despite the criticisms of Cicero, practical augury, divination and the geomantic arrangement of sacred sites were flourishing practices.

Technically, the augurs were concerned with the interpretation of signs which had been observed by special magistrates who watched the sky at certain times for various signs. These signs were viewed from a special location – the *templum* – which was not, as its name might suggest, a temple, but an outdoor viewing mound located with regard to the intrinsic qualities of the site. The magistrate sat at the prescribed location, invoked the appropriate deity under whose aegis the sought-for sign would appear, and watched the sky. Around the mound, which had been located with regard to natural and artificial features visible on the horizon, the sky was divided into 16 equal areas. These were viewed using the *lituus*, a ceremonial staff, forerunner of the pastoral staff carried by Bishops in the Christian church. The head of the staff was in the form of a sickle-shaped crook, which, when held at arm's length, divided the horizon into 16. By the use of this staff in relation to known direction markers on the horizon, the viewer could determine in which sixteenth of the sky the phenomenon manifested itself. The augur himself did not see the signs, for he sat blindfold, receiving the information from the magistrate.

The arts of the augurs involved the interpretation of many separate, but related phenomena. One of the most important was the flight of birds. The interpretation here depended on the type and number of birds, the sounds uttered by them, the direction, directness and speed of their flight and the sixteenth of the sky in which they appeared. This was, of course, related also to the time of day and the day of the week on which it occurred, and was observed in relation to a specific question or request for information. Aristander, Alexander the Great's principal diviner, was a master at the interpretation of the flight of birds, and many of the conqueror's successes were achieved with the aid of this divination.

As with many forms of divination which seem to have died out entirely, sometimes they resurface in a most unexpected manner. One of these instances is in the lore of Leicester City Football Club supporters. A strange bird omen occurred on December 20, 1928, during a very unusual soccer match between Leicester City and Portsmouth. Leicester forward Arthur Chandler had already scored five goals when a flock of five swans flew over the ground. Later in the match, which Leicester finally won by ten goals to nil, a sixth swan flew over, and almost immediately, Chandler scored his sixth goal. This was taken by many supporters to be an omen.

Although divination by the flight of birds is no longer practised, it may have given rise to something of more direct

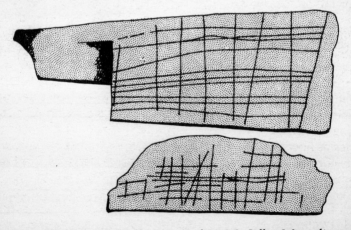

6. *The noted Glaswegian prehistorian Ludovic MacLellan Mann discovered these enigmatic slate slabs in a Bronze Age tomb at Portpatrick, and exhibited them at the Scottish Historical Exhibition in Glasgow in 1911. 'Deposited with the body,' wrote Mann, 'was a small slab of slate, the whole surface of which was carefully prepared and covered with etched lines in a kind of reticular or net-work pattern.'*

use, for the Roman writer Hyginus claimed that the invention of writing was suggested by the flight of cranes, which make letters as they fly. There is a strong element of augury in this statement, and there are many fascinating and subtle connections between the dance of the crane, the ecstatic dance of shamans and the labyrinth. If it is correct, Hyginus's comment places the origin of the alphabet in divination.

Many of the events which the augurs of Rome and the Druids, Magi and Soothsayers of other places were called to comment upon were the sort of things modern news reporters cover. Unusual astronomical events, cataclysmic disasters, runs of bad luck, accidents, assassinations, famines, biological mutations and new inventions were discussed, and their meaning explained. When the Temple of Diana at Ephesus was burnt by arson, the Magi of Ephesus saw the fire as a sign which betokened a much worse misfortune. They ran through the streets of the city, beating themselves and crying 'This day has brought forth the great scourge and destroyer of Asia.' Much later, it was recognized that the day on which the temple was destroyed was the day on which Alexander the Great was born. It was believed that the Goddess had been absent from the temple that day, or it would never have been destroyed. Supporters of Alexander claimed that She had been away in Macedonia, bringing him into the world. The destruction of the temple, then, was seen correctly as a sign of something potentially much worse. When the south transept of York Minster was burnt in 1984, many people saw it as a sign of God's displeasure, whilst others blamed it on random lightning. As in ancient Ephesus, the interpretation of the causes, then as now, depended on one's point of view. Today, there are no *fulguriators* around to interpret the meaning of bolts of lightning.

Haruspicy

The haruspices were specialists in a much narrower field of interpretation and divination than the augurs. Their area of operation included the interpretation of lightning, but they are best known for their examination of the livers of sacrificed animals, a divinatory art known as *hepatoscopy*. This form of divination, adopted by the Romans from Etruscan practice, had a long history before Rome, being used by the Assyrians, the Babylonians and the Hittites. In *The Book of Ezekiel*, Nebuchadnezzar is reported as having 'looked at the liver' to divine which road he should take when he stood at a parting of the ways. The liver, which was believed to be the seat of the soul, was cut from a freshly-sacrificed animal, and inspected according to its divisions. In Babylon, it was divided up by the *baru* (haruspex) into a grid of oracular sections or 'houses' according to a cosmological model. The patterns of the veins and arteries, the ducts and lobes, were interpreted according to this geomantic or astrological diagram. Various terracotta and clay models of divinatory livers have been found at Babylonian and Hittite sites, showing it to have been a popular method of divination. In Europe, a model of a sheep's liver, discovered at Piacenza in Italy in 1877, is divided into sections which correspond to the Etruscan division of the sky, inscribed with the names of the corresponding gods.

Dismemberment of animals or people for internal signs of transcendental messages was not restricted to the pagan traditions of antiquity. The church of Santa Chiara in Montefalco, Italy, contains a rare example of Christian haruspicy carried out on a human being. St Chiara or Clare of Montefalco was an Augustinian nun who died in 1308 at the age of 33. When she died, the nuns saw her age, the same as that of Jesus at his death, as significant, and recalled some words she had uttered on her deathbed: 'If you seek the cross of Christ, take my heart. There you will find the suffering Lord.' Taking her statement literally, the nuns cut open the body of Chiara and dissected her heart and entrails, looking for the images of which she had spoken. When the heart was cut up, the nuns found patterns which were interpreted as a crucifix, the scourge, crown of thorns, the three nails and the lance of Longinus. Elsewhere in Chiara's entrails were found three gallstones, symbolic of the Trinity.

Clearly, in the dismemberment of Chiara for signs of Christian devotion, we have the survival of ancient systems of haruspicial dissection of sacrificial victims. According to the records of the time, the signs were found by precise dissection. If the sister who carried out the divinatory autopsy had misdirected the razor toward the right, or towards the left, even by the thickness of a single hair, so the account goes, or thrust it any deeper, she would have destroyed one or more of the internal signs found in the heart. This indicates that the nuns had considerable anatomical knowledge, precisely that concerned with human haruspicy.

Perhaps the strangest aspect of this whole phenomenon is the preservation until the present day of both the body and heart of Chiara, displayed in glass containers within the church. This divinatory method of interpreting an object according to a predetermined cosmological scheme is an underlying theme that ranges from *hepatoscopy* through augury and divinatory geomancy to game boards. It is the link which connects all forms of divination.

Oracles

Oracles are prophetic revelations usually associated with specific places and/or times. Traditionally, it has been found that oracular utterances have been possible only at certain privileged places, occurring in conjunction with ceremonial rites dedicated to the *genius loci* of the place. Such a place was known as an oracle, more properly the interaction of the power of the place, the time, the rite and the individuals involved, producing insights into the nature of future possibilities. The word *oracle* has the meaning of *the place of invocation*, or *the place of the sacred word*. Places chosen for or discovered to possess oracular powers generally had certain physical features which modern earth mysteries research recognizes as characteristic of places of power.

The major Greek oracles were located at Delphi in Phocis, Dodona in Epirus, Lebadea in Boeotia and Tenarus in Laconia. The oracle at Delphi is perhaps the best known of them all, not least because it was associated with the *omphalos* of Greece, said to be the centre of the world. In its earliest form, the shrine had been sacred to the Minoan Mother Goddess whom the Greeks called Ge-Themis, later Gaia. Like many key places of power, the site appears to have undergone several conversions from one deity to another, or perhaps a process of accretion occurred, where the devotion of new deities was added to the old one. There is some evidence that oracles of Gaia were given at Delphi, and perhaps also Poseidon. According to Plutarch, the oracular cave at Delphi was discovered accidentally. Goatherds looking after their flocks in the rocky terrain noticed that toxic gases emanating from a crack in the ground had caused some of their animals to be seized with convulsions. Approaching the aperture, the goatherds and others experienced similar sensations, producing in them a sort of delirium associated with garbled but prophetic utterances. Priests were consulted, and they deemed the site sacred to Apollo.

When the priesthood of Apollo had taken over the site, it became customary for a woman past the age of childbearing, designated the Pythia, to give the oracular pronouncement. At first, the pronouncements were made only on the seventh day of one springtime month, but later, the privilege was extended to the nine months of the year that were not in wintertime. On one occasion in each of these months, she would appear in long robes, wearing a golden headdress, white woollen bands and a laurel-leaf wreath, and go to drink at the sacred spring called Kassotis. Then she descended into the cavernous aperture known as the *Adyton*. Seated there upon a tripod, sacred stool of Apollo, the seeress would perform appropriate rituals and inhale the fumes, after which she would answer questions put to her by the priests, or by upper class visitors. In her capacity as oracle, she was a medium, the mouthpiece of Apollo. Over the years, the associated rites and observances increased, and many famous people, including the great Pagan holy man Apollonius of Tyana, visited the shrine. This latter event disproves one of the major myths concerning oracles in the ancient world. When the Christian church gained ascendancy in the Roman Empire, as part of the claim to exclusiveness, it was put about that oracles had ceased suddenly at the time of the birth of Jesus of Nazareth. That this is not true is evident from the visit to the Delphic Oracle of Apollonius, who was born in the early part of the first century, after Jesus, and died in the year 96.

The Delphic oracle was the local version of the prophethic tradition associated in Greece with Apollo, but which was rooted in the shamanistic practices of northern Europe. As a central *omphalos*, Delphi was seen as the place where the underworld, the world of humans and the upperworld were in

specially close contact, a location where ecstatic trance could
gain access to the will of the gods and give a knowledge of
things to come. The linking of the wild traditions of shamanism with a more settled, organized priesthood at Delphi

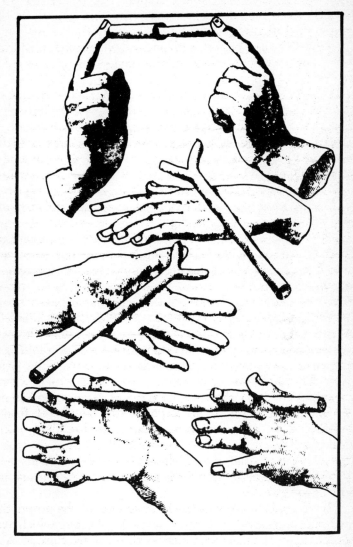

7. *True* rhabdomancy *used various versions of a single stick or rod, as
recorded in this seventeenth-century engraving on the art.*

marks a transition between unbridled ecstatic revelation and controlled divination under the aegis of a priesthood.

The oracle at Dodona was another celebrated shrine which almost equalled Delphi in sanctity and fame. Ancient commentators considered it to be the first of the oracles, dating back to around the eighth century BCE. This oracle, located at the foot of Mount Tomaros, near to the modern town of Jannina, was close to the ancient holy town of Epirus, dedicated to Zeus. The oracular sanctuary at Dodona was in an ancient Oak forest through which ran fast-flowing mountain streams. At the centre of this grove was a clearing in which stood a single tree. This tree had been singled out, it was said, by an Egyptian priestess from Thebes who had gone as a missionary to Europe. At the foot of this venerable Oak was an intermittent spring which dried up at midday and ran again at midnight. Like the gaseous emanations at Delphi, such an aberrant geological phenomenon was bound to attract practitioners of natural religion. At Dodona, the pronouncements came in a calm manner without the hallucinogenic frenzy associated with the Pythia. The priestess, who slept on the ground and never washed her feet, observed the subtle alterations in the sounds emitted by the sacred Oak. These sounds may have been the wind passing through the leaves and branches of the tree and the altering sounds of its attendant spring. Equally, a more intuitive rapport with the tree may have existed, where the actual internal sounds emitted from the fluids flowing in the wood, or the ultrasonic fields emitted by the Oak, were interpreted. The priestess's essential closeness to the earth at this shrine is a typical requirement, the feeling that too much 'civilization' removes our closeness to the earth and consequently our intuitive faculties. Excavations in modern times have uncovered numerous folded strips of flattened lead. Dating from the sixth to the middle of the third century BCE, they are offerings containing questions which could be answered by 'yes' or 'no'.

The location of a sacred oracular tree by an Egyptian priestess reflects the importance of trees in ancient divination. In northern Europe, both the Celtic *Ogham* system of divination and the *runes* were originally based on using the wood of sacred trees (see Chapter 4), and there are several recorded instances of a famous divinatory Oak in ancient

Israel. This 'oak which giveth oracles', the Oak of Meonim, was, like that at Dodona, understood from the rustlings of the wind in the leaves and branches, a survival of the pre-Jewish Canaanite religion. This succumbed at the time of the extirpation of ancient shrines by Josiah in about 621 BCE.

Another important Greek oracle in a mountainside shrine was the sanctuary of Trophonius. This oracle was named after the locator and architect who had built the Temple of Apollo at Delphi. The sanctuary of Trophonius was associated with a temple of the goddess Fortuna, tutelary deity of divination and gambling. The oracle was in an inaccessible cave into which supplicants had to crawl at night, after several days of fasting and being plied with various herbal drinks of unknown composition. The experience seems to have been particularly unnerving, being accompanied by hallucinations and other terrifying experiences from which most visitants never fully recovered. Clearly, the character of this oracle was quite different from the others. When Sir Francis Dashwood created the Hell Fire Caves at West Wycombe in the eighteenth century, they were a conscious recreation of the terrible subterranea of Trophonius.

Wherever they are, the shrines of oracles have common features. The national oracle of Madagascar was similarly inside a cave on the holy mountain of the island at Andringitra. Inside the cave was the image known as Ramahavàly (*The One Able to Answer*), and the prophetic pronouncements themselves were uttered by a member of the family of hereditary guardians. This oracle was suppressed by the Christian queen Ranavalona II in 1869, but on the re-establishment of Paganism several years later, was reinstated. Ramahavàly was a national oracle, and, like the Pythia at Delphi, the spiritual patron of serpents.

The hereditary guardian of such places is well known in Britain. St Elian's Well, (*Ffynnon Eilian*) situated close to Llanelian Church in Denbighshire had a 'priestess' named Mrs Hughes in charge of the waters as late as the end of the eighteenth century. She was the penultimate guardian of the ancient lore at that site, for at her death she was succeeded by a tailor, John Evans, popularly known as Jack Ffynnon Eilian, last of the magical tribe. The well of St Elian was remarkable for being, like the oracle of Trophonius, 'the most terrible of the Welsh Holy Wells', its main use being for cursing. In addition to the more unusual use of cursing people, it had the usual function of healing and prophecy. In common with holy wells in many countries, it was surrounded by rags tied on the bushes as offerings. Eventually, the authorities suppressed the site and its practices, and in January, 1829, the well was filled in on the orders of the local magistrate, and the stones forming the wall around it were moved to make a drain to carry the waters away to the river nearby.

Many of the old holy wells of Celtic Britain retained the oracular function almost into the modern age, so the phenomenon must have been much more widespread in former times. In Cornwall, until about the same period, St Gulval's Well had an accompanying wise woman, who, for a small offering, would drink the waters and then make an oracular answer to a question. In Wales, next to the holy well of St Peris (*Ffynnon Beris*) at Llanberis, which was a shrine whose waters were reputed to cure childhood rickets, was a cottage beneath a rock outcrop known as Tynyffynnon. There lived a woman whose employment was to care for the two sacred trout which were kept in the well. The trout were the living agents of the oracle, the Welsh equivalent of the *Salmon of Knowledge*, which the woman interpreted. Some other Welsh holy wells had fish, eel being common. Invariably, these inhabitants of the sacred waters were treated with great respect. The snake-like appearance of the eel was doubtless connected with the general ascription of sacred oracles to serpents, and the complex chthonic mythos of serpent/dragon lore.

2

NUMBER AND PATTERN

Nothing exists apart, everything has a share of everything else.
Anexagoras, *Fragment, 6*

Oracular pronouncement depends on many uncontrollable factors: the health and capability of the person acting as the mouthpiece of the oracle, the vagaries of the spirit or geophysical energy which creates the oracular effect, and the interference of unexpected omens. Because of this unreliability, people sought more readily-available means of gaining knowledge of the will of the gods, the state of the universe and shapes of things to come. Whatever the form of its manifestation, divination has carried with it the imagery of the eternal, formal structure underlying the universe. This ranges from numerical sequences to geometry and the topographical patterns of knots and threads.

The Three Fates and the thread of life

In many cultures, spinning thread on a spindle and weaving on a loom have an allegorical or direct connection with fate and destiny. Spinning is a creative act which transforms the diffuse and chaotic fibres of wool or flax into a coherent, and usable, thread. The physical act of spinning involves the spindle, which is rotated to spin the thread, and the distaff, onto which the spun material is gathered. The spinning of thread has obvious similarities to the apparent motions of the starry heavens rotating around the pole star, and in northern climes, where this is a very visible phenomenon, the spinner has been associated with the heavens, and by association, the seasons and the passing of time. The ancient astronomy of northern Europe had constellations quite different from those used today, derived from Babylonian, Greek and Islamic sources. One important constellation, now part of Orion (the 'belt'), was known as Frigg's Distaff, and the pole star God's Nail or the Spindle.

Spinning thread was one of the earliest manufacturing technologies, where time was obviously associated with the amount of material produced. The length of thread produced was thus a measure of the amount of time spent in making it, creating the symbolism of the thread of time which exists in many cultures. The Three Fates of the Greeks – Clotho, Lachesis and Atropos, daughters of Zeus and Themis – and the Three Norns – Urd, Verdandi and Skuld – of the northern tradition are depicted as sitting at the centre of the world, spinning the fates of humans, and cutting off lives as one would cut thread. Clotho spins the thread, Lachesis measures its length, and Atropos cuts it when she will. Old illustrations of witches show them spinning, and cord magic is an important part of modern Wicca. In medieval Italy, the power of witchcraft was thought to be so potent in spinning that women were forbidden on pain of severe punishment from spinning whilst walking along the highway. To do this would prevent the crops from growing vigorously!

Psychic researchers believe that the symbolism of the thread spun by Clotho or Urd represents the cord which links the astral body to the physical in out-of-the-body experiences (OOBE). After separation from the motionless physical body, the astral body appears to be floating above it, connected by a 'luminous cable', a cord or thread. This *silver cord* is mentioned in the Biblical book of *Ecclesiastes*, and is reported independently wherever an OOBE is undergone. It appears to be connected to the physical body at the centre of the forehead, the position of the *third eye* in eastern esoteric physiology, and the place where the cord-like serpent known as the *Uraeus* was placed on the headdress of ancient Egyptian monarchs. People experiencing OOBE believe that if this cord is cut, then the physical body would die, releasing the spirit. In the Greek legend of Theseus in the labyrinth, the hero carried Ariadne's *clew*, a ball of string, which enabled him to return to the world once he slew the dreaded Minotaur. Had this been cut, his death would have been certain.

Once spun, the thread is placed on a loom and woven into a grid pattern, creating many more possible patterns. Linguistically, the word *weave* is connected with old Celtic words which have the meaning of a serpent, or more subtly, the serpentine powers detected in the ground by sensitives and dowsers. As the *Wouivre*, it is the quintessence or fifth element, the vibration of energy at the fundamental level of matter. The repetitive motions of the loom, the oscillating, wavering motions can describe the weaver's shuttle, the gyrations of the rhabdomantic rod, or the writhings of the world serpent.

Astragali and dice

We figured the odds as best we could, and then we rolled the dice.'

Jimmy Carter, XXth President of the USA, *New York Times*, 10th July, 1976

Some of the earliest divinatory objects that have been found are *astragali*, knuckle bones of various animals, the forerunners of dice. In Assyria, these astragali, known as *kisallu* were used for gambling, and also to allot the shares from an inheritance, to apportion shares of income in the temples, and for the election of officials. The Assyrians also used clay dice, called

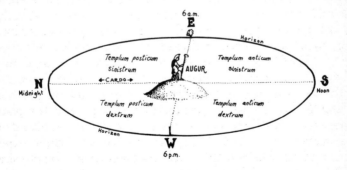

8. *The central location of the* augur, *whose southward-orientated vision automatically divided the circle of the horizon into four areas.*

puru. A divinatory die was inscribed with the name of the candidate for a position, and a prayer to the gods Adad and Assur that the die should roll right.

Astragali were readily available, and so it is to be expected that, once recognized, they should find a widespread use. Many have been found in divinatory contexts in Asia, Europe and Britain. Often, they were buried as grave-goods with the dead. A set of astragali were discovered during excavations of the Anglo-Saxon cementeries near the former Roman town of Caister-by-Norwich, Norfolk. They were almost all identical, except for one which was much larger than the other. It came from a roe deer and bore a runic inscription which transliterates as *raihan*. This word is believed to mean *set in line*, or *that which marks*. It is possible that this piece played a major part in divination, for astragali were the medium for many diviners throughout Europe and the Near East.

Astragali are rather irregular and it is sometimes difficult to interpret which way one has fallen. Dice, however, are unequivocal, and took over from astragali as a preferred method. The original use of dice in divination is embedded in the word *die* and its plural *dice*, which come from the Low Latin *dadus*, meaning 'given', that is 'given by the gods'. In the time before the idea of randomness was discovered, it was considered that everything that happened was part of the will of supernatural beings, whether the gods or the demonic empire. This idea transcended religious barriers, for it exists as much in Christian as in Pagan belief. The throw of dice, then, was not seen as a random, chance event, but as controlled by and accessing the will of the gods. The underlying belief which ascribes the outcome of games of chance to the goddess Fortuna, now more secularized into Lady Luck, is that the fall of the dice is not random, but under the direct control of Luck personified.

In Pagan northern Europe, the invention of dice was attributed to Odin, the god of wisdom, prophecy and the dead. In fact, Odin was believed to be the discoverer of many means of divination, including the Runes and the northern European board game called *Hnefatafl* (see Chapter 7). Similarly, in ancient Irish tradition, the board game of *Fidcheall*, a version of Hnefatafl, was ascribed to the god Lugh, the Irish equivalent of Odin. According to the Icelandic historian Snorri Sturluson (1179–1241) in his great history known as *Heimskringla*, it is

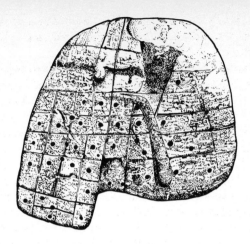

9. *Ceramic model of a sheep's liver, Babylonian, c. 1700 BCE, now in the British Museum. The model is divided into gridded areas showing the different zones of meaning to be encountered and interpreted by the* haruspex (see p. 21).

recorded that Odin was a person who came to Scandinavia from 'the land in Asia east of the Tanakvisl (the River Don in Russia) ... called Âsaland or Âsaheim'. The chief town of Âsaland was Âsagarth or Asgard, whose location is now unknown. Odin and his followers left their country and migrated to Sweden, where they founded the town of Gamla Sigtuna, near the modern Stockholm. 'When Odin and the *diar* (priests) came to the north lands, they brought in and taught others the sports and crafts which were employed there for many years afterwards.' After his death, Odin, like so many larger-than-life humans, was deified, and worshipped as a god.

After Christianization, when people were told that the old gods were devils, dice, recognized as having a Pagan origin, were criticized by the new priesthood. The expression 'The Devil's Bones' comes from this belief. Less fanatical Christians gave mythological humans the credit of creating games and writing. 'Attalus Asiaticus was the first man in Europe to play *Kotra* (backgammon) and dice', wrote Jón Dadason in a work entitled *Gandrei* (The Witches' Ride), 'and, likewise, as some say, *Riddarskák* (Knights' Chess), soon after the Battle of Troy'. Dadason, who died in 1676, was Rector at Arnabaeli in South

Iceland, and at that time it was customary to ascribe the origin of games to classical sources. The use of lots has an important place in the Christian religion, however, for, after the suicide of Judas Iscariot, the 11 remaining disciples of Jesus chose the new twelfth disciple, Matthias, by lots.

Lots or dice have always played their part in the allocation of land. The words *allotment* and a *lot* of land retain the old meaning of a piece of land whose ownership or leasehold has been selected by drawing lots. An important instance where national ownership of a piece of territory was decided by dice took place at Konungahella in Norway in the year 1020. King Olaf of Norway met the King of Sweden to decide which country owned the Hising district. The kings threw dice to decide the ownership. According to tradition, they each threw a six twice in succession, but on the third throw, the Norwegian king's die split in two, showing four and three, and so he won with a seven! Even if the details of this tale are fanciful, the essence of kings divining with dice who should be the owner of land is not. In Tibet, dice were employed in a form of divination known as *Sho-mo*. Three conventional dice were employed, as in the European game of Dicing Nine Men's Morris. Three dice give rise to sixteen different numbers, in various combinations. Tibetan *Sho-mo* compares the numbers with divinatory tables connected with traditional texts. As in western systems like Kirchenhoffer's famous *Book of Fate* ascribed to Napoléon, the texts are divided into sections apposite to questions concerning different aspects of human life. As in many other branches of divination, the number 16 is important here, with not only 16 numbers being available for each question, but human experience being divided into 16 separate aspects. Cubic dice have been known for several thousand years, having been found in Egyptian tombs dating from before 2000 BCE. Modern dice have a standard number arrangement, where digits are located in such a way that each pair adds up to seven. In this case, there are only two possible arrangements, which are mirror images of each other. If a die is looked at so that the faces bearing the numbers one, two and three are visible, the numbers are arranged in ascending order anticlockwise. This is the standard form found all over the world, except in Japan, where a mirror image of this is employed in the game of *Mah Jongg*. Japanese and Korean dice have the ace or single spot red, as well as the four. These are used in determining which player has the first move in a game. Stewart Culin believed that this Asiatic red spot was derived from earlier Indian divinatory practice. There are, however, 30 possible arrangements of the spots on a cubic die, and the degree of uniformity reached today throughout the world is suprising. Octahedral dice, numbered from one to eight are known from ancient Egyptian tombs. Dodecahedrons with 12 faces and even icosahedrons, with 20, have been used in fortune telling. The dodecahedron was popular with mountebanks in France in the sixteenth century. Although no longer used in games or divination, icosahedral dice numbered from nought to nine twice, are used by the Japanese Standards Association for the generation of random decimal digits.

Dice are so much part of our culture that they have their own idioms and literature. The everyday English expression 'dicing with death' may be a survival from times when dice were used to decide who of a group of prisoners should be executed or sacrificed. The irrevocable nature of dicing is recalled in the saying 'The die is cast'. It is usually used in a pessimistic fashion. Dicing has always been equated with the road to ruin. In *Gargantua and Pantagruel*, Rabelais's heroes land on Sharper's Island, a strange terrain formed of two gigantic cubic blocks of white bone. Pantagruel remarks that 'Our navigator told us that these cubic white rocks had been the cause of more shipwrecks, occasioning a greater loss of life and property than Scylla and Charybdis.' Sharper's Island is occupied by 21 Devils of Chance, one for every combination of two dice, from the least Devil, Two Aces, popularly known as Snake's Eyes, to the most powerful, Double Six.

The imagery of dice has proved a fertile ground for philosophy, too. The heartless randomness of the world is at odds with some religious views of a loving, caring God, and the imagery of dice has been used to express this state. The eighteenth century Icelandic mystic Jón Jónsson has just such a pessimistic view of the deity: 'God plays at *Forkjaering* with man in this world', *Forkjaering* being a dice game. In the twentieth century, the rationalist mathematician Albert Einstein stated exactly the opposite, that God does not play dice with the universe. These impressions of God playing dice with people were close to the truth, for we are all subject to those

10. The Pythia *oracular priestess at Delphi, seated on her tripod, being consulted, shown on an Attic red-figure vessel dating from around 440 BCE in the Staatliche Museum in East Berlin. The surrounding ornament incorporates the nine-square grid widely used by the seeresses of northern Europe, and the tripod has the eightfold symbol of the directions (see p. 24).*

unavoidable random happenings in life, which could be interpreted as the roll of a die.

Arrow and stave divination

All over the world, arrows have been used for various kinds of divination. In England, we have three well-known legends where a special site was divined with an arrow. In the legends of the outlaw Robin Hood and the Hertfordshire dragon-slaying hero Piers Shonkes, a deathbed arrow-shot divined by its fall the place where the heroes would be buried. If we are to believe the legend, the relocation of the Cathedral of Sarum to Salisbury in 1219 is another example. According to local lore, an arrow was shot from the ramparts of Old Sarum, and where it fell, Merrifield, the present cathedral was built. There is an element of shooting-magic in these legends, the miraculous ability to hit the correct target, ascribed to the Pagan Lord of the Hunt, symbolized in Robin Hood as the Hooded Man.

Even later, when archery had been replaced by firearms, we find vestigial elements of the old divination in the magic projectiles used by the shooter-magicians of central Europe known as *Freischütze*, immortalized in Johann Friedrich Kind and Carl Maria von Weber's opera *Der Freischütz*.

In traditional archery, the feathers of the arrow's flight were taken from specific birds whose qualities were believed to be manifested in the arrow itself. The flight of a bird is often seen as the shaman in an out-of-the-body state, or as the guardian spirits in avian form. This belief is another version to that which tells of witches travelling the night landscape in the guise of hares. The legend of the death of Robin Hood can be interpreted as his external soul being projected before the body to an appropriate place for his burial, the fletching of the arrow symbolizing his bird familiar. Perhaps by some shamanic empathy, the dying man had a vision of his resting place. The myths of far-seeing messenger birds is found in many traditions, including those let out of Noah's Ark and Odin's ravens, and perhaps this belief was transferred to arrows.

The arrow is a symbolic sacred protector in native American religion. The prayer sceptres of the Huichol of Mexico known as *muwieri* are believed to be derived from scared arrows. They are used to adjust imbalanced body fields of the sick, and to open invisible sacred gateways on the ground during pilgrimage. These are made with eagle feathers, and have a magically protective function. For harmful magic, a *muwieri* of owl and vulture feathers is used. In Tibet, the Lamas used arrows as one of their techniques of divination. The method known as *Dahmo* uses two arrows. One is wrapped in a black scarf, and the other a white, symbolizing the two polarities. An amount of barley grain is tipped into a while woollen cloth on a table top, and the arrows are pushed, point downwards, into the barley. Seated at the table, the querent concentrates on the question and recites mantras. The arrows are supposed to move by a telekinetic effect produced by the concentrated mind of the diviner, or the sound of the mantras may cause chiadni patterns to form in the grain pile, moving the arrows. However they move, their motions are noted carefully, and interpreted according to the question being asked.

The great American expert on games, Stewart Culin, believed that both card games and Chess were derived from arrow divination. Culin pointed out that the national game of Korea, known as *Nyout*, uses sticks about eight inches in length instead of conventional dice. On the fifteenth day of each month, the game was used for divination, and books, titled *The Correct Planet Rule* were sold, explaining the divinatory meaning of the numbers thrown in Nyout. The technical language used to describe the throws is archaic, being neither Chinese nor Korean, but of the 'mountain people to the west'. Culin stated that it was likely that the game was a formalization of arrow divination, the arrows being cast into the magic ring which had been orientated and consecrated according to the correct form. The form of the Nyout game board, which is the quartered square known as the *Holy City Plan* could well have been a diviner's board, with the divinatory results being marked on it by moving the counters around it until, at the end of the divination, their position was read off as the result. This was then compared with the book of results known as *The Correct Planet Rule*. In this way, it is somewhat comparable with the Chinese *I Ching*, and may have a common origin in arrow divination. Culin also believed that there is a connection between arrow divination and playing cards. He noted that traditional Korean playing cards, which are narrow strips rather than the broad rectangles commonly used in most of the world, bear a picture of an arrow on their backs, a relic of ancient divination. Culin believed that the Korean 'cards' were the origin of Chinese playing cards, whose patterns reproduce those of ancient paper money.

Arrows were used for divination also in pre-Islamic Arabia. The Ka'aba at Mecca, the most holy shrine of Islam, is the site of a pre-Mohammedan sanctuary which formerly contained the image of a god brought there from Hit in Iraq. This image, known as Hubal, was surrounded by a circle of 360 lesser images, all of which were destroyed by Mohammed when he took over the place of power. In Pagan times, to settle disputes or to make important decisions, lots were drawn before the image of Hubal. The form of divination employed used seven arrows known as the *Qidh*, a technique employed at several other shrines of the pre-Islamic deities of ancient Arabia, including Ilumqah and Ta'lab. The guardian of the Mecca shrine (known as the *sadin*) shuffled the arrows. In ancient Arabia, seven arrows were used for divination, and also in the betting game known as *Maysar*. Here, the two versions – sacred divination and profane gambling – were distinguished only by the location, the divination taking place at a sacred shrine. When used for divination, the arrows had certain words written upon them, which could affirm or deny ownership, the success of a venture, paternity or other important issues. Arrow oracles were also used to find water. They were then shuffled at the sites and when the 'water' arrow appeared, so did water.

Rods, wands and staves

This form of divination, using seven arrows, sticks or rods, appears to be identical with the form known today as the *Saxon Wands* or *Saxon Rods*, and occasionally, mistakenly, as *runes*. The earliest known versions of these are Scandinavian stave almanacs, which consisted of seven long flat pieces of wood pierced at one end and tied together with a leather thong. Thirteen of the fourteen sides were inscribed with *wend-runes*, (written from right to left), signifying the 28 days of the lunar month, the whole array representing a quarter of the year. As for each quarter, each 'moon' had a specific name and quality. The use of these calendar staves in divination provided a useful lunar oracle. The modern versions of this seven-stave oracular calendar are simplified, without the wend-rune inscriptions. They exist in several forms, and are readily made. They can range from expertly carved symbolic rods of similar length to plain pieces of wood with different lengths which distinguish one sort from another. Their number is always seven. In the simplest form of divination with the Saxon Wands, three shorter and four longer rods are employed. One of the longer rods is distinguished from the others by some sort of marking, or is painted another colour. This is the main wand, known variously as the Master Rod, the Witan Wand or the Agreement Rod.

These rods may be cast according to a ceremonial form, similar to, but less complex than the rune-casting described in Chapter 4. After appropriate self-composure by the caster, and asking the question to which an answer is required, the Master Rod is laid on the ground, oriented north–south, and

11. *The astronomical imagery of the spindle and distaff was a powerful symbol in the northern tradition.* Left: *An eighteenth century* Sinterklaas-Gebärck, *(Yuletide Biscuit) from East Frisia. These traditional designs, moulded from carved wood blocks, contain Pagan imagery. This one has the goddess Freya or Bertha, bearing distaff and spindle and with the lunar horns on her head.* Right: *A medieval mural from Hallingdal, Norway, showing the Lord and Lady of the Elder Faith, surrounded by stars. The Lady holds spindle and distaff aloft to the heavens whilst her male consort tills the earth with a mattock (see p. 29/30).*

the other rods are cast over it, allowing them to slide through the fingers so that only one is retained. Excluding the Master Rod, if more short rods than long ones are on the ground, then reading is a negative answer to the question. If more long rods are on the ground, the answer is positive. If any rod is in contact with the Master Rod, then the answer is unqualified. Conversely, of some rods are resting on others, and not in contact with the ground, this indicates uncertainty. The orientation of the Master Rod is important, for it is along the *Sacred Axis*, the primary direction of prayer of the Elder Faith of northern Europe. If all of the other rods come down pointing towards this rod, and hence to the Sacred Axis, then the resolution of the question will be within the power of the caster or the querent for whom the caster is operating. If they are in alignment with the Master Rod, then it is a matter for the Fates.

There is a more complex variant of this divinatory system. Here, each of the rods is assigned a name and a character. The rods are divided into two genders, and the Seventh (the equivalent of the Master Rod) is here given androgynous qualities. The rods are numbered alternately, beginning with a male rod known as First or *Cæghierd*, the Key-Holder. The first female counterpart has equal status and is called Other, *Scurfoga*, the Rainbow.

The other male rods are called Third and Fifth, having the names *Wyn* (Joy), and *Hærfest* (Festivity). The other two female rods are Fourth, *Guthcwen* (Warrior-Queen), and Sixth, *Halignes* (Holiness). The last rod, Seventh, is called *Radnes*, Agreement. There is sometimes an eighth rod in this, the more complex, system, which is unnumbered, and shaped like a serpent. This is *Dethwic*, Darkness, the principle of negativity, which in certain readings has an influence over the meanings of the other wands. As with all systems of divination, there are is a complete array of numerical and symbolic correspondences in both of these versions of the Saxon Wands. Each of them can be assigned to a day of the week, a divine power, a time of day and a compass direction, and used in divination accordingly.

The last fully-fledged Pagan usage in Europe was in the lands bordering the Baltic, where in Lithuania, the final temple was extirpated in 1386. The Temple of Svantovit on the holy island of Rügen was destroyed by the Danish king Valdemar I in 1169 during his war against the Pagan Wends. Before this, the Wendish shrine kept a white horse sacred to the god, which none but the priest was allowed to ride. This was used in spear divination, which is closely allied to both the arrows and the Saxon Rods. The shrine of the god Triglav at Stattin (Sczezin, Poland) had a sacred black stallion, and a similar horse was kept at the other chief Wendish holy place, Rethra. When the priests wished to know the god's will, they laid spears on the ground. At Rethra, two crossed spears were used; three pairs at Ancona; and nine laid in a row at Stettin. The horse went to the spears, and was watched to see if his hooves touched them, and whether he stepped over them with left or right hoof first, each of which movements had a specific interpretation.

The broomstick or besom was once used for divination, as its symbolism encodes several important principles. In an article title 'Broomsticks', published in the magazine *Albion* in 1979, High Priestess Prudence Jones explained the symbolism:

The staff of the broomstick is traditionally made of Ash, sacred to the World Goddess, although this was later taken over by Woden Allfather. Its twigs are from three trees: Birch, for purification; Hazel, for initiation; and Rowan, for healing. They are bound with Willow.

In the Bardic tradition, the besom has a relation to the ancient Ogham alphabet, which is based on the twigs and branches of sacred trees (see Chapter 4). It is known as the *Dasgubell Rodd*, the *gift besom* which sweeps away that which conceals the truth. The ancient Welsh Bardic work known as *The Book of Symbols* gives the following text:

Question   What is the Dasgubell Rodd?
Answer   The key to the primitive Coelbren.
Question   What is it that explains the primitive Coelbren?
Answer   The Dasgubell Rodd.
Question   What else?
Answer   The secret of the Dasgubell Rodd.
Question   What secret?
Answer   The secret of the Bards of Britain.

In Bardic tradition, the besom or broomstick is the key to an encoded mystery, the *Coelbren* which may be interpreted as a literal cryptographic key, or as the mystical, symbolic grasp of the entire mystery. The composition of the besom from various woods, having certain canonical dimensions has a direct connection with Oghams and runic staves, making the besom, like the knotted strings of the Peruvian Incas known as *quipu*, readable in a direct as well as a symbolic way.

Yarrowstalks and the Book of Changes

One of the major methods of divination used in Chinese culture is the consultation of the *I Ching*, the *Book of Changes*. The principle used is the formation of *hexagrams*, patterns of six long or broken lines or stems, 64 of which are possible. The principle is similar to that of divinatory geomancy, being patterns created by binary combinations.

The diviner starts with 50 stalks of the Yarrow plant (also known in English as Millfoil – 'a thousand leaves'). These are used similarly to the arrows of many cultures or the Saxon

12. *The board of the Korean game of* Nyout *is the classic fourfold division of the world around the sacred centre, 20 outer places surrounding the central nine. This 29-fold division of space occurs also in the Anglo-Saxon runes (see p. 38).*

Wands. One is removed at once, leaving 49 (seven by seven), a square number which is of recurrent significance in sacred geometry and certain board games. The 49 are then divided randomly into two piles, and then each group has four stalks removed at a time until three, two, one or no stalks remain. The diviner counts the stalks, and produces a line, either solid or broken, taking notice of the actual numbers generated, which have further effects. This manipulation is conducted a further five times, until a hexagram is formed. Taking account of the inherent effects noted above, it is occasionally necessary to create another hexagram. The appropriate hexagram is then read off against the book, and, according to the nature of the question, the answer is obtained. An alternative method uses three coins. Some practitioners use nineteenth century Chinese *cash* coins, which were originally ordinary currency, but which are sold now by occult suppliers for oracular puposes. Any coins will do, as long as there are distinguishable obverse and reverse ('head' and 'tail') sides. The divination is conducted by concentrating oneself in the usual manner, and casting the coins onto any convenient flat surface. The coins are tossed six times, totalling the mystic number eighteen, which we will meet again. 'Heads' are taken as positive, whilst 'tails' are negative. If three heads are cast, this is a *Moving Yang* line, drawn as a single line. Two 'heads' and a 'tail' are a weak line. Similarly, three 'tails' are a *Moving Yin* line, drawn as a broken line. As in old Chinese writing, the lines are accumulated from the bottom up.

It is important to note when comparing the hexagrams of the *I Ching* with the *tetragrams* of western divinatory geomancy that in the *I Ching*, even numbers produce a solid line, whereas in the variant form of western geomantic notation, a solid line represents the even number, and a single point the odd.

The sacred pathway

Every religious system has within it in greater or lesser measure the concept of spiritual evolution, and this has been depicted in various ways. The image of the ladder or stairway to heaven is an important archetype upon which much psychological research has been conducted. It has been the subject of religious art, has added to the repertoire of architectural ornament, as at Bath Abbey, and is inherent in many visionary experiences. Seemingly profane, but directly related to this image is the game of Snakes and Ladders. This western game is a modification of the ancient Indian game of *Moksha-Patamu*, whose grid is very similar in appearance to contemporary representations of the planets, the signs of the zodiac and the constellations, where the eight-petalled flower representing the sun is at the centre. In India, the game is one of religious instruction, which may be the remains of a form of divination. In the West, it is purely a game of play. As a game, *Moksha-Patamu*, or the Game of Heaven and Hell displays the law of the unity of opposites in this world, and that of right actions. In this game, right actions, known as *pap* are denoted by a ladder, signifying spiritual evolution, whilst wrong actions – *punya* – are denoted by a snake. The ladder leads to virtue, and upward reincarnation, whilst the snake leads to downfall, and reincarnation in animal form. Many of the squares bear images of deities and demons, animals and constellations. Descent along the snake is always from the head towards the tail.

In some versions of *Moksha-Patamu* there are 100 squares,

and either ascent or descent is from specific squares, whose numbers relate symbolically to vice or virtue. In the 100 square version, ascent is gained from square 12, signifying faith; 51, reliability; 57, generosity; 76, knowledge; 78, self-denial. Descent falls from square 41, which is disobediance; 44, vanity; 49, vulgarity; 52, theft; 58, lying; 62, drunkenness; 69, debt; 73, murder; 84, anger; 92, greed; 95, pride; and 99, lust. The worst evils are at squares 73 and 99, and sins outnumber virtues. A larger version has 24 snakes and only nine ladders. This is divided into panels with 40, 48, 7, 8 and 40 spaces respectively, 143 in all.

The whole game is highly redolent of the Cosmic Axis mythos, with the serpent coiling around the axial tree, or shaman's pole (see Chapter 6). As a race game, where two or more opponents attempt to be the first to get their piece or pieces to the end, *Moksha-Patamu* and Snakes and Ladders are related to one game which is earlier in origin and another which is later. The earlier game's name is now lost, but several original boards, discovered during archaeological excavations, are known. It is a race along a board in the form of a spiral snake, now known as the Egyptian Serpent Game. Information on the game exists in a wall-painting in an Egyptian tomb of the third dynasty (*c.* 2700 BCE), which shows it with a box in which there are six sets of marbles and figures of animals. An alabaster board from Meheu, Egypt, now in the Fitzwilliam Museum in Cambridge, has 125 points or 'stations' between the beginning and the serpent's head, which is at the centre of the board. It is not known whether the direction of play was from the centre to the outside, the direction of 'sliding' in *Moksha-Patamu*. Points 19, 44, 51, 65 and 84 have cross-hatching. In Indian board games, crosses on squares denote places where pieces are immune from capture, a parallel would be the hatched areas on the Egyptian Serpent Game.

The other related game in the pastime goes under the grand title of The Royal and Most Pleasant Game of the Goose, known as the Game of Goose for short. It forms a link between medieval symbolism, the unicursal labyrinth, and modern race games. Invented in Florence, the Game of Goose is another race game, played with dice. It was devised or developed from an earlier race game in the 1570s. Francesco de Medici of Florence (1574–87) is known to have sent a set to

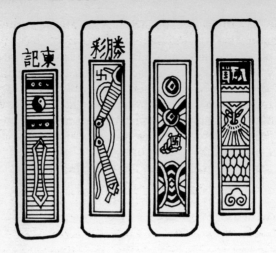

13. *Classic oriental playing cards, such as these* Kwan P'ai *are long strips which Stewart Culin believed were derived from arrow divination (see p. 38).*

King Philip II of Spain, hence its 'Royal' epithet. After this publicity, the game spread rapidly through Europe. One June 16, 1597, John Wolfe entered the game in the Stationers' Register in London, a sort of early copyrighting of the game in England.

Like *Moksha-Patamu*, the Game of Goose has certain squares or spaces distinguished from the rest. When a playing piece falls on one of these, certain penalties are due. Goose has 63 points arranged in a spiral, like the Egyptian Serpent Game. Various versions of the Royal Game of Goose are known, but all use an anticlockwise spiral with 63 points or stations. Each player is provided with a marker and 20 counters (making 42 in all), and two dice are used. In Goose, there are a number of important points, distinguished by pictures. Points 14, 18, 23, 27, 32, 36, 41, 45, 50, 54 and 59 have a picture of a goose. When a piece lands on a goose. When a piece lands on a goose, the value of the dice throw is doubled, and the piece is moved accordingly. If a piece lands on point 6, which has a picture of a bridge, the player must pay a toll and then go to point 12. On point 9 and point 11, certain dice must be thrown to continue. Square 19 has an ale house, when the player must pay one token; whilst on 31, there is a well, where the piece is delayed two turns. On square 42 is a maze, an indication of other, more esoteric connections. Landing here, the player's piece must go back 13 spaces to point 29. Point 52 is the prison house, where a forfeit must be paid for release, and on 58 is death, which results in the player having to start again at the beginning. The player reaching point 63 first, by an exact score, is the winner. This number, 63, was held to be the culmination point in a person's life, the summation of the *Seven Ages*, each of which comprised nine years' duration.

There are several similarities between the Egyptian Serpent Game, *Moksha-Patamu* and the Game of Goose, which may or may not be coincidental. In the Game of Goose, the number nine is important. There are 63 (seven by nine) points on the board. In addition to point 9, points 18, 27, 36, 45 and 54, the multiples of 9 are all marked with something. All except point 9 itself have a goose, and a goose is on every square 5 points on from each of 18, 27, 36, 45 and 54. Points 52 and 58 in Goose are harmful positions on which to land, and these numbers are among the snake squares in *Moksha-Patamu*. Point 84 is a snake square, and 51 a ladder square. These are two of the five hatched squares in the Egyptian Serpent Game. The shorter version of *Moksha-patamu* has 11 snake squares, whilst the Game of Goose has 11 goose points.

In the Game of Goose, station number 42 is called *The Labyrinth*, and here the player unfortunate enough to land on it is delayed. The number 42, (seven by six) is an important mystic number, being the number of the Judges of the Dead in the Egyptian *Book of the Dead*. They had to decide whether the judged soul was innocent of 42 specific sins. 42 is the number of Biblical generations from Adam to Christ. The *Wild Huntsmen* of Odin numbered 42, and Odin himself had 42 by-names. The German antiquary and landscape researcher Josef Heinsch, who deciphered the meaning of the medieval cosmographic mosaic in St Viktor's Cathedral at Xanten in the Rhineland, refers to the number in the astrological poem known as the 'Grimnismal' in the *Edda*. 'In the northern tradition of ancient revealed wisdom,' he wrote, 'there remained a knowledge of a 42-stage descent and re-ascent from the heavenly to the earthly.' Labyrinth symbolism is certainly within this area.

Some English examples of the Game of Goose have an

illustration of what appears to be a turf maze at station 42, whilst continental ones often have a rectilinear maze or a sort of mountain path. Appropriately, and without reference to this, Heinsch showed that the number 42 is the number measuring the *Holy Hill*. This mountain path is reminiscent of the Christian tradition of constructing the Stations of the Cross along established mountain pathways, or even whole new pathways, to make Calvary Mountains. Here, small shrines containing images of Christ's passion are arranged at intervals along a steep pathway, with a chapel containing images of the crucifixion at the top. Pilgrimages to Calvaries take place each Good Friday, when the devout worship at each image in turn, retracing the travails of Jesus.

If they ever existed, Calvaries are no longer extant in Britain, but in many Catholic countries, they are still used by the devout. Calvaries originated in northern Italy, the first being constructed at Varallo in 1491, about a century before the Game of Goose was popularized. When the Game of Goose was popularized, it was the era when Calvary construction was in full swing, such as the famous examples at Orta (1583) and Varese (1604). Perhaps the Game of Goose was a secularization of these Calvaries, using in a new way the

14. *Consulting the rune-staves in ancient Scandinavia (see p. 39).*

popular theme of visiting various stations at which certain events would take place. In the Game of Goose, some of these stations are hazards, and many Calvaries' designers introduced deliberately difficult sections, such as steep or precarious pathways. Of course, to make the *Via Dolorosa* of Christ into a board game would have been unthinkable blasphemy in 1600, and would have received the immediate attention of the Inquisition, but the similarity between the Calvary and the Game of Goose must have some connection.

The Game of Goose was the forerunner of many later race games which were most popular in the nineteenth century. Among these are the English Royal Game of the Gathering of the Nations, commemorating the Great Exhibition in London in 1851; the Dutch *Tramway Spel* (*c.* 1864), where horse-drawn tramcars, then the latest modern advance in urban transportation, race one another; and Up to the Klondyke, cashing in on the gold fever of the Yukon at the end of the nineteenth century. Even in a secularized form, these games still attempt to reflect the ups and downs of life.

3

MICROCOSMIC OR DIVINATORY GEOMANCY

Geomancy is an art of divination, whereby the judgement may be rendered by lot or destiny, to every question of everything whatsoever ...

H. C. Agrippa

The term *geomancy* refers to two distinct but connected arts or sciences. One use of the term is the technique described here, the use of 16 mathematically related configurations of dots, seeds, stones or other available units to answer questions, make decisions and foretell the future. The other usage of the term *geomancy* refers to inspection of the surface of the earth for divinatory purposes or the placement of human artefacts in relation to one another, the cardinal directions, and the features of the landscape. The earliest uses of the word *geomancy* by Latin writers are applied to inspection of patterns in the earth. This form includes the Chinese art of placement known as *Feng-Shui*, Indian *Vastuvidya* and the arts of ancient European *locators*. This aspect of geomancy is dealt with in detail in Chapter 5.

Literally translated, the word *geomancy* means divination by earth, from the Greek words μαια (Gaia, the Earth Goddess) and μαντεια (divination). The inference of the word is at once twofold: it is divination by *means* of earth, and by the *agency* of Gaia, the goddess who is the planet. Although it is thought that originally microcosmic or divinatory geomancy was conducted by throwing handfuls of earth onto the ground and examining the patterns formed there, for many centuries it has involved the casting of objects, such as beans, grains, stones and shells, creating patterns in the dust with a stick or with a pencil on paper, or using special apparatus and even, in modern times, printed cards showing the figures.

Divination by geomancy has various national or cultural divisions across Africa, Europe and part of Asia. It is believed to have originated in forms of Arabian sand divination, and to have spread into Africa with Islamic expansionism and thence into Europe, though its mathematical basis could well have ancient Egyptian or Greek origin. The present word *geomancy* was first applied to this form of divination by the twelfth century translator Hugh of Santalla, who was reporting on the Arab practice. Before that, geomancy referred to other means of divination by and on the earth. One fascinating fragment which indicates an ancient Greek knowledge of the art is the report that during the siege of Syracuse, the great geometer Archimedes (278–212 BCE) created figures in the sand to foresee or affect the outcome of the battle. This may have been a sort of *psammomancy*, a divination by geometry, or a forerunner of the classical divinatory geomancy described here. Perhaps, like many great systems, divinatory geomancy as we know it is a masterly synthesis of various distinct elements.

Divinatory geomancy is an oracular system which gives the person who asks it a question an insight into present or future conditions. It is based upon the formation of certain patterns, which have a name and a meaning which can be interpreted either by itself or in combination with others. These patterns, or *geomantic figures*, are composed of four lines which may have either one or two dots, points, or stars. Sometimes, they are drawn using a straight line for two points and a dot for one. The points may also be connected to produce geomantic sigils. There are 16 possible geomantic figures. These are:

Populus

Via

Tristitia

Laetitia

Fortuna Major

∴
∴

Fortuna Minor

·
∴

Acquisitio

∴
·

Amissio

·
∴

Puella

·
∴

Puer

·
∴

Carcer

∴
·

Conjunctio

∴
·

Albus

∴
∴

Rubeus

∴
∴

Caput Draconis

·
∴

Cauda Draconis

∴
·

There are only 16 figures, the maximum possible when combining odd and even in this way. Traditionally, the top line is referred to as the head, the second as the neck, the third as the body and the fourth as the feet. Each of these figures possesses a quality reflected by its name, and a relationship to other figures depending on its place in the sequence of generation.

The paraphernalia of divinatory geomancy

The full method of divinatory geomancy involves several

procedures in sequence which produce a number of figures, all of which may be taken into account when interpreting the whole divination. The equipment used in geomantic divination ranges from sand or earth to pen and paper. The method considered most authentic by many practitioners is the use of a square box containing a shallow layer of dry earth or sand brought from an inland place (thus containing no salt, as would seaside sand). Like any magical equipment, the materials are consecrated according to the rites of whichever system the practitioner belongs to. Western magic of the present day invokes the elementals of the Earth, and the planetary spirit concerned with the subject matter of the question, whilst traditional Pagans associate geomancy with the Earth Mother Gaia or any other of her many names.

In this sand, marks are made at random with a stick, and the figures generated that way. Pricking paper or a wooden board with a sharp bodkin is an alternative method derived from the use of sand. The traditional African equipment is a board, often carved with magical symbols and images of certain gods, including Ifa and Eshu, upon which the figures are made by casting palm nuts and recording the figures in flour or termite

15. The Chinese Emperor Fou Hi (2000 BCE), who is believed to have formalized the eight trigrams and the 64 hexagrams used in Yarrowstalk divination (see p. 42).

dust. Sometimes a slate and chalk are used. In Madagascar, the geomantic system known as *Sikidy* uses seeds of the *Fano* tree (a species of Acacia) which are thrown into small enclosures made in the dust of the ground. The use of beans was formerly widespread in Europe, but the most popular for many centuries has been with pen, ink and paper.

The binary mathematics underlying the creation of geomantic figures lends itself to any method of determining oddness or evenness at random. Modern geomantic diviners have drawn stones or marbles at random from a bag or bowl, recording the odd or even numbers as a single point or two points, respectively. Finally, it is possible to use objects which have not been designed expressly for geomantic divination. Dice, whose original use was divinatory, atuomatically produce odd or even numbers. Although their use in Europe is not common, Islamic *Raml* has a version which uses special geomantic dice.

In addition to dice, there are several ways of casting and counting dominoes to produce geomantic figures. Although their origin remains unrecorded, it is possible that dominoes originated as a formalized means of geomantic divination. The common British dominoes are numbered only up to double six, but in central Europe, dominoes numbered up to double eight are used, which can be used appropriately to read off pairs of geomantic figures. Central European dominoes are numerically related to the 16 figures of geomantic divination. A complete set of 'eight-point' dominoes has 45 stones, 9 doubles and contains a total of 360 points, all significant numbers in traditional lore. Perhaps nearest to the earliest forms of geomantic divination is the reading of such symbols, or their many variations, from cracks in the ground or even the pavement or floor! This last method, however, involves no manipulation, being direct observation and interpretation of pre-existent patterns, and perhaps ought to be classified with those forms of divination in which shapes are perceived.

The meanings of the geomantic figures

Each of the 16 geomantic figures has a name and attributes. In European divinatory geomancy, these names are in Latin. In

Hebrew geomancy, the figures' names are nearly all the direct equivalents of the Latin forms used today, but in west Africa, the names are less generalized, and reflect more specific ailments or benefits.

The European names and meanings are as follows:

Populus: an assembly, the people, union, society, crowd, gang, congregation. This figure has a mutable character, sometimes good and sometimes bad, depending on circumstance. Ruled by the waning side of the Moon's cycle, the west and night.

Via: path, way, street, highway, journey, direction, ways and means, the way of (one's) life. Affects other good figures unfavourably, but is beneficial when the question concerns journeys. Ruled by the waxing side of the lunar cycle, the east and day.

Tristitia: sadness, misery, melancholy, humiliation, diminution, poverty, damnation, the bad side of all things, change for the worse, the-world-turned-upside-down, severity, debauchery. Also, seemingly unconnected, but with reference to Saturn, cities, earthworks and fortification. Tristitia is a bad figure.

Laetitia: joy, delight, gladness, beauty, grace, sanity, health, matters of the head, bearded. A very good geomantic figure.

Fortuna Major: the Greater Fortune, good luck, fortune, safeguard, success, victory, property, position in society, entry. Ruled by the Sun during its daylight period. An extremely good figure.

Fortuna Minor: the Lesser Fortune, external aid, protection. Ruled by the Sun at night. Beneficial, but not as good as Fortuna Major.

Acquisitio: acquisition, extension of existing property, success, absorption, profit and gain, receipt as the result of a request or investigation. A figure of great benefit.

Amissio: loss, taken away, loss through death, theft, bankruptcy. A bad figure.

Puella: a girl, daughter, young wife, nurse, pleasant, pure, clean, immaculate. Unfortunate figure, as beneficial external appearances may hide an underlying harmfulness.

Puer: a boy, son, servant, employee, beardless, rash, inconsiderate, liberal, a fighter. A malevolent figure, except in combat or love.

Carcer: a prison, cell, enclosure, confinement, arrest, delay, servitude, bondage. If Carcer, a malevolent figure, appears in the first house, the chart is to be destroyed, and no divination attempted that day.

Conjunction: uniting, connection, recovery of lost things, gathering together, reunion, collection, treaties, contracts, marriage. Conjunction is on the positive side of neutral.

Albus: white, fair, dazzling beauty, illumination, wisdom, sagaciousness, profitable. Good in business and entering somewhere.

Rubeus: redness, passion, vice, temper, destructive fire, bad omen, a stop sign, slaughter, rape. An extremely bad figure.

Caput Draconis: the Dragon's Head, in astrology, the northern node of the Moon, an entrance, the upper threshold, the upperworld,

Cauda Draconis: the Dragon's Tail, the exit, the underworld, harbinger of evil and disaster. An extremely bad figure.

Geomantic divination – the technique

Firstly, as in all divinations, a state of meditation, prayer or mental calm must be attained. Many occult writers including Gerard of Cremona and H.C. Agrippa have warned against undertaking divination in unfavourable conditions. These

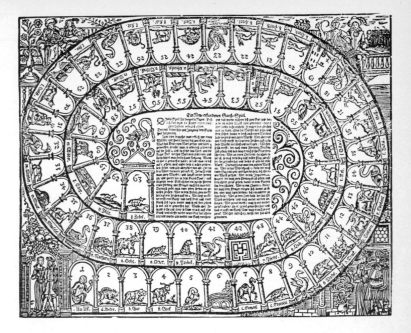

16. *A seventeenth-century woodcut of the* Ganss-Spiel *(Game of Goose) from Germany. In Goose, the direction of progress is anticlockwise from the outside towards the middle. Boards of the Egyptian Serpent Game are also coiled in this direction (see text p. 46).*

include certain states of the weather: windy, stormy or rainy days; certain states of mind, such as being disturbed by anger or cares; and certain 'negative influences' – people whom Gerard called 'tempters or deriders'. As with the runes, tarot cards and other methods of divination, erecting geomantic figures should never be undertaken as a joke or out of frivolous motives, or the results may be more than the joker bargained for.

Before anything is done, the questioner should think seriously of what the question is that is to be put to the oracle. If paper is being used, this question should be written out. Then, keeping the question in mind, a line of dots is made on the paper (or in the sand, etc.), rapidly, without counting. This is repeated until 16 lines of dots are present. The number of dots in each line is then counted and recorded. Where there are an odd number of dots in the line, a single dot is indicated for the final figure, and when an even number, two dots. The results of the first four lines are the south figure; the next four the east; the third four, the north; and the last four, the west. These are known as the four *mother* figures. From these four *mothers*, four further figures, known as *daughters*, are constructed. The topmost point of the first *mother* becomes the 'head' or top point of the first *daughter*, the 'head' or first row of the second figure becomes the 'neck' of the first *daughter*, the 'head' of the third *mother* becomes the 'body' of the first *daughter*, and the head of the fourth *mother* becomes the 'feet' of the first *daughter*. The second row of points of the four *mothers* likewise become the second *daughter*, the third row, the third *daughter*, and the fourth row the last *daughter*.

When the *daughters* have been formed, four further figures, known as the *nephews* are generated. The first *nephew* is derived by adding the corresponding points of the first two *mothers* together, and the second one by adding the other two *mothers*. The manner of generating the figure is the same as with the counting of the original dots: even = two dots; odd = one dot. The final two *nephews* add the first two *daughters* for the third *nephew*, and *daughters* three and four for the last one. We now have 12 geomantic figures. Finally, two *witnesses* are generated. The first *nephew* is added to the second *nephew* to make the first *witness*, and the second *witness* is derived from the other two *nephews*. The final figure commonly erected is the *judge*, created by the addition of the two *witnesses*. Occasionally, if the divination produces an ambiguous result, then another figure, the *reconciler* can be erected by adding the first *mother* to the *judge*.

The mathematics of geomantic divination are such that the *judge* can only be one of eight figures, which are Acquisitio, Amissio, Carcer, Conjunctio, Fortuna Major, Fortuna Minor, Populus, or Via, whose total of dots add up to four, six or eight

Example: the generation of geomantic figures.

Row	Points or marks	odd or even	Figure
1	••••••••••••••••••••••••	odd	•
2	••••••••••••••	even	• •
3	••••••••••••••	odd	•
4	••••••••••••••	even	• •

The figure generated here is Amissio.
When repeated a further three times, the four *mothers* might be:

	Amissio	Caput Draconis	Populus	Albus
1	•	• •	• •	• •
2	• •	•	• •	• •
3	•	•	• •	•
4	• •	•	• •	• •

The *daughters* are generated from the *mothers*, *daughter* number one from row one, and so on, giving:

	Laetitia	Rubeus	Puer	Rubeus
1	•	• •	•	• •
2	• •	•	•	•
3	• •	• •	• •	• •
4	• •	• •	•	• •

The *nephews* are generated from the *mothers* and the *daughters*, by addition. First two *mothers*:

	Amissio		Caput Draconis			Puer
1	•	plus	• •	make	odd	•
2	• •		•		odd	•
3	•		•		even	• •
4	• •		•		odd	•

The first *nephew* is therefore *Puer*.
By the same method, the other three *nephews* are derived, making the four *nephews*:

	Puer	Albus	Fortuna Minor	Carcer
1	•	• •	•	•
2	•	• •	•	• •
3	• •	•	• •	• •
4	•	• •	• •	•

The two *witnesses* are derived by addition of the *nephews*: the first *witness* from the first two *nephews*, and the other one from the last two:

```
1    •        •
2    •        •
3    •       • •
4    •        •
    Via     Puer
```

Finally, the *judge* comes from the two *witnesses*, by addition:

```
1   • •
2   • •
3    •
4   • •
   Albus
```

If a *reconciler* were required, it would be by addition of the *judge* to the first *mother*:

```
1     •              • •              •
2    • •    plus     • •    make     • •
3     •               •              • •
4    • •             • •             • •
   Amissio         Albus          Laetitia
```

The whole geomantic divination should be drawn up in a diagram. As with all systems of divination or play, interpretation of the disposition of the figures is the difficult and essential part without which the whole exercise would be useless. There are two basic systems commonly in use. The first takes the final figure produced, the *judge* as the answer to the question. This is tempered by the two *witnesses* which produced the *judge*, whose examination may show more subtle of Geomancy.

The greater Fortune.	The lesser Fortune.	Solis.
Via.	Populus.	Lunæ.
Acquisitio.	Lætitia.	Jovis. ♃
Puella.	Amissio.	Veneris. ♀
Conjunctio.	Albus.	Mercurii. ☿
Puer.	Rubeus.	Martis. ♂
Carcer.	Tristitia.	Saturni. ♄
♌ Dragons head.	♑ Dragons taile.	

B 2

17. *The 16 figures of divinatory geomancy according to Agrippa, from his* Fourth Book of Occult Philosophy, *published in London in 1655.*

elements underlying the final 'judgement'. If these do not give clarity, then the *reconciler* may be resorted to for further information.

Alternative methods

Because human beings have always tired of complicated procedures, and want fast results, more rapid, mechanical, methods of creating geomantic figures were developed. Among these are cards, unknown before the twentieth century, and divining chains, a much older technique. Divining chains are a common feature of the west African forms of divinatory geomancy known as *Ifa*. In essence, this system is the same as classical western geomancy, but produces double figures which give 256 combinations instead of the 16 available using single figures. One of the *opele* or divining chain is a brass chain about a yard in length, upon which eight halves of the *opele (Schrebera golungensis)* pod are strung, with weights in the form of coins, talismans or beads on strings with a different number at each end of the chain. Alternative markers are used sometimes: shells of the seed of the *Oro* tree, the African Mango, or seeds of the *Apuraga* fruit. Additionally, artificial markers can be cast from various metals including brass, copper, gunmetal, iron, lead and silver. Sometimes, a rope strung with appropriate markers substitutes for the chain. Variant numbers are found in divination chains and strings from different cultural areas. One important variation has four strings bearing four markers, which produces at an instant the four *mother* figures.

The diviner is seated on a mat on the ground, and performs appropriate cleansing rituals and invocations of the god Ifa, the west African parallel of the European gods Hermes, Mercury and Odin, patrons of medicine, writing, divination and the spirits of the dead. The chain is flung in the air, and falls to the ground, giving a reading of so many shells upwards and so many downwards, the top and bottom of the figure being defined by the differing numbers of weights at each end.

Chains bearing charms of different types, such as the *charm bracelets* popular today in European countries can be used for this type of divination, and may well have originated in forms of divinatory geomancy now forgotten. At the time of the Roman Empire, divination markers or dice were often made in the shape of animals or human figures which could stand in several ways when thrown, giving different readings. The stylized images on charm bracelets are similarly useable. Even the Christian Rosary may have originated as a divination string, now used in prayerful devotions. The *Witches' Ladder*, a cord bearing 40 knots or the same number of beads is used by modern practitioners of Wicca for their meditational devotions. The red string or rope bearing nine knots, used in traditional Wiccan magic, is another present-day connection between the use of ropes or chains for divination and the construction cords of sacred geometry. Here, the cords have a close connection with the thread-spinning symbolism of the *Three Fates* or *Norns*. It is possible to use knot-tying of the

Populus	⠿	☽	▽	♋	N	𝄞𝄆𝄇𝄈	Monday Thursday n.	Moses
Via	⠇	☽	▽	♋	N	⯊⯊⯊⯊	Monday night	Abachim
Tristitia	⠒⠄	♄	△	♒	E	𝄆𝄆𝄆𝄆	Saturday	Jacob
Laetitia	⠂⠒	♃	▽	♓	N	⯊⯊⯊⯊	Thursday Sunday	Adam
Fortuna major	⠅	☉	△	♌	S	♀♀♀♀	Sunday	Noah
Fortuna minor	⠡	☉	△	♌	S	⯊⯊⯊⯊	Saturday n. Noon Thurs.	Mohammed
Acquisitio	⠌	♃	△	♐	S	𝄆🗙🗙🗙	Thursday	Ousmane
Amissio	⠡	♀	▽	♉	W	🗙🗙🗙🗙	Friday	Jesus
Puella	⠈⠡	♀	△	♎	E	♈‡♈♈	Friday Monday n.	Ladari
Puer	⠠⠄	♂	△	♈	E	♈‡♈♈	Tuesday	Jonah
Carcer	⠒⠄	♄	▽	♑	W	♀♀♀♀	Saturday Wed. n.	Solomon
Conjunctio	⠒⠂	☿	▽	♍	W	▯𝄆𝄇⊕	Wednesday Sat. n.	Ali
Albus	⠂⠒	☿	△	♊	E	♀♀♀♀	Wednesday Saturday	Idris
Rubeus	⠒⠂	♂	▽	♏	N	𝄆𝄆𝄆𝄆	Tuesday Friday n.	Amar
Caput draconis	⠒	♃♀	▽	☊	W	♀♀♀♀	Friday	Madi
Cauda draconis	⠠	♄♂	△	☋	S	△△△△	Tuesday	Lassima al-Houssein

18. Diagram of geomantic correspondences. Left to right columns: Name of
figure; geomantic figure; planetary attribute; element; astrological sign;
quarter of the earth; alternative sigils derived from geomantic figures;
corresponding days; corresponding Jewish and Islamic prophets.

traditional witches' cord in combination with geomantic
divination, the knots being distinguished from one another in
some way by the addition of coloured threads, ribbons, or
charms.

When used in magic, the witches' cord has nine knots, tied
according to a set ritual. Concentration whilst knotting the
rope is attained by chanting or singing certain ceremonial
words whilst the act is performed, and although the words
may alter from tradition to tradition, the following formula is
typical:

Knot
1 By knot of one, the spell's begun.
2 Knot of two, the spell comes true.
3 Knot of three, so must it be.
4 Knot of four, the power will store.
5 Knot of five, the spell's alive.
6 Knot of six, the spell to fix.
7 Knot of seven, the power to leaven.
8 Knot of eight, ties up the fate.
9 Knot of nine, what's done is mine.

Connections with astrology

The alternative method which relates divinatory geomancy directly to astrology dispenses with the *witnesses* and the *judge*, and lays the remaining 12 geomantic figures out on a chart of the astrological houses. There are propitious times for performing geomantic divination. These depend upon the nature of the question being asked, and its planetary ruler(s), which will determine the most appropriate planetary hours for the performance of the divination. All magical systems are based upon the law of correspondences, and the 16 geomantic figures are no exception. They have been assigned correspondences with astrological signs, planets and planetary spirits. Although several systems of correspondence have been used over the years, the system most popular today is that employed by the Hermetic Order of the Golden Dawn. This was derived by S.L. McGregor Mathers from *Theomagia* by John Heydon (1664), and has been described by Israel Regardie and others:

Figure	Element	Zodiac sign	Planet	Spirit
Populus	water	Cancer	Moon	Chasmodai
Via	water	Cancer	Moon	Chasmodai
Tristitia	air	Aquarius	Saturn	Zazel
Laetitia	water	Pisces	Jupiter	Hismael
Fortuna Major	fire	Leo	Sun	Sorath
Fortuna Minor	fire	Leo	Sun	Sorath
Acquisitio	fire	Sagittarius	Jupiter	Hismael
Amissio	earth	Taurus	Venus	Kedemel
Puella	air	Libra	Venus	Kedemel
Puer	fire	Aries	Mars	Bartzabel
Carcer	earth	Capricorn	Saturn	Zazel
Conjunctio	earth	Virgo	Mercury	Taphthartharath
Albus	air	Gemini	Mercury	Taphthartharath
Rubeus	water	Scorpio	Mars	Bartzabel
Caput Draconis	earth	Caput Draconis	Jupiter/Venus	Kedemel/Hismael
Cauda Draconis	fire	Cauda Draconis	Saturn/Mars	Zazel/Bartzabel

The astrological house system

The fixed system of division of the heavens known as houses are the sectors of the twelvefold division of the heavens. Being based upon 12 and not 16 makes the direct reading of each house as a geomantic figure impossible, so it is traditional to use only the *mothers, daughters* and *nephews*. The 12 houses have their own qualities and character, and the position of planets in the sky can be described in terms of the house it occupies as well as the sign of the zodiac. The first house is situated on the left side of the chart, immediately below the eastern horizon, and the others succeed it counterclockwise. House 12 is just above the eastern horizon. The characters ascribed to the houses are as follows:

House	Quality and reference
First	The querent's own person, life, health, habits, behaviour, character.
Second	Property, money, wealth, personal worth, gain and loss.
Third	Relatives, sisters and brothers, communication, news, short trips, language.
Fourth	Home, male forebears, inheritance, possession, conclusion, including death.
Fifth	Reproduction, children, food, luxury, amusements, speculation.
Sixth	Aunts and uncles, sickness, employees, domestic animals.
Seventh	Love, marriage, partnerships, fornication and adultery, conflict, theft, dishonour.
Eighth	Death, pain, anxiety, wills, legacies, poverty.
Ninth	Voyages, long journeys, pilgrimage, science, faith, portents and auguries.
Tenth	Mother, rank, reputation, authority, fame and notoriety, worldly position.
Eleventh	Friends, acquaintances, hopes, patronage, philanthropy.
Twelfth	Fear, sadness, punishment, prisons, asylums, secret societies, espionage, hidden dangers, restrictions.

Each of the houses is assigned a figure created in the process of geomantic divination, and there are several ways of doing this. In astrological theory, the planetary qualities act upon

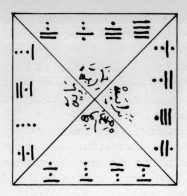

19. *Diagram showing the Islamic ascription of the directions, linking divinatory with locational geomancy.*

humans, the zodiac signs affect their modes of action, and the houses are the locations where their action is experienced. Being related to the planets and their tutelary spirits, the geomantic figures act and are interpreted in the houses as planets would be in true astrology. In geomantic divination, these are often drawn out in the square chart now obsolete in astrology, but equally the modern circular chart may be used.

In the Golden Dawn system, the first *mother* is entered into the tenth house. The second *mother* figure goes into the first house, and then the other two *mothers* counterclockwise in the angular houses (at right angles to the first two houses: houses 4 and 7). The *daughters* are placed in the succedent houses (the houses immediately counterclockwise of the first four, i.e. houses 2, 5, 8, 11). Finally, the *nephews* are entered in the cadent houses (the four unoccupied houses). The sequence is thus 10, 1, 4, 7, 11, 2, 5, 8, 12, 3, 6, 9. The two *witnesses*, the *reconciler* and the *judge* are omitted.

If the very harmful figures of Cauda Draconis or Rubeus occupy the first house or the ascendant, then the whole divination must be abandoned. Cauda Draconis or Rubeus in these positions are considered to portend the impending death of the querent. Amissio, Carcer and Via also generally portend bad things when they fall here, but they do not render the whole divination worthless.

Raml: Islamic divinatory geomancy

It is thought that the various local variants of divinatory geomancy as practised today have a common origin round the tenth century in Arab practice. Modern divinatory geomancy superseded the practice of *Raml*, and took over its name. This form of sand divination, otherwise *'ilm al-raml*, the science of sand, or psammomancy, is a technique where patterns formed randomly in sand are the indicators of the message. However, psammomancy is not very precise, and types of divination like that have usually been superseded by more understandable forms. The random patterns first produced in the sand were then joined up as appropriate to create forms which fitted in with some pre-arranged system, such as alphabetic, geometric or occult sigils. When modern geomantic divination arrived, the making of lines in the sand with a stick or the finger, the original practice of *Raml*, became the preliminary mark-making of divinatory geomancy. When the modern form of divinatory geomancy became associated with *Raml*, it seems to have been added to, and then superseded, a pre-existing system. The Arabs ascribed the origins of divinatory geomancy to the prophet Idris, who received the art by divine revelation from the Archangel Gabriel. Despite this ancient origin, the main practitioners of Islamic divinatory geomancy lived in the twelfth and thirteenth centuries, and it is through them that the art was transmitted to Europe by monkish translations from Arabic into European liturigical languages like Greek and Latin. Islamic divinatory geomancy lies within the mainstream of western occultism, having strong connections with astrology, alchemy and the other major arts.

The human body

In astrology, certain parts of the body are believed to be ruled by corresponding planets and signs of the zodiac. Various traditions extend these correspondences to metals, jewels, woods, herbs and colours. Similarly, in Islamic geomancy, each of the 16 geomantic figures has been allocated to the appropriate bodily organ. These can be used in divination to locate the seat of an illness, or in the creation of talismans to protect vulnerable parts of the body, as below:

Head	Laetitia
Neck	Rubeus
Right shoulder	Puella
Left shoulder	Puer
Right hand	Amissio
Left hand	Acquisitio
Right side of chest	Conjunctio
Left side of chest	Populus
Heart	Carcer
Stomach	Via
Solar plexus	Albus
Genitalia	Tristitia
Right thigh	Fortuna Major
Left thigh	Fortuna Minor
Right foot	Cauda Draconis
Left foot	Caput Draconis

Madagascar

A very important example of a meeting point between divinatory geomancy and the geomancy of landforms and placement is in the Vintana of Madagascar, where elements of African magic, Islamic divination, Malay religion and Chinese *Feng-Shui* were melded into a system unique to the island kingdom. Vintana, a word meaning 'fate', covers sophisticated local versions of ritual magic, astrology, the geomantic divination known as *Sikidy*, locational geomancy and the sacred divinatory board game called *Fanorona*.

The system of divinatory geomancy known as *Sikidy* is a very complex and sophisticated version of the art, having local names for the figures, and local meanings. *Sikidy* is seen as a manifestation of the supreme creator, Andriamanitra, acting through a chain of cause and effect. This is in keeping with the Islamic concept of the geomantic art, which is attributed to the prophet Idris as having been devised as a means of gaining knowledge of the will of Allah.

In Madagascar, the *mpsikidy*, or diviners, use the seeds of the

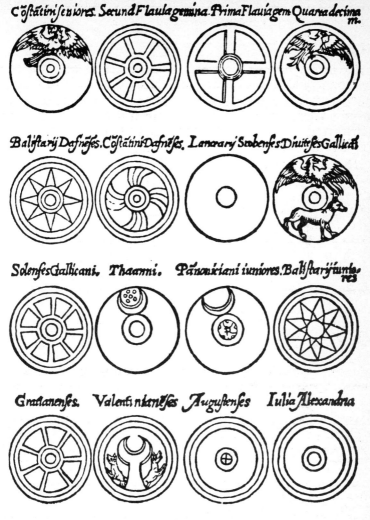

20. *The sixteen shields of the Thracian legions, used in divination. Illustration from* Notitia Dignitatum *by Guido Pancirolo, published at Lyon in 1608 (see p. 73).*

Fano tree, a species of Acacia, manipulated in a way similar to that of European divinatory geomancy, but setting the odd or even numbers of seeds in grids whose components are then added in certain fixed sequences to achieve the final result.

Madagascar's system of correspondences is one of the most sophisticated and complex to have survived in everyday use into quite recent times. Almost every aspect of time, place and name were related to one another. Unlike western astrology, in Madagascar the interaction of heavenly aspects with the specific day is very important.

Such a complex system required expert practitioners, and when the system was still intact, these were two further kinds in addition to the *mpsikidy*: the *mpanintana*, experts in astrology, and *mpanadro*, the 'day makers', practitioners in calendar lore and other matters. When a person's Vintana, the overall aspects of their life-situation and destiny, was being investigated, a consultation of both types of practitioner was required.

21. *There are many uninterpreted prehistoric inscriptions from all over the world. This disc of lignite (brown coal), found in Scotland by Ludovic MacLellan Mann, and dating from around 1000 BCE, bears a deliberate but undeciphered legend (see p. 77).*

In the western tradition, the days of the week are associated with and bear the names of various deities who are associated with planetary powers, colours, and qualities. The tradition of Madagascar has its own attributes of the each day of the week. These are taken into account when geomantic divination is undertaken.

Sunday	the appropriate day for everything white, especially white stones.
Monday	the day for everything green and blackish, grass, forests, etc.
Tuesday	the day of people with many scars, the survivors of smallpox.
Wednesday	the day of women and everything female.
Thursday	the day of slaves.
Friday	the day of nobles and everything red.
Saturday	the day of young people and everything young.

Geomantic divination in Madagascar is concerned with averting trouble foreseen by the oracle by means of various sacrifices or prophylactics prescribed by the figures. The practice of *Faditra*, sacrifices to avert predicted ills, is fundamental to the working of *Sikidy*. In the case of a certain figure, *Mati-Roa*, for instance, the predicted two deaths may be turned into a *Faditra* by killing two locusts. This carries out the spirit of the prediction. The sacrifice is made, but not in the manner expected. In other *Faditras*, a pumpkin is smashed, money is cut up, or ashes are scattered to the winds. The seeds themselves from certain appropriate figures of the *Sikidy* are sometimes used as medicines to avert predicted illnesses, having gained their virtue by appearing in the right columns. In this case, it is the belief that the seeds with the healing power have been selected by the *Sikidy* for use in this way, literally a form of divine intervention. As in other parts of the world, the figures generated by geomantic divination may be used as sigils of protection, carved or painted onto buildings or sacred objects to protect them against harm and to bring in good fortune.

Geolocation

The sixteenfold division of the horizon practised in European navigation and augury is directly related to divinatory geomancy. The erection of the figures in fours begins with the first four representing the group of fire (south), air, water and earth in sequence. The second is east, (air), the third north (water) and the fourth west (earth). In 1558, Christopher

Cattan wrote 'everie Pricke (point) signifieth a Starre, and everie Line an Element, and everie Figure the foure Quarters of the World.' Traditionally, as with the astrological allocation of the figures to the houses, the figures can be assigned to the directions, four for each quarter of the heavens. The allocation in Madagascar *Sikidy* is rather aberrant, however, as one group (*Kizo* or *Alakarabo* = Puella) was assigned to a different quarter at a certain date after it had offended the diviners in some way! (It was removed from the east quarter or *Trano – Tantianana* – to the west *Trano – Tahandrefana*). The Malagasy divinatory geomancy of directions is called *Andron-Tany*, the *Days of the Land*. In whichever system it occurs, the assignment of geomantic figures to a direction can be used as a means of deciding which direction to go, if lost, the location of a lost object or buried treasure, or in which direction something should be orientated. This form of geomantic divination is allied with the finding of beneficial places in which to perform a ritual, construct a dwelling or bury the dead. In Madagascar, it was used at a very sophisticated level, being consulted not only for the location of the appropriate place, but also in the design of the building and in the timing of its construction and use. It is at this level that the two strands of geomancy – the microcosmic, divinatory geomancy of figures, and the geomancy of finding beneficial places for human activities on Earth – come together.

4

FIGURE AND SEQUENCE

Divination can be accomplished by assigning qualities, values and meaning to almost any set of objects, natural or artificial. All that is required is that they are readily distinguished from one another, and are easily available or created. Being one of the more esoteric arts undertaken by human beings, divination naturally sought out the more unusual or symbolic elements for use in its practices. Because of this, objects of intrinsic symbolic quality, or those which, through traditional usage, had such qualities, have been chosen. These include characters of various alphabets, numerical systems, objects bearing symbols, such as the shields of the Thracian legions, and finally specially created divination pieces and cards like the tarot.

Defensive magic has been part of the military arts since antiquity. Soldiers have always worn lucky charms, carried magic talismans and amulets, and borne heraldic devices imbued with protective meaning. Over 2000 years ago, the Thracian legions in the Roman army were divided into 16 divisions, each of which had its own symbolic shield, rather like the regimental colours of the present day. The 16 designs on the Thracian shields had a complex set of correspondences with planets, metals, modes of combat and deities. These designs were used in a form of divination which has some connections both with divinatory geomancy and tarot, when, by manipulations, a single shield or combinations of shields were selected. The outcome of the divination was read from the symbolic meaning on the appropriate shield. This connection between heraldry and divination is very obscure, yet the use of divination in military affairs has been a common feature in combat since antiquity. From ancient China, where generals conducted wars according to the *I Ching*, the *Book of Changes*, to Napoléon Bonaparte, who is alleged to have used some form of geomantic divination, perhaps the enigmatic *Napoléon's Book of Fate*, military men have 'trusted to luck'. The defeat by the French army of the forces of Ranavalona III, the last queen of Madagascar in 1895 certainly involved divination, this time by the Malagasy. The part that luck plays in any conflict is still a major factor in the outcome, and divination has still a part to play, even if it only serves to randomize tactics and confuse the opposition.

Alphabets

Because they contain the potential to describe and transmit all the knowledge in the universe, alphabets have a magical quality, especially to the illiterate. Several ancient alphabets have names for each character which are descriptive of an object or quality, and to which magical and divinatory possibilities are attached. Perhaps the best known of these is Hebrew, whose use in the magical Qabalah is one of the main supports of the western tradition of occultism. The Roman alphabet in use today is not usually considered to be of any magical or divinatory significance, but under certain conditions in the past, this was not so. In former times, when literacy was a rare thing, to write the entire alphabet somewhere was considered to be a magical, protective formula. This tradition survives in the Christian church, where, during consecrations carried out according to full ritual form, the letters of the Roman and Greek alphabets are written by the bishop with his pastoral staff in ashes forming a cross on the floor of the new church. Although it is rationalized as being symbolic of Christ, who is described as α (alpha) and ω (omega), the beginning and the end, in Greek alphabet lore, both characters have the meanings of riches and abundance. This rite is a survival of the divination conducted by the Pagan priesthood of ancient Rome when laying out a sacred site for a temple.

Closest to the Roman alphabet is the Greek, which does have a complete system of attributions to the 24 letters, which

22. Hällristningar *characters from Scandinavian rock-faces form the basic figures of the Rune-Hoard (see p. 77).*

can be used in divination. Unlike Roman, but like Hebrew, the Greek characters also represent numbers, giving the alphabet a considerable potential for magical use. In fact, a major area of sacred symbolism is the art of *Gematria* where each word in Greek or Hebrew has a number produced by adding the numerical equivalents of the letters together. These numbers, of which the notorious *Number of the Beast*, 666, from *The Revelation of St John the Divine* is the best known, are the hidden side of scripture. Different words with the same numerical equivalent may be used to encode a meaning only apparent to practitioners of *Gematria*, whilst dimensions or numbers in sacred buildings may have a specific meaning when decoded by *Gematria*. The Greek alphabet has the following attributes, some of which appear to have been derived from Mithraic sources:

α Alpha, has the meaning of a bull or cattle. This is interpreted as mobile wealth. It is interesting that in Hebrew and Runic, two other alphabets with symbolic equivalents, the first character has the same meaning.

β Beta, the second letter has demonic connotations. In the Mithraic religion, the demonic God of Wrongdoing, Angra Mainyu, has the epithet, 'the second', being a challenge to and breaker of unity.

γ Gamma, has the meaning of godliness, the sacred.

δ Delta, stands for the four elements, the four directions, the four horses of the chariot known as the quadriga, and (in Christian eschatology) the Four Horsemen of the Apocalypse.

Ε Epsilon, stands or the *Aion*, or ether, the fifth element known as the *Quintessence* in alchemical lore.

ζ Zeta, means an offering or sacrifice.

η Eta, stands for joy and love, the divine harmony of the seven plants and seven spheres of pre-Copernican cosmology.

ϑ Theta, the eighth character, symbolizes the eighth, crystal sphere, upon which, in the former cosmology, the fixed stars stood.

ι Iota, represents destiny, being sacred to the Three Fates.

κ Kappa, brings bad luck, disease and death, sacred to the god Kronos.

λ Lambda, is connected with plant growth, and the mathematical progressions associated with the figure in classical geometry, upon whose principles organic growth proceeds.

μ Mu, signifies the stars, more specifically the *Fourteen Stars*, those given magical sigils in medieval astrology.

ο Omicron, is the Sun.

π Pi, symbolizes the Sun in its glory, surrounded by 16 rays of light, identified with Apollo, Mithras and Christ.

ρ Rho, represents fruitfulness, the power of vegetative growth and reproduction.

σ Sigma, is the Lord of the Dead. As the eighteenth figure, it has connections with the mysterious *eighteenth rune* of Norse magic.

τ Tau, represents the human being.

υ Ypsilon, stands for water, and flowing qualities.

φ Phi, is the phallus, the male generative principle.

χ Chi, signifies property, and is related to the Runic stave *Gyfu*, as a of or for the Gods.

ψ Psi, is the heavenly light embodied in the sky-god Zeus.

ω Omega, the final character, stands for riches and abundance, a successful conclusion to business.

The Origin of the Runes

Runes are far more than simply phonetic signs used to write down prosaic information in the ancient languages of the peoples of northern Europe: their symbolic, sacred and cryptic meanings go far beyond the modern conceptions of practical necessity. The *rune* is a special concept in its own right. The word itself has meanings concerned with *mystery*, in Old Celtic *run* and Middle Welsh *rhin*, the Old English *to rown* and the modern German *raunen* meaning to whisper, give indications of the occult nature of the script. Fundamentally, a *rune* is a mystery, containing hidden and fundamental secrets pertaining to the inner structure of the world. Each hieroglyph which we call a rune is a unit encapsulating a wealth of secret lore, a storehouse of knowledge and meaning which is apparent only to those with knowledge of runecraft. As a sign, a rune represents a formless yet eternal reality which is manifested in the world as we experience it as the objects, powers, feelings and attributes represented by and controlled by that sign.

Runes, like many alphabets, were derived from pre-alphabetic signs. The use of runes as a script is later and somewhat distinct from their use in magic and divination. Runes are interesting because they are derived from two separate sources, melded together so well that it is obvious that the common, deeper, level of the two origins has been tapped. In late Bronze Age and early Iron Age northern Europe (1300 – 800 BCE), especially in Scandinavia, pictographic rock-scribings known as *Hällristningar* were created for magical and sacred purposes. This collection of signs, sigils and symbols is sometimes called the *Rune-Hoard*. From these pre-runic inscriptions came forms which were incorporated in the *Futhark*, the runic 'alphabet', created in about 350 BCE. The *Rune-Hoard* contained many other signs which were not incorporated in the runic *Futhark*, and these survived as calendar symbols, protective and sacred sigils, many of which have survived to the present day in talismanic magic, heraldry and earth harmony techniques. The entire *Rune-Hoard* comprised many forms and meanings which are interpretable today, and also many which are now barely comprehensible.

Although it is certain that these symbols were used for divination before the creation of the *Futhark*, it was when some of the signs were taken and identified with certain characters from the alphabets of southern Europe that the runes came into being. This act of genius is recorded in the *Edda*, where Odin, the shaman-god of magic, poetry, divination and inspiration (among other attributes), makes this synthesis, or rather act of realization, occurred. In the song of *Havamál* (The Utterances of the High One), stanzas 138 and 139 read:

> I know that I hung on the windswept tree,
> Through nine days and nine nights,
> I was stuck with a spear, and given to Odin,
> Myself given to myself,
> On that tree, which no man knows,
> From which roots it rises.
> They helped me neither by bread,
> Nor by drinking horn.
> I took the runes,
> Screaming, I took them,
> Then I fell back from there.

Odin's reception or realization of the runes came through a shamanistic revelation. In ancient society, the holy man was very different from the modern priest in church, temple or mosque, for he had direct access to the worlds beyond by means of dangerous, sometimes lethal, practices of self-torture often involving the use of natural hallucinogenic or trance-inducing herbs and fungi. Initiation into the shamanistic experience was one of the experience of death, dismemberment and (hopefully) reassembly, after which the person returned to the everyday world was possessed with powers of seership. Sometimes, the initiation was spontaneous, through accidental injury, disease or other near-death experiences. The shamanistic experience undergone by Odin seems to have been one of self-crucifixion for the magical period of nine days and nights, nine being the number of completion in the northern tradition. Nine is three times three, and understandably, each rune has a threefold or triadic nature. The threefold structure is in the form, symbolic content and numerical value of each rune.

The symbolism of the tormented flash of realization which enabled Odin to release the full potential of the runes for the benefit of humans describes a rare moment in history where the two sides of the brain were linked by a unified response to a single sign. Modern research into the difference between the left and the right side of the brain has demonstrated that it is the left side which possesses the functional abilities needed for reading and writing. The alphabet, and the *Futhark* in its use as a script, symbolizes a fully phonetic representation of language in a manner qualitatively different from that of hieroglyphic, ideographic or other non-phonetic systems of language notation. In the western, alphabet-dominated, linguistic system, physical injuries to the left side of the brain are associated with impairment or total loss of writing and reading skills.

Studies on the relative abilities of either side of the brain have shown that logographic characters, such as ancient Egyptian hieroglyphics, or the symbols used in traditional crafts in Europe on calendars, for example, are more efficiently recognized by the right side of the brain. Similarly, the non-phonetic *Kanji* writing of the Japanese, is processed by different areas of the brain than is *Kana*, the phonetic system used alongside *Kanji*. People suffering from brain damage in certain different areas have been found to understand only one or other system, depending on the location of the injury. The representation of non-phonetic hieroglyphs in the right side of the brain in opposition to the left may be even superior to the use of the left side for the phonetic system. Certainly, the modern pictograms on road signs are easier to recognize than written instructions. If pre-alphabetic systems of writing and divinatory encodement were handled by the right side of the brain, then the differences between the non-phonetic and phonetic means of communication may be more fundamental than previously recognized. The transition of the use of runes from their state in the ancient *Rune-Hoard*, where each character was non-alphabetic and non-phonetic, to their use in an alphabet, marked a changeover in the use of the sides of the brain from right to left, from the intuitive to the analytical. The genius of the runes lies in the person who first connected the two sides of the brain simultaneously.

The origins of the runic *Futhark* have been the cause of considerable discussion, but it is well established historically that as an alphabet the signs known as runes are derived from North Italic script, but that their divinatory meanings are mainly derived from the *Rune-Hoard*. North Italic was the writing of the Etruscans, and it is believed that the script was carried northwards to the Baltic by Etruscan amber traders. Archaeological evidence for the Etruscan–Runic link came in 1812, when 26 bronze helmets of the fourth century BCE were dug up at Negau (now close to the border between

ᚠᚢᚦᚨᚱᚲᚷᚹᚺ(᛭)ᛏᛁᛃᛋᚴᛉᛊᛏ
ᛒᛖᛗᛚᛜᛞᛘᚠᚨᚪᚦᛣᛟᛇᛥᛝᛤ

23. The 33-character runic row, as used in Northumbria, contains the earlier 24- and 29-rune rows.

Austria and Yugoslavia). The helmets bear inscriptions in Germanic words written in North Italic script.

It is largely the runes' connection with right-hand side of the brain that concerns us here, for runes have a powerful link with decision-making, which at the last resort is intuitive. The leaders and counsellors of Anglo-Saxon England called their secret deliberations *runes*, and the use of the runes in divination at such meetings is well known. The earliest known runes are those from what are now German-speaking countries. They ranged in number from 19 to 23 characters, with a consistent order comparable with, but different from, the Greek or Roman alphabets. The characteristic runic order begins *F U Th A R K* ..., whose sequence gives order to the whole row. The number of runes soon stabilized at 24, divided for divinatory purposes into three *eights* known as *ættir*, each of which is ruled by the first rune of the eight. This row, which is the main one used today, is known as the *Elder Futhark*.

When the Angles, Frisians, Jutes and Saxons migrated to England in the sixth century, they brought with them their adherence to the Elder Faith and their experience and expertise with the runes. The Frisians, whose magical system was based on the Druidic pattern, added four new runes to the row of 24 in accordance with their linguistic and esoteric requirements. The earliest known example of this 24 rune row is on a wooden rod dating from the period 550–650 CE, discovered in 1895 at Arum in West Friesland, the Netherlands. This rod bears the runic inscription ᛖᛞᚨᛒᛟᛞᚨ which trans-literates as *edaeboda*, 'return, messenger'. In Frisia, runes have been found scribed on amulets and ceremonial rods, often made of Yew wood. These had various protective functions inside buildings and for travellers. The amulet found at Britsum is a wooden stave with the runic inscription 'always carry this yew in the host of battle', magical protection for a warrior. Another, later stave, dating from around 800, which has a ritual function of giving power over the waves, is probably the only surviving maritime amulet, whose powers echo those lost by King Canute.

The Saxons in England added further runes to the row; first it was increased from 28 to 29, and finally to 33 characters, divided into four *eights* plus one central rune. A 29-rune row is engraved upon a short sword known as a *scramasax* found in the River Thames in 1857. A complete rune row, inlaid in silver, formed the magical protection of the sword. It is accompanied by the name or formula *B EA G N O H*. The final rune-row used in Northumbria around the year 800, had 33 characters. In Scandinavia, the reverse process occurred. The 24 runes of the *Elder Futhark* were cut down to 16, which underwent stylistic simplifications until they became a sort of shorthand. Today, the most commonly used runes are the *Elder Futhark*, but in German-speaking countries, the *Armanen Runes*, consisting of 18 staves, are popular. These are a nineteenth-century reconstruction by Guido von List of what he held to be the original runic system.

The names and the meanings of the runes

Each runic character or stave has a specific meaning which indicates its character. The names are related to physical objects, and the interpretation of the divinatory meaning of each rune comes from this. Although the 24-rune *Elder Futhark* is the row normally encountered in runic divination today, the late Northumbrian 33-rune row can be used to give a greater breadth of meaning in divination. It is this row that I describe here. The meaning of the first 24 runes is identical to that in the *Elder Futhark*, except that the fourth rune here is altered. The fourth rune of the *Elder Futhark* reappears here as the twenty-sixth rune. The first 29 characters of this row are identical with the early Anglo-Saxon 29-rune row.

ᚠ FEOH is the first rune in the row, and the primary rune of the first *ætt*, that sacred to the god Frey. Its meaning, *cattle*, carries with it the traditional concept of mobile wealth, negotiable property (unlike the homestead, which is immutable property). It represents the collection together of power, either in terms of the herd itself or of its possession. Involved with this possession is the concept of responsibility, that ownership requires correct stewardship and not wastefulness or greed. In modern life, this rune refers to money, worldly success and great wealth.

╻ UR or URUZ is the second rune, representing the mythological Primal Ox, Audhumla, who in northern mythology licked the block of salt to form the progenitor of humankind, Buri. The power represented by property in FEOH is here the raw, untamed energy of the Primal Ox, the force necessary for creation. Perseverance and strength are combined in a fearsome unity of creative power. Unlike FEOH, UR is not a personal power owned by an individual. It symbolizes collective power, 'our' power. The form of the rune echoes the horns of the ox. In divination, it refers to good fortune, personal success which is not at the expense of others and the advancement of the common good.

▶ THORN or THURS is the third rune, representing the defensive power of the god Thor, the Thorn tree and the legendary giant Thurs or Thurisaz. Primarily, it is Thor's personal rune, embodying the power resistant to all things inimical to right orderliness. As the rune of fertilization and empowering, thorn is also the lightning, the sudden change which brings forth an immediate alteration in atmosphere. As such, it represents a change of fortune, good news, or the necessity for an important and far-reaching decision.

▷ OS is the fourth rune of the 29- and 33-rune row, replacing the fourth rune ASA or ANSUZ of the 24-rune *Elder Futhark*. This latter rune, sometimes confusingly also called OS, is the twenty-sixth rune in the longer rows. The meaning of ASA and OS are intimately connected. Here, OS, the rune of Odin, is the mouth which utters the divine sound, signifying the creative power of words and wisdom itself. It is the necessity for communication and information which underlies the very processes of life, also the wisdom of human society in song, legend, lore, custom and knowledge.

ᚠᚢᚦᚨᚱᚴ᛬ᚼᚾᛁᛄ᛫ᛁᛏᛒᛦᛚᛟ

24. *In Scandinavia, the longer rune-row was progressively reduced until a standard form with 16 runes emerged, appropriate for both inscriptions and divination.*

ᚱ RAD is the fifth rune, signifying both riding and the wheel. In addition to the rider or the vehicle, it represents the road itself, the way forwards and the means to get there. RAD represents the transformation of energies, a transference of spirit, matter or information from one place to another, with emphasis on personal transformation. It is the channelling of energies in the correct manner to produce the desired results, with the emphasis upon being in the right place at the right time performing the appropriate act.

ᚲ CEN is the sixth rune, representing the flaming torch within the ancient royal hall, or the Pine tree from which it was made. CEN stands for the mystery of transformation, regeneration through death, the destruction of the Pine wood giving heat and light. It is the creative fire, the hearth, the forge where material is transmuted by the will into something which reflects the human intellect, the mystical creation of a third which formerly did not exist from the union and transmutation of two others. CEN represents protective energy, positive action and regenerative power, the positive aspects of sexuality immanent in the goddess Freyja and the god Frey.

ᚷ GYFU is the seventh rune. This sign, originally carved or painted upon objects to mark them out as to be sacrificed to the gods, has the meaning of *gift* or *giving*. By the use of this rune, unification is achieved, binding together members of society, or the human with the godly. This fusion of people and deities can also be the fusion of two individual wills to a common intent, a business partnership or a magical working. It is the unity between the giver and the person to whom the gift is given.

P WYN is the eighth rune. It represents joy, the mystery of harmony within a disharmonious world. It is the rune of balance, the mid-point between opposites necessary for a sane and happy existence, the removal of alienation either from shortage or excess. WYN stands for the creation of harmony, comfort, the transformation of life for the better, well-being and fellowship.

H HÆGL or HAGAL is the ninth rune, marking the commencement of the second *ætt*. HÆGL signifies hail, the icy primal seed of transformation, the sacred geometry whose patterns underly the universe. In its earlier form,✳, this rune had a sixfold form which signified the four directions, the zenith and nadir, and also the primary geometry of frozen water in the snowflake, something unknown scientifically when the rune was created. It signifies the process necessary for anything to be accomplished, and because of this is often interpreted as delay. In its structure it signifies the grid of nine squares which lies at the centre of the sacred grid. It is used as a talisman of protection on house doorframes in Westphalia and as a *hex* sign by the 'Pennsylvania Dutch'.

✝ NYD or NEED is the tenth rune, symbolizing necessity and need. This may not be the need of absence or scarcity, and the rune's meaning contains the idea of the power of release from need being within the need itself. NYD calls for caution in action, and the old adage 'know thyself' is particularly applicable to this rune. The Austrian runemaster Guido von List's reading for this rune was 'Use thy destiny, do not strive against it.'

| IS is the eleventh rune, the principle of static existence as manifested in ice. Ice is the cessation of flow by a change in state of water from liquid to solid, and IS represents a cessation of progress or the end of a relationship. It is the opposite of the runes CEN and CWEORTH, being the principle of inertia and entropy, but in conflict with fire, it brings forth matter.

◆ GER or JER is the twelfth rune. Its meaning, *season*, or *year* expresses the cyclic nature of time and life. GER is the fruition of right orderliness, the completion of the process in HÆGL, the harvest gained by correct husbandry. If actions are performed according to the correct principles, that is, in accordance with natural law, then the outcome will be favourable, with 'a bright abundance for both rich and poor'. A rune of Frey, its form echoes the mystic marriage between earth and the cosmos, or the transition through the seasons.

♪ EOH is the thirteenth rune, representing the Yew tree and its wood. The Yew is a tree sacred to the dead, found growing today in many ancient churchyards. The wood of sacred staves, such as the Frisian amulets from Britsum and Westeremden, Yew had the dual funtion of protecting the dead and giving access to the other world through shamanistic practices. The very dangerous shamans' incense made from the resin or leaves of the Yew (which has led to deaths) has made the Yew the rune of death, carrying with it also the unlucky connotations of the number 13.

𐰲 PEORTH is the fourteenth rune, symbolizing the pawn or playing-piece, whose dance upon the gameboard parallels the vagaries of human life. It signifies the force of destiny operating in the world, but not predestination. In the board game, the form of the movements of the pieces is prescribed by the rules and the board itself, but their actual movements are not fixed, being the result of the players' skill and interaction. Likewise, in life, destiny has placed us in our situation, but we have free will within the great pattern of cosmic evolution.

Ψ EOLH, EOLX or EOLHSECG is the fifteenth rune, representing the resistant power of the Elk (or in the case of EOLHSECG, the hardy plant Eelgrass). It is a rune of protection, related to the Gothic word *alhs*, a sanctuary, and as if to emphasize this, a double version of the rune is carved in one of the caves in the Pagan sanctuary at the Externsteine, Germany. It is optimistic power, protection and even offence against those forces or influences which would attack us.

ϟ SIGEL is the sixteenth rune, signifying the Sun and its light, both physical and divine. SIGEL is the magical will manifested as the power of good throughout the world, the spiritual force which counters the forces of destruction and death. It is the harbinger of victory and ascendancy over darkness, also the jewel known as *The Mountain of Light* which emanates the power of the sun for guidance and healing.

↑ TYR is the seventeenth rune, the first rune of the *ætt* of Tyr. It is the rune of Asa-Tyr, who gave his right hand to facilitate the binding of the demonic Fenris-Wolf. The rune of positive regulation, it is manifested as the necessity that to rule justly one requires self-sacrifice. As the rune of Tyr, it signifies victory, success and happiness.

ᛒ BEORC is the eighteenth rune, the rune of mystery. Representing the Birch tree, symbolic of purity and purification, BEORC is a rune which links to the primary character BETH of the Ogham tree alphabet. Birch is also symbolic of rebirth, As the eighteenth rune, it is the symbol of completion, double the sacred nine (as in the number of men in Nine Men's Morris – see Chapter 7), and new beginnings.

ᛗ EH or AIHWS is the nineteenth rune, meaning horse. A rune of combination, it is associated with twins, or the inseparable bond between horse and rider requiring trust and loyalty. The horse is a sacred animal in the Elder Faith, and this rune represents the sacred journey, either as a spiritual path or a physical pilgrimage, the movement necessary to commence the task of life. This may be manifested more prosaically as a move of house or an alteration in lifestyle.

ᛝ MAN is the twentieth rune. It represents the archetypal reality of humanness which exists in every person, male or female. Its divine attribute is the god Heimdall, under his alternative name of Rig, progenitor of the traditional classes of ancient society, symbolic embodiment of the cosmic order. The rune MAN presents the human as the microcosm of the universe, the shared experience of every person's humanness.

ᛚ LAGU is the twenty-first rune, representing water, fluidity, mutability and the uncertainties of existence. A rune of unified opposites, like water, a necessity of life which can flood and drown, LAGU symbolizes the life force inherent in matter, organic growth and waxing force. It is the medium by

25. *The final runic row, shown in this sixteenth-century engraving, contained equivalents to all of the letters in the Roman alphabet.*

which passage may be gained, but not without risk.

⧲ ING is the twenty-second rune, representing the god Ing, the male consort of the Earth Mother goddess of fertility and nurture Nerthus. ING is god of the hearth, the Inglenook, and this rune has a protective quality for households. ING is a symbol of light, firebrand or beacon, transmitting a message far and wide. ING stands for potential energy, the capability of limitless extension reflected in the geometrical form of the rune itself.

◊ ETHEL or ODIL is the twenty-third rune, signifying the immutable ancestral property of the family – the homestead. Its Frisian name, *Eeyen-eerde*, meaning 'own earth' or 'own land' is a perfect expression of the qualities of this rune. It symbolizes innate qualities, material and spiritual heritage. Its character represents Odin, its form the enclosure necessary to delimit possession. On a house gable, it draws in currents of beneficial energy, and in divination it signifies property or ancestral influences.

ᛞ DAG is the twenty-fourth rune, the last in the *Elder Futhark*. DAG means day, the rune of light and awakening, and is used today as a protection on doorframes and window shutters. It is a beneficial rune, of light, health, prosperity and openings. Sometimes these last two runes, ETHEL and DAG are reversed, ETHEL becoming the final rune in the row. Where 24 runes only are used, sometimes a twenty-fifth, blank, rune is introduced.

ᚠ AC is the twenty-fifth rune, the first in the *ætt* of the Æsir, the gods. Its meaning is Oak, the sacred tree of Jupiter, Thor and the Taranis of the ancient Druids. The Oak bears the acorn, which is symbolic of the primal cosmic egg, that which contains within it the growth potential of the universe. Its meaning is thus of strong growth and support, for Oak beams are the structural fabric of the traditional timber-framed houses of northern Europe.

ᚠ ÆSC is the twenty-sixth rune, representing the Ash tree. The Ash was the most sacred tree in the Norse religion, being the Cosmic Axis Yggdrassill, its black buds and horseshoe-shaped leaf scars making it sacred to the god Odin and the goddess Eostre or Ostara. ÆSC stands for eternal stability: 'In a firm position it holds well to its place, though many foes advance to fight it.' ÆSC is identical with the fourth rune of the *Elder Futhark*, ASA, ANSUZ or OS, which has its origin in archiac Indo-European tradition in the Sanskrit primal sound which preceded the manifestation of the universe. This powerful rune signifies the divine force at work.

ᚣ YR is the twenty-seventh rune, meaning the bow. The bow, made from the wood of the fatal Yew tree, is an instrument of protection, death and divination. It symbolizes the creative skills of craft at all levels of physical ability, intuition and esoteric knowledge. Apart from being a weapon, the bow was an instrument of divination, both from the fall of the arrow, and as a sort of dowsing rod. The rune signifies defence, protection at the expense of others, and finding the right place – hitting the target.

✳ IOR or IAR is the twenty-eighth rune, representing a sea serpent, primarily the world serpent Jormungand. This rune takes the form of the early HAGAL, symbolizing the dual nature of matter, as in the amphibious habits of legendary wyrms and dragons. The world serpent is a dangerous beast which threatens the stability of the world, yet its removal would presage a far worse disaster than its continued presence. This rune is the embodiment of the necessary evil which must be accepted for life to continue tolerably.

ᛡ EAR is the twenty-ninth rune, representing dust, symbolically, the grave. This is the anthesis of life, its cessation, yet without it, there would be no life in the first place. It is the unavoidable end of all things, the return of human beings to the undifferentiated material of which their bodies are made. As such, its interpretation is very material – *earth–grave* – the abode of the dead, incorporating elements of the location of tombs and the reverence which ought to attend the resting places of the departed. This is the final stave of the Anglo-Saxon 29-rune row.

ᛢ CWEORTH is the thirtieth rune, representing the swirling flames of the ritual fire, kindled at one of the Fire Festivals of the Elder Faith (Samhain/All Saints'; Midwinter; Imbolic/Candlemas; Spring Equinox; Beltane/May Day; Midsummer; Lughnasadh/Lammas; Autumnal Equinox). The rune embodies the concepts of ritual cleansing by fire, the sacred hearth, celebration and joy, opposite to the fire of the tenth rune, NYD, the need-fire, kindled in hard times.

ᛣ CALC is the thirty-first rune, meaning the offering cup or ritual container. In this form, it is an inversion of the fifteenth rune, EOLH, symbolizing the death of the individual. In this aspect, CALC signifies the inverted, empty cup whose contents are poured on the ground as a libation to the gods, and not touched by humans, equally the memory of absent friends or the departed in an act of remembrance. The mystery of CALC is that which is full, yet empty, that which appears to be accessible, yet cannot be touched – the unattainable and the sacrally prohibited.

ᛤ STAN is the thirty-second rune, signifying stone. This may be the stone piece on a gameboard, for the rune's shape, like the fourteenth, PEORTH, resembles traditional forms of pieces used in such northern European board games as *Hnefatafl* and *Tablut*. Equally, the stone may be a megalith set up at a place of numinous power on the Earth's surface, marking celestial and telluric influences, a link between humans, the

26. *The Armanen Runes, explained by the Austrian mystic Guido Von List in the early part of this century, has become the standard system for magic and divination in German-speaking countries. There are 18 runes, and this diagram, dating from the 1920s, shows their arrangement around the Wheel of Time. The legend is the Hermetic Maxim, 'As above, so below.'*

Earth and the heavens.

GAR is the thirty-third and final rune. It represents the

spear, specifically *Gungnir*, the Ash-handled spear belonging to Odin which signifies the Cosmic Axis-tree Yggdrassill. GAR is not in any of the four *ættir*, but acts as a central point to which all may refer. It is the central axletree of the runic wheel, being geometrically the fourfold division of an enclosure which is divided naturally into eight, corresponding with the eightfold division of the horizon in Etruscan and northern European traditions of earth harmony. As the final stave, GAR is the rune of completion, the middle, and at once the beginning and the end, encompassing the other 32 within its sphere of influence.

Divination systems using runes

The earliest known reference to runic divination comes from the writings of the Roman author Tacitus (*c.* 120 CE), who wrote in *Germania*, his account of the Germanic nations of northern Europe:

> They have the highest possible regard for divination and casting lots. Their procedure in lot-casting is always the same. They break off a branch from a fruit tree and slice it into strips; they distinguish these by certain runes and throw them, as fortune will have it, onto a white cloth. Then the state priest (if the divination is a public one) or the family father (if it is private), after a prayer to the gods and a strong heavenward gaze, picks up three of them, one at a time, and reads their meaning from the runes carved on them.

Naturally, Tacitus was observing as an outsider without the inner knowledge necessary to give more than a basic outline of the procedure. However, several viable methods of rune-casting have survived in oral tradition, passed down from ancient times to the present day. Modern rune-casting can be done in a similar way using the stones or wooden runic tablets manufactured by various producers, or, preferably, using runes made by the user.

The method of casting runes is known as *Raed Waen*, literally *riding the wagon*, that is, placing oneself in the position of the god on the sacred wagon from which all things, past, present and future, may be viewed. *Raed Waen* is a ceremonial act, in which the actual casting, or *shoat* takes place. When undertaking *Raed*

Waen, the locational aspect is considered first: the orientation of the room or *heathen* (outdoor) place where the casting is to take place. Indoors, the axis of the room is the first thing to be determined. This is a line across the room or ground where the energy of the earth is at its optimal power for rune-casting. This alignment is largely intuitive, being a dynamic interaction between prevailing local conditions and canonical rules, but there are simple rules-of-thumb which can be used. In a building or room correctly oriented to the cardinal directions, the axis should lie parallel to the longer wall and divide the floor space in two. According to tradition, the direction of energy flow is always *towards* the Sun, and in ideal conditions, the work is aligned towards the Sun itself, which can be achieved by direct observation, or by the use of a magnetic compass. Indoors, this is towards the east in daylight, and to the west during darkness. Thus the cast of the runes will be at right angles to the *presence*, the place of the gods in the north, which will lie to the left of the runemaster in daytime, and to the right at night. The cast is undertaken at right angles to the *presence*, as its outcome is not a matter concerning the gods directly.

The positioning of the *shoat* along this axis is now determined. The *shoat* or *shoot* is the area in which the runes will be cast. This is a white cloth whose dimensions are defined by natural measure, being the runester's own length from feet to fingertips at full stretch above the head, and in width the distance between the runester's outstretched arms. The old definition of the English foot and yard from measures of the king's body is a similar geometric formula, encapsulating some essence of the person in the sacred measure. The *shoat* is the body space of the runester in space and time, and is situated so that indoors the *navel* point, the centre of the *shoat*, is located one third of the way along the axis so that the view of the rune-caster is along the longer portion. The wall in front of the runester is known as the positive wall, and that behind, the negative.

Various ceremonial objects are arranged on the white cloth prior to the rune-casting. These are the *stol*, which is a cushion placed at the negative end for the runester to sit upon and the *weofod*, a small ceremonially-embroidered white cloth located at the opposite end, on which the *mearomot*, a personal talisman of

Rune	Tree	Colour	Rune	Tree	Colour
Ⱨ	Elder	Red	↑	Oak	Red
⋂	Birch	Green	ß	Birch	White
Þ	Thorn	Red	M	Ash Oak	White
⋈	Ash	Blue	⋈	Holly	Red
R	Oak	Red	⌐	Willow	Green
⌐	Pine	Red	⌧	Apple	Yellow
X	Ash Elm	Dark Blue	⋈	Thorn	Gold
P	Ash	Yellow	⋈	Spruce	Blue
H	Ash Yew	Light Blue	⋈	Oak	Green
⟊	Beech	Black	⋈	Ash	Blue
I	Alder	White	⋔	Yew	Brown
⟡	Oak	Light Blue	✳	Ivy	Black
⌡	Yew	Dark Blue	⋓	Yew	Dark Brown
⋉	Beech	Black	⋔	Bay	Orange
Ⴤ	Yew	White	⋏	Rowan	White
⌐	Juniper	Yellow	⋈	Blackthorn	Grey
			⋇	Ash	Dark Blue

27. *Table of runic correspondences used by practitioners of the Northumbrian system.*

the runester containing the essence of the whole person, is placed. At each of the four corners, consecrated symbols of the four elements are placed, making the entire *shoat* a microcosm of the world. When the paraphernalia have been located correctly, the runester goes through appropriate personal mental cleansings before charging the runes by symbolically passing the stones through each of the elements in turn.

Finally, the runes are cast along the *shoat* towards the positive end. There are several ways of casting the runes along the *shoat*. One popular method is to take a handful from a bag, in the 'conscious randomness' manner of diviners, and throw them along the *shoat*. Then, leaving the *stol*, the runester examines what has turned up, literally, as only those runes-tones which fall face up are taken into account.

There are several ways of completing the divination, based upon a threefold principle: the past – the present – the future, as manifested in the northern European version of the Three Fates or Norns. There, they are *Urd, that which was*, representing past actions and events which have led to the present; *Verdandi, that which is becoming*, the eternal present in which we exist; and *Skuld, that which should become*. The first rune (or group of three if multiples of three are taken), stands for influences acting on the past, the second, for those acting on the present, and the third for those which will come to pass as a result of the foregoing if no appropriate action is taken to prevent their happening.

If the 24 runes of the *Elder Futhark* (with or without the twenty-fifth blank stone) are used, then these have 'reversed meanings' if inverted. This applies to the 29-rune system, but with 33, there is only one reading for each rune. The combinations of possibilities and complex interpretations make the runes an ideal system of divination or problem-solving.

Runic divination in ancient times

The runes were held in great regard in the ancient north, being used for the selection of sacrifices or victims for execution when most of a party were to be spared. Here, the runes were seen as the agents of the gods, who chose those to die. Although the documentary evidence we have was written by monks, and so is expected to be largely hostile to rune-casting, several practical applications of runic divination are recorded. An important example of this is recorded in the monk Alcuin's work entitled *The Life of St Willibrord*. Willibrord was a Christian monk sent as a missionary to Frisia, a stronghold of Pagan belief. During his progress through the country, Willibrord was unmolested until he committed an act of sacrilege by baptizing Christian converts in a holy spring, and slaughtering the sacred cows kept there. Brought before the king, the Christians were convicted, but the monarch ordered that every day for three days, runes should be cast to select three of them for execution. Though others were killed, Willibrord was not selected by the runes, and was released to continue his mission. This was seen by Christians as being God's intervention through the runes on behalf of the preacher.

In addition to choosing who should live and who should die, the runes ere consulted as a normal part of military strategy. In the ninth century work *The Life of St Ansgar*, the use of runes by the Swedish and Danish military is recounted. Anund, the exiled king of Sweden and his Danish allies had occupied the holy town of Birka in east Sweden. The town had been evacuated, and only the Prefect Herigar was left, with the intention that he should offer the victors a ransom so that they should not sack the town. The Danes decided to cast the runes to discover if it was the will of the gods that a town where great and powerful deities were enshrined and worshipped.:

> They determined that it would not be possible to achieve their aims without endangering their own welfare and that the gods would not permit the place to be sacked by them. They asked further where they should go in order to obtain money ... they ascertained that they ought to go to a certain town which was situated at some distance, on the borders of the lands belonging to the Slavonians. The danes, then, believing that this order had come to them from heaven, retired from this place, and hastened to go *by a direct route* to that town (author's emphasis).

This runic divination obviously contained the necessary locational and directional information for a direct route to be planned. Whatever anyone's opinions of the efficacy of runic divination, it is certain that in both of these instances, the direction of history was changed by the casting.

The Oghams

The Ogham or Ogam system of divination is mainly associated with Celtic Britain and more especially Ireland, where it attained the most widespread and long-lived use. Ogham (or the *Oghams*) is a tree alphabet, each character having a correspondence primarily with a tree, and secondarily with various other plants, animals and natural objects. Like the runes, with which they have an affinity, the Oghams originated in an age of wood and stone, a time when the intuitive realization of human unity with the natural world was an everyday reality. Unlike runes, which are alphabetic characters, the Oghams are composed of single strokes cut against a line or across the corner of a wooden object or worked stone. Beside stone, there were four special forms upon which Ogham characters could be cut: *Tamlorga Filidh*, the Staves of the Poets; *Taball Lorga*, tablet staves; *Taibli Filidh*, the Tablets of the Poets; and *Flearc Fili*, the Wands of the Poets. The wood from which these magical tablets and staves were made were of certain sacred woods, prescribed by Bardic tradition. The Oghams upon them were cut at the ritually-prescribed times, and according to correct canonical form.

Like the runes, the Oghams were reputed to have been devised by one of royal blood named Ogma. An ancient Irish text, preserved in *The Book of Ballymote*, gives the story in the form of an answer to a question, a common didactic method of Bardic times:

> Q: From whence, from what time, and what person and from what cause did the Ogham spring?
>
> A: The place is Hibernia's Isle, which we Scots inhabit; in the time of Breass, the son of Elathan, then King of All Ireland. The person was Ogma, the son of Elthan, the son of Dealbadh, brother to Breass ...

Like Odin, brother of Vili and Vé, Ogma was one of three brothers. *The Book of Ballymote* continues:

> Ogma, being a man much skilled in dialects and poetry, invented Ogham, its object being for signs of secret speech known only to the learned, and designed to be kept from the vulgar and poor of the nation ... It is called Ogham from the inventor, Ogma. The name derivation is from *Ghuaim*, i.e. the wisdom through which the Bards were able to compose; for by its branches the Irish Bards sounded their verses.

Great wooden 'books' of Ogham existed in ancient Pagan Ireland. It is recorded that at the feast of Samhain in the year 166 CE, King Art, son of Conn of the Hundred Battles

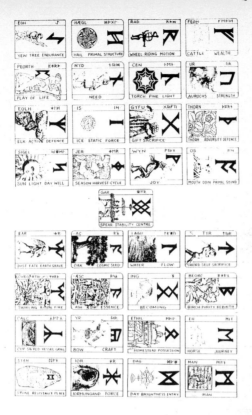

28. *Set of Northumbrian system divinatory rune cards designed by the author.*

gathered together the Bards and Druids and professors of all the arts, together with their Ogham Tablets. Two tablets of venerable antiquity were brought to Art, and, as he was reading them, they closed together and it was found impossible to separate them, which was read as an omen. These books were wooden stave tablets which took the form of a fan, which could be closed up to form a staff. Comparable calendars composed of seven flat staves were in use in Scandinavia up to the seventeenth century, and the modern divination known as the Saxon Wands may well be derived from these tablet staves.

The Oghams are named after different trees, which like the *Elder Futhark*, are arranged in three sets of eight, plus 'shrub' trees for the rest, which may have been added later. These are the eight Royal or Gentle trees; eight Kiln trees; and eight Spiral trees. The Royal trees are Alder, Blackthorn, Furze, Hazel, Heath, Ivy, Oak and Vine. The Kiln or Peasant trees are Apple, Ash, Birch, Hawthorn, Holly, Rowan, Whitethorn and Willow. The attribution is rather complex, and various scholars have attempted to reconstruct what is forgotten or lost. According to Robert Graves, whose system, derived from Roderick O'Flaherty's *Ogygia*, and significantly composed of 18 letters, is now the most widely followed among Ogham users, the attributions are as follows:

> Beth (B), Birch; Luis (L), Rowan; Nion (N), Ash; Fearn (F), Alder; Saille (S), Willow; Uath (H), Hawthorn; Duir (D), Oak; Tinne (T), Holly; Coll (C), Hazel; Muin (M), Vine; Gort (G), Ivy; Pethboc (P), Dwarf Elder; Ruis (R), Elder; Ailm (A), Silver Fir; Onn (O), Furze; Ur (U), Heather; Eadha (E), White Poplar; and Idho(I), Yew.

Variants of these attributions have been suggested by various Ogham researchers, and for the additional characters up to the full complement of 25. Although it may originally have been intended as a ceremonial script for memorials, or as a cryptic way of passing information among initiates, the final and present-day use of Ogham is in divination. The cryptographic symbolism of the Oghams allows the diviner to use them in a manner very similar to that of the runes. Colin Murray, late chief of the Golden Section Order, a Druidic organization which holds the *Bardic Chair of Caer Llyndain* (London), produced a set of Ogham divination cards which can be used with spreads rather like the tarot. In his system, each letter represents a tree, and each tree a month on the lunar calendar, each letter being a key and a talisman to the inner worlds. The complete set of cards comprises 25 characters, the whole Ogham alphabet, with a chart of attributes to be read off.

As a cryptic system of notation, each character of the Ogham script was assigned numerous correspondences with trees, birds, and colours, each of which could be used in symbolic language and as a means of divination in its own right. For example, the Ogham letter corresponding with 'F', *Fearn*, is symbolized by the Alder tree. This produces dyes which can be used for clothing. The bark makes red dye, which signified fire, the flowers green, symbolizing water, and the twigs brown, emblematical of earth. A red, green and brown garment thus symbolized the power of fire to free the earth from water. The tree is related to the raven, the sacred bird of the hero-king Bran, and is aid to be proof against water. Alder piles were used as foundations for sacred buildings which, for reasons of earth harmony, had to be built in water meadows, such as Winchester Cathedral. Alder as the Ogham stave *Fearn* signified the time period from March 19th until April 14th, and the corresponding compass direction. The time of the year is symbolic, because the spiral arrangement of the buds represents the power of growth, which is very apparent at that time of year. This sort of series of correspondences exists for every stave in the entire Ogham alphabet. A few are detailed below:

Letter	Tree	Bird	Colour	Dates
B	Birch	Besan (Pheasant)	Ban (White)	Dec 24 – Jan 20
L	Rowan	Lachu (Duck)	Liath (Grey)	Jan 21 – Feb 17
N	Ash	Naescu (Snipe)	Necht (Transparent)	Feb 18 – Mar 18
F	Alder	Faelinn (Gull)	Flann (Crimson)	Mar 19 – Apr 14
S	Willow	Seg (Hawk)	Sodath (Fire-colour)	Apr 15 – May 12
H	Hawthorn	Hadaig (Night Crow)	Huath (Thorn-colour)	May 13 – Jun 9
D	Oak	Droen (Wren)	Dub (Black)	Jun 10 – Jul 7
T	Holly	Truith (Starling)	Temen (Dark Grey)	July 8 – Aug 4
C	Hazel	Corr (Crane)	Cron (Brown)	Aug 5 – Sep 1
M	Vine	Mintan (Titmouse)	Mbracht (Multicolour)	Sep 2 – Sep 29
G	Ivy	Geis (Mute Swan)	Gorm (Blue)	Sep 30 – Oct 27
Ng	Reed	Ngeigh (Goose)	Nglas (Green)	Oct 28 – Nov 25
R	Elder	Rochat (Rook)	Ruadh (Blood-red)	Nov 26 – Dec 23

In addition to these periods of the year, the four cardinal directions are represented through the equinoxes and solstices. Here, there is a beginning winter solstice and an end winter solstice, expressing the ancient Celtic cycle of completion of the *Year-and-a-day* still observed in modern Wicca. The vowels are used for the time-directions:

A	Fir	Airdhircleog (Lapwing)	Ahad (Piebald)	Winter Solstice (1)
O	Furze	Odorscrach (Cormorant)	Odhar (Dun)	Vernal Equinox
U	Heather	Uiseog (Skylark)	Usgdha (Resin-colour)	Summer Solstice
E	White Poplar	Ela (Whistling Swan)	Erc (Red)	Autumnal Equinox
I	Yew	Illait (Eaglet)	Irfind (White)	Winter Solstice (2)

Ogham characters have a numerical correspondence as well, related to the symbolic functions of number which existed before the appropriation of number by mathematicians.

A = 1; O = 4; U = 5; E = 2; I = 3.

In this arrangement, the vowels signify the annual cycle. A is one as the New Year Goddess of Inception; 0 is four as the Spring Goddess of Increase, Eostre; U, five, is the leafy centre of the year, the midsummer balance point at the centre; E is the autumnal goddess of Combat and Rutting; and finally I is the Threefold Goddess at Midwinter. This correspondence of letter with time also exists with the shorter time-cycle of the week:

Letter	Tree	Day
B	Birch	Sunday
S	Willow	Monday
T	Holly	Tuesday
N	Ash	Wednesday
D	Oak	Thursday
Q	Apple	Friday
F	Alder	Saturday

As a form of divination, the Oghams have a less well documented and less developed tradition than the runes, which have some sort of continuity from ancient times, but as a reconstructed system, the Oghams are of great interest, and to people of the Celtic tradition, must be an essential means of divination. The correspondences given here can be used as a basis for one's own meditation and divinatory praxis.

5

THE ORIENTATION OF
PATTERNS

Our place in the cosmos, both in space and time, is related largely to the form of our physical bodies. We are bilaterally symmetrical beings, with a front and a back, a left and a right side, and, naturally, we envisage the world in terms of these directions. Whether or not we recognize this perception consciously, it is innate in our constitution, and automatically affects our interpretation of the nature of reality. The natural fourfold division of this perceived field centred upon our bodies appears in the patterns we perceive. It is fundamental to astrology, divination and geolocation, for at the centre of this fourfold division is the individual person. In the landscape and on game- or divining-boards, this central point is the navel, known in geomantic terminology under its Greek name of *omphalos*. In the human being, the navel is the vestige of the umbilical cord which connected the unborn baby to the placenta in the mother's womb. Through the *omphalos*, the material world is linked upwards to the creative upper world and downward to its complementary opposite, the destructive underworld. This sacred cosmology existed throughout the world, and in Europe these concepts permeated the religious systems of the Germano-Norse and Celtic peoples.

The physical artefacts which stem from the application of this concept are visible in the traditional layout of the countryside and urban settlements. According to the ancient principles of earth harmony, these are structured with a local Cosmic Axis at the centre of a fourfold or eightfold area. The location and management of such powerful centres were among the most important tasks of the *augurs* and *locators* of old Europe. As the individual's spirit is centred in the physical body, and that body must have a location in space, so the spirit of the place, the *genius loci* was seen as localized at a specific place, the local navel. Just as the individual's spirit is separate in its own right, but part of the divine spark, so the local spirit of place is as individual as the local centre, but also identified with the archetypal central point. In the landscape, these central navels are the fixed points at which other states of consciousness and spiritual evolution may be attained by those attuned to such things.

The most powerful centres in any area have become the major shrines of the nation, seats of monarchs and governments and shrines of the chief deities. Important national *omphaloi* such as Delphi are often also associated with shamanistic practices such as ceremonial state divination and oracular pronouncements. The means by which this may come about varies as much as the character of individual sites varies from one to another. The medieval pavement labyrinths in French cathedrals are quite different from the Delphic shrine, yet they are a later manifestation of the same phenomenon. They have a design which is related directly to the fourfold division of the earth, with numerical and geometrical affinities with the layout of gameboards. Located on major places of power, and protected within sacred buildings, the labyrinths have the overt symbolism of progress along the spiritual path, paralleling the ascent of the Cosmic Axis towards God, encapsulating the whole symbolic message in one masterly synthesis.

The discovery of such a *place of power*, its definition and the *Geomantic Act* is enshrined in the mythos of dragon-slaying in the stories of the Pagan heroes Siegfried and Beowulf, the Christian saints Beatus, George, Leonard, Martha and Michael and the secular knight Lord Lambton. Each of these legends have general or specific locations and appropriate connotations. In these legends, a dragon, wyrm or serpent symbolizes the spiritual energies which roam, bewilderingly and dangerously, free, in the soil and the underlying rock formations at these places of power. The determination of the most powerful and appropriate location for the fixation of these spiritual forces was the task of the *locator*, who, after long and meticulous scrutiny of the site, would decide upon the correct place and time to undertake the *Geomantic Act*. At that designated instant, when the spiritual forces were at their most malleable, and when they could be best taken under control, the *locator* would drive a spike, peg, lance or sword into the earth as the culmination of the foundation ceremony. Factors including local custom, electional astrology and other arcane methods and techniques, would be applied to ensure the efficacy of the *Geomantic Act*.

Piercing of the ground at the optimal location was believed to fix this hazardous wandering spirit in a permanent, accessible, place. In many depictions of the *Geomantic Act* the hero is shown transfixing the dragon with a stave, sword or spear, which frequently runs through the head to pin it to the ground below. The font in the church at Avebury, Wiltshire, England, a village built within a massive megalithic complex, shows this, with a bishop's crozier despatching the reptile. A later representation of the act, Paolo Uccello's celebrated painting of St George and the Dragon in the National Gallery, London, shows the reptile being slain by a mounted St George, who pins it to the earth with his lance. The dragon is tethered lightly on a leash by the virgin whom the knight is ostensibly rescuing from its clutches.

The binding or immobilization of the dragon, perhaps prior to pinning it down permanently, is paralleled by several myths of the binding (or attempted restraint) of other demonic beings. In the Norse tradition, these include the trickster-god Loki, the monstrous Fenris-Wolf and Jörmungand, the world serpent. In ancient British legend, there is the water monster known as the Addanc, and in Judæo-Christian tradition, Satan. In mythology, many of these monsters and demons are the cause of earthquakes. A hero overcomes them in combat, and they are cast down into the underworld, where their periodic writhing in the torment of their bondage still occasions earth tremors. In Norse legend, one of these monsters, the world serpent Jörmungand, lies untamed along the ocean bed, causing disastrous tidal waves and earthquakes by its movements. Although Thor attempts to fish it out, his expedition fails, and earthquakes continue.

Geological research in this century has shown that submarine earthquakes and their associated tidal waves are caused by the movements of the mid-oceanic ridges, which could be described poetically as having a serpentine form. On the other side of the world, Japanese tradition says that earthquakes and *tsunamis* (tidal waves) are caused by demonic giant catfish, the

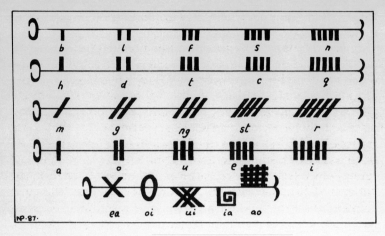

29. *The Ogham characters (see p. 96).*

namazu. In order to prevent repeats, after every earthquake, the God-Superior of the Kashima Shrine ordered the *Daimyojin* to hammer the *Rivet-rock of the World (Kaua-mi-ishi),* shaped like the western *omphalos* stones, through the appropriate catfish's head. The connection we can find all over the world linking the bound serpent or demon and earth tremors had definite connections with techniques of earth harmony. The traditional associations, and the actual location of an important Swiss dragon-slaying legend at the St Beatushöhle, a cave on a major alpine fault near Interlaken, shows some considerable intuitive geological acumen in antiquity.

The geophysical connection

These natural sites of oracular facility and places of prophetic character have common features which hint at some geological reason for their choice. Many of the places where sybils or saints experienced revelations or where oracles have been consulted are at springs where water comes up from the ground, or underground sites of intense geological activity. The oracle at Delphi was sited over a geological fault, a place known now to be prone to geophysical disturbances, and the curious behaviour of the spring at Dodona indicates an aberrant geological formation there. Near Interlaken in Switzerland, the cave of St Beatus, reputed site of a dragon-slaying, is the emerging-point of an underground river, located on a major geological discontinuity.

There are many instances of human responses to anomalous geological phenomena, which have close parallels to the oracles of old. The occurrences which took place in the district around Barmouth in Wales at the beginning of this century give us an important insight into this connection between place, phenomena and religious experience of the more traumatic kind. In his book *Earth Lights*, among many instances of geological light phenomena, Paul Devereux details the remarkable series of manifestations. He recounts that between Christmas, 1904 and July, 1905, there were a considerable number of sightings of unidentified lights of various shapes and forms above and close to the ground in the area around the town of Harlech and the villages of Egryn, Duffryn, Llanfair and Tal-y-Bont. Brilliant rays of light, balls of 'fire', some deep red in colour, and columns described as composed of light or fire were seen by many reliable witnesses. Many of these were seen starting at ground level, several in close proximity to the chapel at Egryn and another chapel, at Llanfair. The chapel at Egryn, which was the focus of a religious revival led by a local prophet named Mary Jones, actually had a light appear over it. This was witnessed by a reporter for the London newspaper, *The Daily Mail*. 'Suddenly, at 8.20 p.m.,' he wrote, 'I saw what appeared to be a ball of fire above the roof of the Egryn Chapel. It came from nowhere, and sprang into existence instantaneously. It had a steady, intense yellow brilliance and did not move.' Joined by another witness, the reporter continued, 'We watched the light together. It seemed to me to be at twice the height of the chapel, say fifty feet, and it stood out with electric vividness against the encircling hills behind. Suddenly, it disappeared, having lasted a minute and a half.'

In *Earth Lights*, Paul Devereux demonstrates the close correlation between this class of phenomenon and tectonically active fault lines in earthquake zones. Although the precise mechanism of the generation of these lights is not fully understood, it appears that the lights around Barmouth were activated by an earthquake which had occurred along the Bala Fault in 1903, triggering off the anomalous geophysical phenomena. Lights associated with earthquakes and tremors have been documented in many places since then, and are the subject of scientific study.

There are many recorded interpretations of these geologically-related light phenomena as human forms, perhaps seen as gods, angels or other divinely-inspired beings. This leads to the conclusion that the original geolocation of many sacred places, such as *omphaloi* and the Egryn Chapel itself were in response to such spontaneous phenomena. Paul Devereux's analysis of this complex of cross-connections is very apposite. In ancient times, he wrote:

> The sites with optimum confluences of conditions would have been divined. Studies of the motions of the Sun and Moon would have been made, and their effect on the human mind and the Earth's body would have been noted and matched over the generations. The spectres and strange lights flitting through their environment would have been observed by these great people. The places in the landscape where they could sense the powers coursing most strongly through their beings would be studied. The nature of such places would be recognized by well-tried acts of divination by people with keenly sensitive sense perceptions. The occasional glows and currents of force emanating from certain hilltops would have long identified such sites as holy, as places for magical and spiritual gatherings. A place to talk with Nature; a place for the spirit to depart from the body.

These places of power, where the boundaries between the material and non-material, the living and the dead, past, present and future, are thin or confused, are the places where shamanism, the oracular arts and sacred rites are best performed.

The connection between the cluster of light phenomena around Egryn and a religious revival is important, for in the Barmouth district, we have documented instances of both phenomena occurring in the same place at the same time. 'Exceptional electromagnetic elements accompanying tectonic events,' wrote Paul Devereux, 'may have triggered mental processes producing the contagious religious zeal she [Mary Jones] was experiencing ...' Although she was already a devoutly religious person, there was certainly some connection between the prophetic religious revivalism led by Mary Jones and the electromagnetic phenomena happening at and around her chapel in 1904-5. The fields of force associated with the vast stresses generated in seismic movements appear to trigger off these phenomena, which have direct, if subtle, effects on the human organism. There is scarcely any information available on these effects, but modern documentary evidence, historical and legendary sources indicate that there is a geniune connection between these phenomena and religious experience, including the more prophetic, revivalist and shamanistic elements. If, as seems likely, great oracular centres like Delphi and Dodona were places of anomalous phenomena, it is apparent that at oracular locations, ordered emanations of energies can link into human brain patterns to create states of altered consciousness.

Scientific research on the effects of electrical fields on the human body has given us an insight into the sort of experiences likely at a place of electromagnetic flux. It is in the area of what are known as athermal effects of electrical fields that we find a fascinating clue to oracular visions and voices. Athermal effects are the results of the action of electric fields on the human body which do not involve heating, and therefore usually go unnoticed. Of athermal electrical effects, the phenomena known as *phosphenes* are the most noticeable. These occur when people in low frequency magnetic fields experience a sensation of flashes of light, when none is present. These flashes are usually white or with slight tinges of blue or yellow. They are believed to be caused by electromagnetic eddy currents acting directly upon the retina of the eye. Obviously, such phosphenes would not be noticed in daylight, but at night, to people expecting them, they might occur readily at places of magnetic disturbance. These effects have certain perceptual consequences which resemble the experiences of shamans and oracular people at their places of power. This leads to the speculation that these places may indeed be locations where measurable electrical effects would be found, if looked for with the right instruments. In the past, before the proliferation of electrical generating plant, transmission lines and universal radio broadcasting, which create enormous amounts of electrical pollution throughout the world, human beings experienced a totally different electromagnetic environment to that of today. These effects would have been localized in their occurrence at just the sort of places

30. Swiss medieval engraving of St Beatus driving the dragon from the sacred cave by the Lake of Thun near Interlaken (see p. 104).

where the earth lights phenomena were encountered.

Another phenomenon which could be connected with sites of prophecy are what are known as *radiosounds*. The researches of Allan H. Frey showed that people can hear electromagnetic energy. It is heard as buzzing, hisses and clicks, appearing to be coming from behind the head, like the experience of hearing music on sterophonic headphones. Over a long period, people have reported mysterious hums and buzzes coming seemingly from nowhere. This phenomenon has been dubbed the *hummadruz*, a portmanteau word derived from hum-drone-buzz. This appears to be part of a phenomenon reported by psychics which they have connected specifically with sacred places. Their experience has been dubbed *the singing* because it is a continuous vibrant sound heard only to the percipient. It is described as a humming, high pitched vibration like the sound of a distant dynamo, but which, as in the scientifically-monitored radiosounds, is perceptible as coming from round the back of the head. The singing has most often been reported at places of sacred power, especially consecrated sites where ritual observances take place, such as in churches. The noted psychic Rosalind Heywood described its effect in church as if it came from an inner force streaming from the altar. To her, this was more marked in churches where the reserved sacrament – a consecrated host – was kept. To those who are aware of it, this sound is most noticeable at natural places like mountaintops and in forests, where the 'spirits of nature' are said to be at their strongest. To the trained diviner, such noises may have been interpreted as the voices of spirits or the gods. The sounds heard by seers at Dodona, for instance, may have been radiosounds generated from the Earth's natural electric fields. Some people are more sensitive to these radiosounds than others, and there have been instances of people 'hearing' natural discharges such as the Aurora Borealis and meteors entering the Earth's atmosphere.

When we look for ancient artistic renderings of these earth lights phenomena, we cannot fail to be struck by the similarity between the light patterns and the ancient forms used in structures marking the central point of the ordered landscape. The *omphalos* and its associated Cosmic Axis or world tree are both forms which have been seen as light phenomena associated with places of tectonic activity. Many modern documented sightings of earth lights have included forms which would have been recognized as such by the ancients. The characteristic forms of this phenomenon, reported from many separate places, are in the shape of a ground-based hemisphere, a floating sphere, a single column of light or several columns together. Sometimes these columns have cross-arms at the top, in the shape of the letter 'T' or like the trilithons of Stonehenge. In certain circumstances, the columns appear to be in humanoid form, interpreted by night as 'white ladies', but seen by day as darker, smoky, shapes.

The usual reports of such earth lights tell us that they are pulsating, ever-changing and transient phenomena. Some-times, witnesses of ground-based lights have beheld hemispherical or globular forms containing flickering 'tadpoles of light', or pulsating iridescent strips. For example, in November 1940, a man working in his garden at Coventry, witnessed a ball of pale green light about two feet in diameter, which he described as being made of 'a mass of writhing strings of light'. These patterns resemble closely the enigmatic designs on several ancient *omphalos* stones, which have been described variously as 'fillets, leafy branches, netted work, and skeins of wool'. In Ireland, the Turoe Stone, a Celtic *omphalos*, has similar swirling patterns interpreted in *La Tene* style. *Omphalos* stones could well be permanent representations of nodes of energy which once may have manifested at these locations, leading to their recognition and use as places of power. It is probable that such stones were painted once to represent the shimmering, iridescent patterns reported by witnesses of such balls of light.

Among the inhabitants of ancient Cyprus, Venus was worshipped in the form of an *omphalos*, which was shaped like a pillar. This parallels the earth light apparition interpreted as the 'white lady', where a humanoid form is seen in a pillar of light. There was a famous oracle of Apollo at Paphos in Cyprus, which had a statue of the god upon a beehive-shaped *omphalos*. Interpreting the *omphalos* as an earth light, the ensemble of god and stone may have been a representation of the observed phenomenon of a ground-level blob of light which transformed itself into a column of humanoid form, seen by the devout as a manifestation of Apollo.

Depending on the location, and the cultural background of the local people in some places, these visions were seen as dragons who had to be slain by the performer of the *Geomantic Act* so that order might be restored and further earthquakes prevented. Such places became the centres of gods and saints. In Britain, holy hills with ancient churches dedicated to St Michael, or hilltop chapels of St Catherine often have accompanying foundation legends which fit this pattern. In Christian iconography, St Michael is depicted as overcoming the Devil in the form of a serpent or dragon, and St Catherine is associated with the fiery, eight-spoked wheel. St Catherine's Wheel is also the *Wheel of Fortune*, giving her some of the attributes of the Goddess Fortuna. In the north of Europe, she is also the manifestation of the Sun Goddess Sól, for in the Germanic tradition, the Sun is female and the Moon male. The most prominent St Michael's hill in Britain, Glastonbury Tor, which has a history of a spectral castle, strange apparitions and phantom lights, has suffered several earthquakes in the past, including a major one which largely destroyed the hilltop church of St Michael, leaving only the tower which still stands there today.

The interaction between these places of power and human consciousness is what makes them special, and allows human beings to gain oracular knowledge or divine revelation there. According to many theories, the extreme emotions generated at these places are added to the pre-existent qualities of the site to create something special, and are then fixed finally by the rite of consecration. According to the noted Theosophist C.W. Leadbeater:

> ...wherever any tremendous mental disturbance has taken place, wherever overwhelming terror, pain, sorrow, hatred, or indeed any kind of intense passion has been felt, an impression of so very marked a character has been made on the astral light that a person with even the faintest glimmer of psychic faculty cannot but be deeply impressed by it ...

If the occurrence of ghosts and other psychical phenomena can be ascribed to these emotion-charged place-memories, then shamanistic revelation must have the same effect. The consecration of such a place for the re-enactment of oracular acts can be seen as the creation of deliberate, artificial place-memories, making an impression on the astral light of the place. Many occultists have explored versions of this field theory, and have come to similar conclusions. Dion Fortune asserted that whenever a place has had prayers or concentrated wishes directed towards it, an 'electrical vortex' is formed. For a time, this 'vortex' has an independent existence which can be felt and used by people. Fortune believed that shrines, temples, and in later days, churches, were built around such 'bodies of force'. If 'bodies of force' exist, then they must have a structure, and it appears that it is reflected on the earthly plane as the grid, and on other levels as the *Cosmic Axis*.

The Cosmic Axis

In all traditions, the central *omphalos* is seen as the place which links the lower, the middle and the upper worlds. This conceptual alignment is known as the *Axis Mundi*, the World or Cosmic Axis. A coherent system of cosmology, or the geography of consciousness, underlies the Elder Faith of Britain. The ancient traditions of the Bards and Druids, collected together by the great Welsh Bard Llewellyn Sion of Glamorgan (*c.* 1560–1616) from ancient manuscripts he recovered from Raglan Castle, are the most coherent description of this system. In this tradition, the Cosmic Axis links four *circles of being*, which are envisaged as circular planes pierced at the centre by the Axis itself. In effect, only three are accessible to the human spirit, for the uppermost, *Ceugant*, is the sole abode of the transcendent creator god, known by the Bardic name of Hên Ddihenydd.

The circle or plane immediately below that of God (*Ceugant*) is *Gwynvyd*, the *White Land*, whose name translates as the quality of *Felicity*. Here is the abode of the enlightened – the saints, and people who have transcended the reincarnatory cycle of their Earthly lives. Below this is the middleworld, the Earthly level known as *Abred*, which also has the alternative name of *Adfant, The Place with the Turned-Back Rim*. In *Abred*, good and evil are in dynamic balance with one another, and hence here there is free will, for in *Abred* every act is one of consent or choice. Whatever one does, one could do differently, and therefore it is appropriate that one should receive punishment or reward according to one's acts or works. Acting upon *Abred* is the force known variously as destiny, fate, luck, *Vintana*, *Wyrd* or *Ørlög*, which includes all of the forces, events, accidents and ideas which have made the present what it is at this instant. Although here in *Abred*, we cannot avoid the present situation in which fate has placed us, our future reactions with regard to it are important, and divination can give valuable information in that direction.

In Breugel's painting *De Tolle Gret*, the Bardic cosmology is depicted as a typical tree of the *Trained Lime* type one encounters as a *Dorflinde* (literally, Village Tree) in parts of Germany and the Netherlands. As they grow, these trees are cut and trained to form a vertical axis surrounded by two, three or sometimes four circular horizontal layers of branches and foliage, representing the Bardic Cosmic Axis. In the tree of Breugel's painting, on the level equivalent to the Earthly, figures are shown in dance or combat. On one side, a horned being, symbolic of evil or wrong action personified as the Devil, grapples with a human figure. On the other side (the right, customarily the side of good), a hammer-wielding character, perhaps one of the old gods, gestures. Appropriately, this figure seems to oppose the horned being's threatening advances. In a painting created in the symbolic environment of 1564, it is difficult to decipher the precise attributes of the characters, but the triple-tiered arrangement of the tree, and the cage beneath it, emblematical of the abyssal underworld, *Annwn*, is

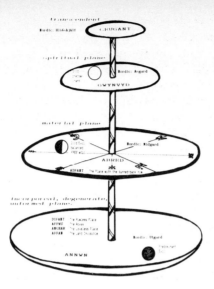

31. The Cosmic Axis, as described in the ancient Bardic tradition of Britain.

apparent. The bars exactly parallel the supports for the first level we can see today on many a continental *Dorflinde*.

The Bardic tradition asserts that at the Earthly level, human beings undergo successive reincarnations. This is reflected in the ancient Cornish saying, attributed to Bardic times, '*Ni fuil an sabras athragad death*' – There is nothing in death but an alteration of life. Here, in *Abred*, a series of lives is led in free will, with spiritual progression or retrogression dependent on action. The perpetration of real evil ends in a fall down the Cosmic Axis into the abyss of *Annwn*, otherwise called The Loveless Place or The Land Invisible. It is important not to equate *Annwn* with the Christian doctrine of hell, for *Annwn* is not punishment in itself, but a state containing lower insensate matter and organisms that have not progressed sufficiently yet to enter *Abred*. The traditional practices of the shaman, who accesses other worlds – or other states of consciousness – by way of the Cosmic Axis, either in physical or astral form, is recalled by the mythic journeys of gods and heroes through this Axis between the worlds.

This Cosmic Axis form is not restricted to ancient Celtic Britain. An almost identical concept exists in the religious system of the Kogi Indians of the Sierra Nevada de Santa Maria in the Andes of Colombia. The Kogi Cosmic Axis links nine worlds, with our world at the centre: four being above and four below. Our world is divided, in the customary manner, into four quarters by the intercardinal directions (NE–SW, and NW–SE). The Cosmic Axis is seen as a spindle on which the Universal Mother works unceasingly in the production of thread, a concept paralleled in northern Europe by the Norse goddess Frigg, the Queen of Heaven, whose spindle is the Axis around which the heavens rotate.

The loom of time

The Kogi tribe have a coherent system of cosmology which relates to the design of temples and also to weaving. The foundation of the Kogi temple is accomplished by a Kogi shaman, known as a *mama*, driving a peg into the ground at the place destined to be its centre, the *Geomantic Act* known all over the world. At the base of this peg, the *mama* fastens a cord, made by his wife. This cord has knots tied in it so that the proportions of the circular temple with its four fireplaces and other ritual features may be laid out according to the correct principles. The knotted cord as a divinatory and magical device has been mentioned above in Chapters 2 and 3. The temple is orientated with regard to the cardinal directions and the solsticial orientations.

Just as the form of the Kogi temple is designed to be a microcosmic image of the universe, so is the loom, upon which cloth is woven. In Kogi belief, the Earth is a vast loom on which the Sun weaves two pieces of cloth a year. The Kogi loom has parallels with the Marshallese navigational stick charts because it, too, is a map of the forces acting on the Earth. The Kogi loom is square with two diagonals. In local geographical terms, the four corners of the squre represent the four Colombian cities at the corners of the Sierra Nevada de Santa Maria, and the crossing-point at the centre represents the holy mountains at the centre. The top bar of the loom is taken to signify the apparent path of the Sun through the sky at the time of the Midsummer Solstice, whilst the bottom bar represents its path at the Midwinter Solstice. The crossing at the centre is the point of intersection of the diagonals of the solsticial sunrises and sets – the central *omphalos* of the temple or village, identified with the shaman himself.

The Kogi temple is seen as a form of loom activated by the Sun. The roof of the temple has an aperture, usually covered by a fragment of pot. At the solstices, this is removed by the shaman, and the Sun's course is tracked as a spot of light on the floor, which travels across the temple during the day. At 9 a.m. on the Midsummer Solstice, the ray of sunlight strikes the fireplace in the south-east, and travels eastwards during the day until it illuminates the south-western fireplace at 3 p.m. Similarly, at the Midwinter Solstice, it shines on the north-western fireplace in the morning and the north-eastern in the afternoon. Colombia is, of course, in the southern hemisphere, and in Europe or north America, these northern and southern positions would be reversed.

The Kogi see these lines as the Sun weaving the fabric of the year on the loom of the temple. The Sun lays down the weft in an east-west direction, whilst the Earth Mother provides the warp of the fabric, but at night, the fabric is black. The black fabric is woven at night in the mirror image of the temple, which is believed to exist simultaneously with the earthly one, but inverted in the Earth. This cloth, however, is woven in the opposite direction from the light one, unifying the opposites.

Traces of a similar concept can be seen in several ancient French ecclesiastical buildings. At Chartres Cathedral, a white pane of glass in an otherwise coloured window allows the rays of the Sun at midday on Midsummer's Day to strike a brass tablet in the pavement, marking the moment of the Sun's apex. At Tonnerre, a brass lemniscate shape (figure-of-eight) in the floor tracks the position of the midday Sun throughout the year. The great architectural symbolist W.R. Lethaby noted in 1891 that 'Even now in some of the French cathedrals – Bourges and Nevers for instance – diagonal lines may be seen right across the floor graduated into a scale of months and days.' The design of sacred buildings, and the grid which underlies those built according to canonical principles, is always related directly to the perceived structure of the world, and its interactions with celestial phenomena. When rays of the Sun are projected onto such a grid, the various portions of it have a specific geometrical relationship to a time of day and the time of year. By these means, a harmonious relationship with the universal order is created.

Sacred space

The Hindu tradition of earth harmony from India known as *Vastuvidya* is probably a very pure survival of the ancient geolocational art which gave rise to both the European and Chinese traditions. An ancient Sanskrit text on temple foundation, the *Manasara Shilpa Shastra*, explains the geometrical techniques for laying out the basic square which is then subdivided into the sacred grid. Having used the rules of *Vastuvidya* to find an appropriate location for the temple, the practitioner erects an upright or *gnomon* at the centre of a water surface prepared at the site. This *gnomon* must be of prescribed canonical dimensions, being either 12, 18 or 24 *angulas* in length. From this centre, using knotted rope to maintain the correct dimensions, a circle is drawn, with a radius twice the length of the gnomon. By observing opposing limbs of the Sun, a true east–west line can be drawn. The two positions of the Sun when it is the same height above the horizon in the morning and the afternoon are marked on the circle, and a line drawn between them. At each end of this equinoctial axis, a peg is driven into the earth, and the rope used to form arcs centred on the two pegs. This makes a geometrical figure known as a *vesica*. A line between the crossing-points of these two arcs, the extreme ends of the *vesica*, is true north–south, crossing the east–west line a little to the north of the centre of the original circle. Taking this as a centre, a new circle the same diameter to the original one is drawn on the ground. From this circle, an east–west *vesica* is created in the same way as the first one. The four intersection-points of the two *vesicas* are joined by straight lines to form a square, the basis of the sacred grid.

Ancient philosophy asserted the unity of all existence, the greater being reflected in the lesser. Certain geometrical forms, which are capable of seemingly limitless expansion or subdivision, are a perfect way of expressing this truth. The human form can be envisaged as a living physical reflection of the hidden patterns of the creation. In the Jewish faith, human beings are created in the image of God, as temples ordained by the supreme creator to enshrine the divine spark, the sentient soul which elevates human beings above the animals. The qualities inherent in the universe are reflected in the human body, which is the microcosmic mirror of the macrocosmos. According to this viewpoint, all things present in the universe

Roga	Ahi	Mukhya	Bhallata	Soma	Bhujaga	Aditi	Diti	Agni
Papa-yaks-man	Rudra						Apa	Pary-anya
Sosha		Rudra-jcya	Prthividhara		Apa-vatsa		Jayanta	
Asura		Mitra		Brahma		Aryaman	Indra	
Varuna				Brahma			Surya	
Kusuma-danta							Satya	
Sugriva		Indra	Vivasvan			Savitr	Bhrsha	
Dauva-rika	Indra-jaya	Bhrngaraja	Gandharva	Yama	Brhatksata	Vitatha	Savi-tra	Anta-riksha
Pita-rah	Mrga						Pusan	Amila

32. *The sacred* Paramasayika *grid of the Hindu tradition ascribes specific places in the grid to specific deities. The central nine squares are the* Square of Brahma, *the Creator's sacred space (see p. 130).*

are encapsulated in each and every human person. The so-called *Hermetic Maxim*, attributed to Hermes Trismegistus, the mythical founder of alchemy, states: 'That which is in the lesser world (the microcosm) reflects that of the greater world (the macrocosm).'

The geometrical form of ground-plans, expressed as the grid, manifests itself as the *Yantra*, a sacred image which is explained as a gathering-point or nucleus of spiritual force. In Tantra, these geometrical patterns act as focal points upon which devotees may fix their meditative concentration. But *Yantras* are much more than aid to meditation, for they are also sacred icons of specific spiritual beings, whose actual images are not present. To practitioners of Tantra, *Yantras* represent the subtle bodies of these *Devatas*, their underlying eternal network of energies. Like Chladni patterns, they are connected with sound. When the appropriate *Mantram* is recited, the corresponding *Yantra* is activated. The appropriate *Devata* manifests in the person saying the *Mantram*, unifying the person with the infinite.

The similarity between the common forms of *Yantra* and gameboards is striking, showing their common origin in the sacred grid. The cosmological design of ancient sacred space was seen as the manifestation of this realm of the sacred around the Cosmic Axis, a limited, circumscribed area within the realm of the profane outer world. Faiths that believe that human order came into being at the inception of the world reflect the cosmos in a reduced version on Earth. A state of sacredness is only achieved through the accurate representation of this celestial archetype. This is put into effect by the transformation of natural landscapes into sacred space, making them images of the cosmos. In the sacred world view, every human artefact which might be seen as an image of the world – whole kingdoms, cities, sacred enclosures, temples, shrines, and even board games – were designed according to this sacred cosmic image.

In this world view, irregularities in the cosmic order are interpreted as having a direct relation to human beings, so that each cosmic event was interpreted as a warning or an admonition. As sacred cities were laid out as a microcosm of the world, it was necessary to maintain the working of these parallels at all levels. This was achieved by the participation of the whole population in festivals commemorating the seasons, which were seen as the necessary human element in the uninterrupted maintenance of the cycles of time. Human participation in cosmic events was achieved by the careful observance of those events, reinforced by the appropriate symbolic ritual. The ancient Chinese view of *Li-Chi* was that: 'In ceremonies of the grandest form there is the same hierarchical relationship as that which exists between Heaven and Earth.'

The cosmological foundation of an important place by geomantic practitioners has an ideal form which reflects the cosmic axial pattern. Etruscan augurs found the correct geolocation for the centre, which was marked by digging a shaft into the ground beneath the future crossroads from which the rest of the area was to be laid out. This pit or *mundus* was consecrated and then sealed with a disc of stone resembling a millstone or a playing piece. According to Varro, this *mundus* was the gateway to the Gods of the Nether Regions. Once this *mundus* has been driven, consecrated and sealed, a stone or other upright marker was erected over the shaft, and the official foundation was deemed complete, equivalent in board game terms to setting up the pieces ready for play. To this day, a *mundus* exists at Royston, Hertfordshire, a perfect cosmological pivot of the four quarters whose structure reproduces perfectly the classical geomantic ordering of the landscape. Here, the cave is located at the crossing-point of two of the Four Royal Roads of Britain, making it the centre of a conceptual grid pattern which overlay the land.

Ættcunning and the lore of the eight directions

The details of the Cosmic Axis are important in our understanding of the cosmological symbolism that underlies the sacred layout of the countryside and its microcosmic reflection, the gameboard. The most significant part of this cosmology is, however, the visible world in which we live. The ancient augurs were always aware of the horizon visible from a site, both for the observation of the apparent motions of Sun, Moon and stars, and to be in harmony with the powers inherent in the shape of the landscape. Their basic layout was organized according to natural measure by the division of the circle into its four quarters by conceptual lines running north–south and east–west. Between these lines, the horizon was divided by further lines running to the intercardinal directions. This created the eightfold division necessary if one is building a square or rectangular building or enclosure facing the four quarters of the heavens. These four quarters are as follows: the southern quarter is between south–west and south–east; the eastern between south–east and north–east; the northern between the north–east and the north–west; and finally the western between the north–west and the south–west. The four cardinal directions are thus the mid-points of the four quarters.

These eight directions are related to the physical structure of the world, the north–south polar axis and the east–west one at right angles to it. But in addition to the fixed structure of the world, there are the variable features, of the apparent motions of the heavenly bodies in relation to the fixed site. Depending on the latitude of the site, the position of the rising and setting Sun at the solstices (the longest and shortest days) and on other important sacred festivals of the year will be at different places on the horizon from the intercardinal directions. Furthermore, the height of the horizon above or below the viewing-point will alter the rising place of the Sun, Moon or star, and unless the site has an equal-height horizon all around it, this will destroy the symmetry of sunrises and sets. On a level horizon, a solar geometry exists in which midsummer sunrise is diametrically opposite midwinter sunset and midwinter sunrise opposes midsummer sunset.

Because the length of day varies with the season of the year, and this season is directly observable by the position of sunrise on the horizon, it is possible to mark the calendar by means of sunrise direction. Between the southernmost sunrise at midwinter in the northern hemisphere, and the most northerly sunrise at midsummer, the Sun rises due east at the equinox, crossing southward in winter and northward in summer to define the two halves of the year, the dark half and

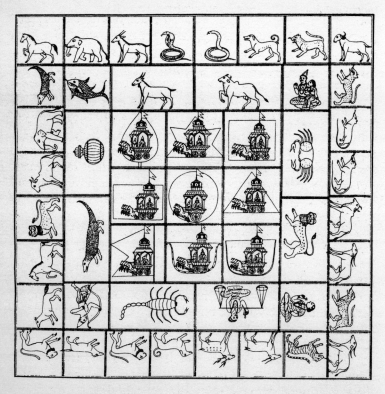

33. This grid from Choultry on the south-east coast of India, has a nine-square grid at the centre holding the seven astrological planets and the Moon's north and south nodes. The Sun is at the centre. Surrounding this are the Signs of the Zodiac, and outside them, the 28 houses or stations of the Moon.

the light half. Between the two solstices, the traditional rural calendar of the north marked the end and beginning of winter at the festivals of Beltane (May Day) and Samhain (November 1). In the harmonized landscapes of the past, these rising and setting points were indicated either by natural features, or by artificial markers such as standing stones or cairns, known in Norse countries as *dagsmark* and *eyktmark*. Where natural features mark these important days, the inference is that the location from which they are viewed was chosen with regard to the configuration of the horizon. This may be seen admirably at many stone circles in the north of England and Scotland, whose masterly geolocation attests to the high technical ability of their constructors.

In addition to the location of sunrise, these direction markers also automatically show the time of day. When the Sun is rising due east at the equinoxes, that is 6 a.m. according to the modern clock reckoning of time, and when it sets due west, it is 6 p.m. When the Sun stands due south at any time of year, it is 12 noon, but the Sun at midsummer stands much higher in the sky – the highest it will ever reach at that latitude – than at noon on Midwinter's Day, when it is at its lowest point. At any time of year when the Sun is above the horizon, it will always be above the same horizon marker at the same time of day. At 6 a.m. on Misummer's Day, the Sun will stand due east from the observer, over any horizon marker, and so on.

Unlike today, when most people are unaware of which way anything faces, the directions played an integral part in traditional ways of life. Not only is the telling of time directly related to the direction of the Sun, but the construction of houses, the construction, ornamentation and orientation of furnishings, the layout of temples and law courts, divination and the playing of board games were all done with consideration of the qualities of the directions. Because of the considerable differences in day length during the year in northern Europe, the science of directions was more highly developed here than in many other parts of the world as a necessary part of survival. The knowledge of the directions – *ættcunning* – was an integral part of the knowledge of priests, builders, seafarers and wise women and men. This awareness of directions has subtle ramifications in all manner of areas, underlying much traditional design, which, in pre-industrial times, combined symbolic and magical content with practical considerations, such as we find today in the stick charts of the Marshall Islands and the looms of the Kogi.

In many cultures, the various directions have been assigned the guardianship of deities, demons or personifications of the winds. Some of these are named and determined by the local conditions under which they were developed, whilst others have deeper, more occult, reasons for their attribution. The traditional European division of the horizon, or space in general, has been by 16 lines running from the centre to the circumference, equivalent to the fourfold division of each of the four quarters. The significance of the number 16 has been seen already in divination using the shields of the Thracian legions and classical divinatory geomancy. The sixteenfold division of space allows the definition of eight regions and their mid-points, sufficient for a relatively accurate recognition of the times of day. This distinction between a direction and a quarter (or eighth) is of great importance in the Etruscan and northern European traditions, but it seems less recognized in those divisions based upon 12, such as the zodiac and the 12 house system of astrology. The fundamental difference is seen in *ættcunning*, where a key distinction is made between the *ætt*, or eighth of the horizon, and the *ætting*, the actual compass *direction*. Thus, in the *ætt* of Uht, the *greying of day* or *small hours*, which occupies the eighth from north-north-east to east-north-east, the *ætting* is the line running towards the north-east, dividing the eighth in two. The traditional reckoning of solar time was used in northern Europe until the arrival of cheap clocks and the imposition of standardized time, first by railway companies, then by governments throughout national areas. Residents of isolated farmsteads in the Faeroe Islands were the last people in northern Europe practising this art hereditarily, but finally it died out around the 1920s. Fortunately, the knowledge of it has survived, giving us a remarkable link with the harmonious knowledge of the ancients.

This eightfold division was important in the design of symbolic pavements in medieval Europe. The pavements which survive at Westminster Abbey and Canterbury Cathedral, several in Italy and that excavated at Xanten Cathedral, Germany, in 1933, have a cosmological symbolism. According

34. The occult powers which traditionally guard the 32 directions.

to the mystical architect W.R. Lethaby, the English medieval alchemist Sporley stated that at Westminster, the circles of the Cosmati Pavement symbolized the four elements. The central *omphalos* of this remarkable medieval cosmogram formerly bore an inscription that the pavement was emblematical of the microcosm, that is, that the sacred geometry encapsulated in the tesserae of the mosaic encoded the mathematics and geometrical structure underlying all matter. Many of the cathedral pavements of France and England contained representations of the Labours of the Seasons and also the Signs of the Zodiac, such as survive today at Canterbury. The pavement labyrinth at Sens Cathedral had an octagonal stone at the centre surrounded by eight keystone-shaped slabs, expressing the combination of the eightfold horizon around the central local navel of the world. This was at the centre of the turning path reminiscent of the world serpent coiled around the Cosmic Axis. We will see the further ramifications of these concepts in Chapter 6. In medieval Europe, this sixteenfold division and its subdivision into 32 was adapted to the use of the magnetic compass, and it remains with us today in the names of the directions. On another level, occultists assigned these 32 directions to various spiritual and demonic powers. The four quarters were allotted the qualities of the four seasons, the four archangels, the four elements, and the four humours. Like the figures in divinatory geomancy, the subsidiary powers or demons were allocated according to their corresponding characters. Thus the demon of the north is Rasiel; that of the east is Pamersiel; the south, Barmiel; and the west, Malgaras. Rasiel, being of the north, is Demon of Midwinter, midnight, darkness, cold, and the meeting-point of earth and water. Barmiel, on the other hand, is the complete opposite, being Demon of Midsummer, bright light, heat, and the meeting-point of air and fire. The other demons are characterized accordingly, having a time of day at which they are most active, related to their position on the compass rose.

Unlike the Etruscans and northern Europeans, who divided the horizon into 16 regions, the architects and geomants of the Græco-Roman culture had a different system. It was still derived from the basic eightfold division of the horizon, with eight winds, but became twenty-fourfold, as each wind had two accompanying lesser winds or 'breezes'. The ascription of compass directions to the winds has led subsequently to much confusion, as many writers have used the two terms interchangeably. In Athens, the Greek architect Andronicus of Cyrrhus built the octagonal structure known as *The Tower of the Winds*. On each side of this building, which was orientated appropriately, was a sculpture representing the presiding genius of the corresponding wind. In his *Ten Books of Architecture*, Vitruvius wrote:

> On top of the tower he set a conical-shaped piece of marble and upon that a Triton of bronze with a rod in its outstretched right hand. It was so designed to rotate with the winds, always stopping to face the breeze and using its rod as a pointer directly over the representation of the wind that was blowing.

Because every natural force in ancient times was personified, or ascribed to a ruling genius, spirit or deity, the powers associated originally with the winds came to stand for the compass directions in their own right. In the Roman system, however, most of the names of the winds were descriptive of the places from which they were believed to originate.

The eight major winds of the southern European directions are:

Auster, south
Africus, south-west
Favonius, west
Caurus, north-west
Septentrio, north
Aquilo, north-east
Solanus, east
Eurus, south-east.

When seen as directions for architectural use, these are 'eighths' as in the northern European system, with the cardinal and intercardinal directions at the mid-point of each 'eighth'. When seen as actual directions, the cardinal and intercardinal directions (*ættings*) were called by these names. There, 16 other points were introduced to make a twenty-fourfold windrose. These extra 16 were the breezes subsidiary to the main winds, one on either side of each wind. The subsidiary breezes are shown in the illustration on p. 126, taken from Fra Giocondo's 1511 edition of the works of Vitruvius.

In his great work on architecture, Vitruvius gave intricate descriptions of the nature of the winds, and their properties. He gave instructions for laying out the streets of a new town, or local development, by means of orienting them with regard to the winds: 'Let the directions of your streets and alleys be laid down on the lines of division between the quarters of two winds.' This, he claimed, would shut out the disagreeable force of the winds from dwellings and rows of houses: 'Therefore, the rows of houses must be aligned away from the quarters from which the winds blow, so that as they come in, they may strike the angles of the blocks and their force thereby be broken and dissipated.' Although Vitruvius's interpretation of the orientation of houses with regard to the winds may work in only a very small part of Italy, the principle of orientation with regard to the winds or the compass directions has been practised everywhere.

In country lore, various rhymes still exist which give some indication of the qualities ascribed to the winds for divinatory purposes. An old Scottish rhyme tells us that the direction of the wind at New Year sets the tone for the future year:

If on New Year's Night wind blow south
It betokeneth warmth and growth;
If west, much milk and fish in the sea;

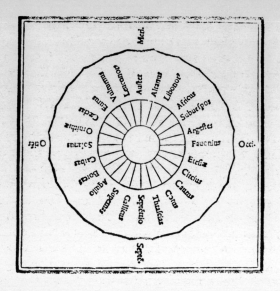

35. *The rose of the winds, showing the eight winds and sixteen breezes, from Fra Giocondo's edition of the works of Vitruvius (1511).*

If north, much cold and snow there will be;
If east, the trees will bear much fruit;
If north-east, flee it, man and brute.

It is apparent that the attributes of the directions were very much conditioned by the local prevailing weather and culture. However, the principle that the wind or the various qualities of the directions have an effect depending on the place is universal. The direct experience of nature preserved in these old adages was applied as a matter of course through every aspect of life. There was no separation.

A very similar system existed in pre-conquest Peru, where the capital city, Cuzco, whose name means 'navel', was the centre of the Inca Empire. This city was divided into four quarters which met at the Coricancha, the Temple of the Sun, where the religious ceremonies of state were performed. From this temple ran out 41 straight lines known as *Ceques* which linked the Sun Temple with sacred sites known as *Wak'as*: temples, single standing stones, fountains, holy hills, sacred images, and places of sacrifice. These lines, which were up to

12 miles in length, were arranged in four 'quarters' with nine lines in three of them and 14 in the other. These areas reflected the structure of the whole Empire, which was divided into four parts, called *Tahuatinsuyu*, meaning 'the four quarters of the world'. These 'quarters' were assigned names: the north-western was called *Chinchasuyu*, whilst the north-eastern was *Antisuyu*. These areas described the northern half of the sky, and the northern half of the area in and around the city, being *Hanan Cuzco*, the upper area. To the south of them was the lower area, *Hurin Cuzco*, which was divided unequally into two areas: the south-eastern (from 90° to 146°), *Collasuyu*; and the south-western, *Cuntisuyu* which had 14 lines. The city of Cuzco was laid out consciously as an image of the Empire by the founder Manco Cápac, first Inca emperor, who ordered that the chiefs of the nations he had conquered should live in houses located in parts of the city corresponding to the positions of their homelands. Associated with the landscape lines and quartering of the land were the four main highways, which ran from the city to the four parts of the Empire.

These straight alignments of sacred sites had various functions. They were tended by families whose hereditary right it was to keep them in good order. This has parallels in pre-1950 Tibet, where eight families guarded the eight directions through rituals, and in ancient Celtic Britain, which had eight noble families whose function was similar. The Peruvian *Ceques* also had associations with the winds, irrigation systems and astronomy. Major alignments of *Wak'as* were orientated upon certain significant solar azimuths. From the Temple of the Sun, astronomer-priests observed sunrises at the solstices and other key points of the calendar, linking the cycles of the year to the layout of the city and countryside, and the structure of society.

Electional astrology – the selection of the right time

The astrological aspects active at the inception of anything, such as a person's birth, are considered to have an effect upon its future, the actual experience depending upon the structure of the horoscope. Electional astrology is the branch of the art which is concerned with setting up and diagnosing charts to

define appropriate times for the commencement of any
project. This can be the foundation of a building, the formation
of a new company, the celebration of a wedding, or the most
suitable time to enter a contest. The astrologer looks at the
charts for the possible dates, and determines the most
auspicious moment in keeping with the constraints on action.
The chart set up is called the *Election Chart*. When an Election
Chart is used to determine the time of, say, the foundation of
a building, that chart becomes its *Inception Chart* which differs
from an accidental chart only in that it has been selected in
advance.

The *Inceptional Chart* drawn up by the Astronomer Royal,
John Flamsteed, for the time of laying the foundation stone of
the Royal Observatory, Greenwich, appears to be in fact an
Election Chart. The stone was laid at 3.14 p.m. on August 10,
1675, seemingly a strange time for the ceremony. It appears
that the chart in fact is an election, calculated in advance. The
Cambridge astrologer, Patrick McFadzean, has analysed Flamsteed's chart and has noted the Sun in the 9th house as
appropriate for astronomy, being connected with philosophical and scientific exploration. The rising sign of the Royal
Observatory's chart is Sagittarius, ruler of the 9th house,
almost exactly at its rising position. Although, like any chart, it
is not absolutely perfect for the function, Patrick McFadzean
sees it as indicating clearly the spirit of looking at the heavens.

Cambridge's King's College Chapel, founded by King Henry
VI in 1446, has a Chart which was most probably elected. The
Chapel, which was constructed according to a complete
system of symbolism and sacred geometry, has both the Sun
and Moon in Leo, appropriate for its royal name and connections. Three other planets are also in Leo, reinforcing the regal
associations. Like all Charts, that of King's College Chapel is
not perfect, for the Moon's south node – Cauda Draconis – is
conjunct Mars. This can have the meaning that a project will
never come to completion. Of the project for King's College, as
drawn up by Henry VI, only the Chapel was completed, the
other buildings remaining unfinished or never started. The
Chapel itself was never completed as envisaged by the King, as
the interior was not painted in the vibrant symbolic colours of
late medieval church architecture.

6

THE ROYAL CENTRE, FAIRS AND SACRED BOARDS

The holy grid

Place and time were of much greater importance to our forebears than they are now in modern society. Large local and national gatherings, such as fairs, pardons and royal courts were, in a real sense, a microcosm of the country itself, attracting together people from afar. This symbolic quality was recognized by deliberately laying out such gatherings according to a cosmological scheme. The temporary courts of old, when kings progressed around the country, collecting taxes and overseeing justice, reflected the nation in its entirety, which was symbolized in the royal person. Democratic assemblies of state, too, such as the Icelandic *Althing*, and the Manx Parliament known as *Tynwald*, were arranged in accordance with the ancient holy city principle as symbolic microcosms of the country. People from the north camped at the north side, in places ritually appropriate to their trade or profession. The other directions were laid out in the same manner. The whole area was thus a ceremonial replica of the kingdom, with the king, or a symbol representing his authority, at the centre. This canonical layout parallels the archaic traditional layout of sacred places of India, from which it is probably ultimately derived.

Although they no longer hold the same social importance as formerly, the great traditional fairs still flourishing today, like the Cambridge Midsummer Fair, were laid out as a microcosm of the country itself, reflecting not only the country but the order of the cosmos, temporarily brought to earth at a specific place for a limited duration. This gridded layout of towns and fairs is part of the locational tradition which includes the assigning of relative positions on a gridded square to various planets, qualities or deities (see p. 117).

From this conceptual layout of sacred space come temple design, holy city and fair layout, and the patterns of game-boards. There is a direct connection, and direct correspondences exist. In the Hindu tradition, which has a venerable antiquity, this layout is based upon the *Paramasayika* grid, which is a square composed of 81 smaller squares (nine by nine). Various parts of the square are allocated to specific dieties, which have protective functions over the various places and directions to which they correspond. The placement of images in a temple, or shrines in a town or the countryside, can be determined by the relative positions of the deities in the *Paramasayika* grid. At the centre of the grid is the *Square of Brahma*, the creator's nine squares which are one-ninth of the total area. This nine-square square is seen as the quintessence of existence, the central core through which all space and time may be accessed. When the *Paramasayika* grid is depicted in terms of the body of the mythic primal giant *Purusha*, slain to make the world, these squares occupy the area of the navel, the energy centre of the body known in the Japanese martial arts as the *hara*. When used as a city layout, the *Square of Brahma* is the location of the central temple complex. The whole 81-square grid is identical with the board of the northern European game *Tablut*, and the Sri Lankan game of *Saturankam*. In both of these games, the central square is most important.

In the temple, city and fair layout of India and Europe, this central point was marked permanently at the foundation ceremony. The Indian technique of earth harmony known as *Vastuvidya* retains the ancient ceremony, of which there were European parallels which might be reinstated yet. A hole dug at the centre of the site represents the navel of the *Purusha*, the primeval cosmic man. His limbs are symbolized by the four streets that run from the navel to the four cardinal directions. Once this has been dug to the correct size in the right place and at the right time, the ceremony of foundation takes place. One of two alternative rites are used. The longer, complete rite fills the hole three-quarters full with earth and then blocks it with a flat stone. Twelve holes arranged in a square around a large central hole are drilled in the stone. A gold plate bearing the image of a bull is inserted in the central hole of the stone. The pattern of the holes is significant. Twelve holes in a square mark the starting-points of the lines which, if drawn, would make a square of nine smaller squares, the *Square of Brahma*, and the golden image of the bull is at the central square of the nine. On this foundation stone is placed a jar and other ritual objects, and then everything is covered over, completing the foundation. A simplified version of the foundation ceremony places a

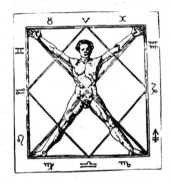

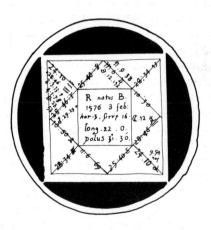

36. *The traditional diagrams used for drawing up horoscopes have a direct relationship with the geometry underlying sacred architecture and board games. Left: The horoscope of Robert Burton, author of* The Anatomy of Melancholy, *on his tomb at Christchurch, Oxford. Right: Man the Microcosm.*

jar at the centre and a stone for each of the cardinal points. The
ritual is said to represent the creation.

The grid of nine squares

It is believed that as a system of land division, this grid of nine
squares originated in a very ancient system of feudal land
tenure, which may have begun in ancient India, and thus be
the basis, too, of the Indo-European system, which is identical.
In China, the nine-square arrangement meant that eight
peasant families tended an area of land which surrounded a
central ninth square which was cultivated communally for the
benefit of the lord. This central ninth square contained the
communal well. This so-called 'well-field' division was considered an ideal, which, in the real conditions of the countryside,
was modified according to local conditions. The Chinese
pattern of nine rooms known as *Ming-Tang*, *Hall of Light*, or *Hall
of the Moon*, symbolizing the cycle of the year, had the nine-
square pattern as its underlying essence. The grid of nine
squares, or a circle divided into nine by straight lines, is often
encountered at the centre of Tibetan sacred diagrams. In
Scotland, the nine-square pattern was used at Beltane (May
Eve/Day) on the ceremonial oatmeal cake, which was circular
with the pattern inscribed on it. The Beltane bonfires were lit
on the central ninth of a ninefold square cut in the turf, the
outer eight squares of which were removed. The Ogham
character of the *Eight Ifins*, equivalent to the phonetic Æ,
signified the *Vineyard* or the *Hurdle of Wrought Twigs*, corresponding to the Witch Hazel tree, with all of its supernatural
connotations. The Eight Ifins bring together the mystery of
eight and nine which underlies the magical use of this
powerful figure. Its phonetic expression is the cosmic primal
sound revered in both the Sanskrit and Runic traditions, being
the God rune Æsc, and the name of the gods themselves – the
Æsir.

Shamanry in the Norse lands made extensive use of the grid
of nine squares and its derivatives. The *seiδ hallr*, or platform of
the seeress, on which the female shaman or *völva* sat to have
prophetic visions, was seen as the centre of the world. This
was a square wooden platform divided into nine squares, with

the seeress seated at the centre, facing north. Sometimes, the platform was covered by an ox hide, with nine squares incised on it. From this *seiδhallr*, the seeress could see things hidden to others. The remains of a ninth century tapestry found in the Oseberg ship burial is believed to represent a seeress's platform.

These platforms were often erected on a high point, such as a holy hilltop or on a burial-mound, being used for the practice of *útiseta, sitting out*. Sitting out was a form of meditation used to commune with the spirits of the departed, to obtain guidance from the gods, or to gain knowledge of future events for oneself or others. The old Norse *Mariu Saga* says if someone wants to gain an answer to a question, the querent must sit outside on a freshly-flayed ox hide in a hidden place in the forest. By drawing nine squares on the skin, the magical procedure will summon the Devil, who will bring him an answer to the question. Although this is a Christian interpretation, with the supernatural knowledge ascribed to the Devil, the gods of the old religion becoming the devils of the new, it records the mantic power ascribed to the nine-square pattern. In the *Færeyinga Saga*, the Magus Thrond sets up a platform outside his hall. On it are drawn a 'four-cornered lattice-work', and coming from this, nine circles drawn out from the lattices in all directions. This grid is used to call up the wraiths of three slain men to discover their murderer. Thrond sits silently by the fire until the wraiths of the three dead men come in and walk up to it. By the way they walk, the wizard knows how they died, and at whose hand, and is then able to apprehend the culprits.

The Norse scripture called the *Hávamál (The Words of the High One)*, a text ascribed to Odin Allfather himself, tells of 'runes and understood signs, signs of great power and great strength, those which the powerful Thul painted'. The seat of this great runemaster Thul, who is identified with Odin, is located at the Well of Urd, namely the centre of the world. The repeated connections made between runic divination, the world tree and the well of the fates at the middle of the world is apparent in the symbolic design of the *seiδhallr*, which microcosmically reproduces the cosmic centre at which prophecy arises. This is an earthly representation of Odin's high seat, *Hliδskjálf*, which gives him simultaneous views of the nine worlds of Norse cosmology. The designs drawn on the *seiðhallr* were the square of nine, or its subdivision into 81 (nine by nine), the *Paramasayika* grid and the basic board of the game of *Tafl*. The seeress sat in the middle, the ninth square at the centre, shielded from the outside by the other eight squares around her. We will meet this recurrent sacred pattern again in the ancient board game of *Tawlbwrdd*. The pattern used by the wizard Thrond is also connected with traditional board games, and also the construction of labyrinths.

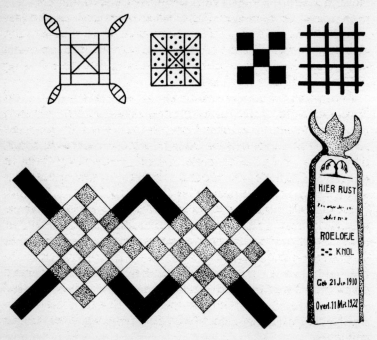

37. The grid pattern. Top left: Protective sigil from an eighteenth-century bucket of traditional design in the Museum für Volkskunde, Vienna. Centre illustrations: Versions of nine-square pattern used as magical protection, from traditional Austrian furniture. Top right: The Eight Ifins, producing the nine-square pattern. Bottom left: Protective sigil incorporating 25-square grids and Ing rune, on a North Tyrolean cabinet in the Museum für Volkskunde, Vienna. The entire pattern is composed of 72 squares (six by twelve). Bottom right: Tombstone of Roelofje Knol, 1920s, from the cemetery at Wanneperveen, Frisia, bearing the Pagan tree of life motifs and the nine-square sigil.

In Scandinavia, the erection of the nine-square platform on top of a mound was forbidden in the twelth century by a 'Great Law' enacted in Norway to suppress Paganism. A very late survival of these seeresses' platforms were used by the *witta wijven* or wise women of the remote Dutch province of Drenthe, until the middle of the seventeenth century. Their earth-houses with platforms, bedecked with skulls, animal and human, are shown in an engraving in Johan Picardt's book *Korte Beschryvinge van eenige verborgene antiquiteten*, published in Holland in 1660. Shortly afterwards, the institutionalized state persecution of non-Christians brought an end to the last remnants of traditional Frisian shamanry. Until well into the eighteenth centruy, the Dutch military organized Pagan hunts known as *Heidenjachten*, with the intention of exterminating indigenous Pagans and Gypsies.

Another use of the grid which is now disused is the medieval European method of accounting using a squared board known as the *Exchequer*. This board usually measured five by ten squares. The name comes from a form of recording rents, tithes or taxes levied on plots of land, and placing them in corresponding areas on a board, which was a conceptual map of the area, a secular parallel of the sacred *Paramasayika* grid. Several modern mathematical terms have come from these chequerboards. The word *calculate* is related to the pieces of stone or *calc* (chalk) which were placed on the board in appropriate positions. When we check something, we refer to the old board as a means of calculation. When the more efficient Indian (so-called 'Arabic') numerals arrived around 1450, such modes of calculation were rendered obsolete, and the mental patterns associated with them were no longer cultivated.

The national grid

The grid pattern of the Eight Ifins, the gameboard, the magic square and the seeress's platform was often applied to whole countries, figuratively or physically. Allegories which compare Ireland to a *Brandubh* board exist in ancient Irish literature. The game of *Brandubh*, played on a grid of seven by seven squares or holes, had a central point on which the king or *Branán* stood,

surrounded by four defending playing pieces. Similarly, the
political and sacred central point of ancient Ireland was Tara, a
central square surrounded by four other squares representing
the four provinces. An old Bardic poem draws the parallel:

> The centre of the Plain of Fál is Tara's Castle, delightful hill; out
> in the exact centre of the plain, like a mark on a parti-coloured
> Brannumh board. Advance there, it will be a profitable step:
> leap up onto that square, which is fitting for the Branán, the
> board is fittingly thine. I would draw they attention, O white of
> tooth, to the noble squares proper for the Branán, let them be
> occupied by thee. A golden Branán with his band art thou with
> thy four provincials, though, O king of Bregia, on yonder
> square and a man on each square around three.

The 'noble squares proper for the Branán' are Tara, Cashel,
Croghan, Naas and Oileach. Another ancient Irish text, *The
Settling of the Manor of Tara*, states that the Green of Tara had
'seven views on every side', alluding to the game of Brandubh,
played on a seven-by-seven board. When the High King of
Ireland held meetings of the chiefs of the land at Tara, they
occupied the appropriate quarters of the hall. As on the
gameboard, the King occupied the centre. The men of
Munster were in the south, those of Connacht in the west;
Ulster in the north and Leinster in the east. In the middle of the
hall, in the appropriate orientations from the High King, sat
the four Kings of the provinces. Tara was thus the
microcosmic symbol of the entire island, and whatever
happened there was enacted accordingly in the corresponding
part of the nation.

The numerical parallels between cosmology, sacred
geometry, canonical numbers and board games runs throughout northern European mythology. In ancient Irish tradition,
the '1 + 8' numerology of the nine square pattern. As in the
board game of *Tawlbwrdd*, which has a king defended by eight
pieces, eight swordsmen guarded the Irish hero Bricriu on his
way to the feast he had prepared in his nine-chambered hall.
Another Irish hero, Cu Chuláinn possessed nine weapons of
each type, one large and eight small. Unlike his Christian
counterparts, who would have had twelve, Cathbad the Druid
had eight disciples. A very important relic was dug up during
the excavation of an artificial island known as a *crannog* at

Ballinderry, near Moate, country Westmeath, Éire, in October, 1932. It is a square wooden gameboard, with a human head at one end, and a handle at the other. The playing part is nine and a half inches square, making it readily portable, like a modern travelling Chess set. Forty-nine holes arranged in a square are drilled in the board, making it the game of *Brandubh*. The central hole, in which the Branán would have been placed, has circles around it, marking it as the navel of the board, which it is in relation to the head. Here, the board is the slain giant underlying the world of Indo-European cosmology.

The central post

The tradition of the central point in the middle of a sacred city or landscape continues today. In many parts of Europe, there are still trees growing which were planted in villages or towns as spiritual markers. The sadly destroyed Merlin's Oak at Carmarthen, Wales, was one such tree, whose legend: '*When Merlin's Tree shall tumble down, Then shall fall Carmarthen town*', reflected the spiritual sustenance that tree afforded the town. Like other town trees, Merlin's Oak was a microcosmic image of the Cosmic Axis, which supported the stability of the heavens, and hence the physical and social order of the town itself. The recently-felled *Murtenlinde* in Fribourg, Switzerland, had an identical function. Planted in 1476 as a commemoration of the foundation of a new order, the overthrow of Burgundian domination at the Battle of Murten, the Linden tree symbolized the foundation of a new, stable order of society, patterned according to eternal laws. For centuries, the *Murtenlinde* stood in a triangular enclosure in the middle of the road near to St George's Fountain and the City Hall. Even when mechanized transport was introduced, the tree was protected. The overhead wires for the trolley buses were curved away from their straight alignment to clear the venerable tree, but traffic was finally its downfall, for on April 13, 1983, a drunk driver rammed his car into it, causing, as it turned out, lethal damage. In 1984, the one or two remaining branches still bore leaves, but in 1985, the *Murtenlinde* was declared dead, and cut down. A new tree, genetically identical with the *Murtenlinde*, grown from a cutting, has been planted, near to the fountain, but not in the street. Even that caused some motorists to complain, as some car parking spaces were abolished for the new tree. However, despite the alteration in the precise geolocation of the new tree, the spirit of the old tree, and hence the city, continues. The fact that in 1985 the citizens of Fribourg continued the tradition of possessing a living town tree shows its psychological, if not its spiritual, importance to them.

The planting of permanent trees as the central axis of a city is reflected in the tradition of a stave putting forth leaves when set up at a place of power. The legend of Joseph of Arimathea at Glastonbury and St Etheldreda at Etheldredestow, are the best known examples of this tradition, which are another version of the *Geomantic Act*. In both instances, a cut stave was rooted to the ground at an important location in the countryside, which became the focus for a shrine. By earthing the stave at such a point, it was revitalized, and in turn, revitalized the surroundings. At Glastonbury, the stave became the celebrated holy Thorn tree, and at Ethedlredestow, a mighty Ash. It is significant that these two trees are members of the trinity of sacred trees, Oak, Ash and Thorn, revered in country lore, and significant characters in Runic and Ogham.

The cutting down of a special tree and transporting it to a sacred site where it is used in sacred ceremonies is very widespread. It is practised by the indigenous populations of central and north America, and in parts of India. The European Maypole is part of this tradition, being the central focus of ceremonial dances which celebrate the end of the winter half of the year, and welcome the incoming of the summer half. The Maypole is the last relic of festivities conducted at various significant times of year which were enacted around a central marker or in a structure which symbolized Earth and the cosmos. The foundation and commencement of traditional fairs, held to commemorate Pagan or Christian festivals, were conducted with symbolic ceremonies, many of them redolent of the Cosmic Axis. At the Honiton Fair, held each Whitmonday, the occasion was inaugurated by the Town Crier, who recited: '*Oyez, oyez, Oyez, The glove is up and the fair has begun. No man shall be arrested until the glove is taken down. God save the King!*' A pole bearing a glove at its top – the emblem of regal authority – was erected, and a special law, separate from that of the surround-

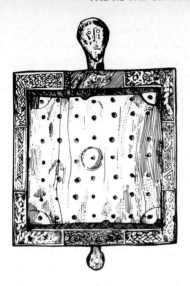 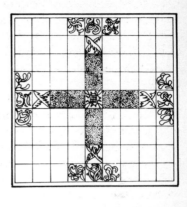

38. Left: The Ballinderry Game Board, found in a bog in County Westmeath, Éire, 1934. The central point on which the king-piece stands is the figure's navel. Right: Lappish cloth for playing Tablut, *as recorded by Linnaeus in 1732. In this game, the king stands on the central square – the* Kónakis – *symbolically at the centre of his army, his country and the world.*

ing town or county, reigned through the fair's duration. The 'kings' of old French playing cards often represent specific monarchs, commonly St Louis and Henri IV, each bearing a sceptre or rod, on the end of which is a hand, symbol of regal authority. Some versions of the Saxon Wands made today bear a hand at one end.

Customary survivals

Like many customs or 'superstitions', the sacred cosmic patterns which underlay towns, fairs and divinatory techniques have continued long after the magical elements have been discarded and forgotten. So long as the customs continue to be observed, the underlying patterns are also preserved as an integral part of the proceedings. One area in which these traditions have continued is in annual fairs, many of which have a very ancient provenance and continuity. Fairs have always had a strong association with fortune-telling and the performance and exhibition of seemingly magical feats. The layout of the traditional fairs of Europe was a deliberate and planned reflection of the cosmic order. At the centre was a pole, known as the *pau* or *pal*, which bore the lordly emblem, such as glove or crest, symbolic of the king in his absence. This post was fundamentally important in the ceremonies attending the foundation of towns and fairs, which were enacted according to identical principles. In the middle ages, the erection of the *pal* marked the foundation of a new town in exactly the same way as the sealing of the *mundus* had to the Etruscan and Roman augurs. The fair was, in effect, a temporary town with its own laws and jurisdiction. As in the traditional town, the fairground booths of various trades and crafts were allocated their own rows.

In several cases, these rows have become permanent buildings, and their successors stand on the same sites, preserving the alignments. The town of St Ives in Cambridgeshire (formerly Huntingdonshire) has a grid-pattern derived from St Audrey's Fair, still held annually in the streets of the town in the week nearest October 17, St Etheldreda's Day. In nearby Cambridge a similar process has occurred. There, in Barnwell, the east side of the city, are streets called Oyster Row, Mercer's Row and Garlic Row, which are a survival of the grid of the once-mighty Sturbridge Fair, whose plan remained unchanged for centuries. The latter row was the principal street of the fair, a *cardo* orientated north–south between the main road to Newmarket and the river, where there was a ferry.

In such fairs, jurisdication, represented by the *pal*, was enforced by the *Court of Pie Powder* (from the French *pied poudre* – dusty feet). This court was a tribunal of summary jurisdiction, where convicted offenders would be placed immediately in the stocks or on the pillory. The court at Sturbridge was sited in a tavern-booth to the west of Garlic Row, the main street. It was at the north end of the row, the position associated tradition-ally with authority. Several such courts continued until 1939, when World War II put an end to them. They included the fairs at Newcastle, Guildford, Ely and Bristol. That at Sturbridge continued until the fair's demise in 1932. They were the last examples of mobile jurisdiction associated with the grid as a symbolic microcosm of the world.

In former times, the grid was a very important symbol of jurisdiction in old Europe. Derived from the grid of the shamanistic Deer God, the medieval grid symbolized the imposition of divine and therefore also state order upon a piece of territory, for the purposes of control, record and taxation. Its meaning of law and order is self-evident. The regard in which the grid, in the form of the gameboard, was held, is apparent from ancient Celtic society. One of the Three Treasures of Éirinn (ancient Ireland) was a *Brandubh* board, and in old Wales, the *Tawlbwrdd* board was a symbol of judgeship (see Chapter 7).

In medieval Germany, the grid was the basis of the *Mystic Plot* of the *Vehmgericht*, the secret and unofficial Westphalian courts of jurisdiction which met out of doors. These courts were the direct successors of the Free Field Court of Corbey, under the jurisdication of the Pagan priests of the Eresburgh, the temple which contained the cosmic pillar known as *Irminsul* (now the town of Ober-Marsberg). When the Pagan shrine was suppressed by Charlemagne in 772 CE, and the Christian religion imposed upon the Saxons, the courts continued, but as a means of suppressing surviving Pagan practices and belief. 'Secret Crimes', such as the practise of magic, witchcraft and poison-making, were particular targets of the *Vehmic* courts. Forcible usurpation of land was also an offence against the *Vehm*, which was entrusted with the maintenance of boundaries, a sacred trust symbolized by the pattern of the *Mystic Plot*.

The court was composed of 16 people, who held their office for life. The senior member was the *gerefa* or *graff* (reeve or count); the most junior was the *fröhner* or summoner, whilst the other 14 were the ordinary members, the *echevius*. When any of them died, a new member was elected by the monks whose monastery had taken over from the Pagan shrine. The members were chosen from among the 22 families of the district.

It was essential that the court should be held in the open, and in daylight. It had to be *'up roder Erde Gemaket'* (made on the Red Earth), that is within the limits of the ancient Duchy of Westphalia, and at specific locations. The seat of Judgement, known as the *Freistuhl* or *Königs-Stuhl*, Free Seat, or King's Seat, was set up at the middle of the *Mystic Plot*, a square measuring 16 feet by 16 feet. The plot was laid out each time by the *Fröhner*, who, after 'proving' the *mete-wand* (measuring stick) against the foot of the *graff*, measured out the area. The central point, where the seat was placed, was first consecrated by the *Fröhner* digging a pit, into which each of the members threw a handful of ashes, a piece of charcoal and a tile, a parallel with the rites of Roman and Indian town-foundation. If on a subsequent sitting of the court there was any doubt that the correct place had been found, the ground was dug for these tokens. If they were not found, then all the judgements which had been passed were null and void. One of the signs of the *Vehm* was an eightfold pattern consisting of eight square tiles overlapping one another, symbolizing the eight directions meeting at the centre and the complete coverage of the area by the court's jurisdiction.

The layout of a plan upon the ground, symbolizing an actual or spiritual building, was formerly a practice also in English Freemasonry, where a plan of the lodge in which the ceremonies were to take place was drawn in chalk on the floor of a room, and erased afterwards. Customarily, this *tessellated pavement* measures 16 by 16 squares. Like the fair and the game board, but unlike the city, the gridded pattern, whilst still reflecting the cosmic order, was temporary. Although after 1850 most fairs gradually altered in character until they became little more than funfairs, complete with mechanized rides and side-shows, the tradition of their layout has remained. Fair people form a close-knit community dealing with the specialized problems inherent in their way of life. Any specialized community must preserve within itself a craft knowledge of how to accomplish the required tasks, and this always includes traditions and rites which are often incomprehensible or just unrecognized by outsiders.

An incident which occurred in 1943 demonstrates the survival of geomantic knowledge amongst showmen. In December of that year, the funeral of Pat Collins, '*The King of the Showmen*' took place. Although in the midst of World War II, a period of dire austerity, it was a major event. It was reported in *The Sunday Express* on December 12, 1943 in a piece entitled '60-Year Ritual Fixed Grave for Showman "King"'.

There was a strange incident at the cemetery when the old man's son visited it accompanied by Father Hanrahan, of St Peter's Catholic Church, Bloxwich, to select a site for the grave. When he came to seek a site for his father's last resting place it was found that the Catholic portion of the cemetery was full. The adjoining land which belongs to the cemetery was specially consecrated. When Mr Collins went to select a place for its first grave, he brought his foot forward, raised it and brought his heel down sharply on the turf, making a deep dent in it, exclaiming as he did so *'This is the spot. I want the exact centre of my father's grave to be over that mark.'* He explained to the priest: *'My father used those words and that gesture for 60 years every time that he inspected a fairground site to indicate where the principal attraction, usually the biggest of the merry-go-rounds, was to be erected. He never measured the ground, but the chosen spot was always in the exact centre of the showground. It was a ritual with him.'*

The fixation of a central point in a newly-consecrated cemetery by the same means as the geolocation of the centre of a fair is very interesting. The rite of bringing down the heel – called in the parlance of Rugby Football *making a mark* – appears to be an authentic geomantic survival from former times. It was fitting that *The King of the Showmen* should be buried, as the first interment in a new cemetery, at the centre. Subsequent burials were to be, as it were, his guardians in death. In laying out fairgrounds, the connection between the centre of the showground, the Cosmic Axis and the rotation of the merry-go-round appears to be another overtly symbolic survival amongst showmen. The possibility that dancing around the Maypole may have been superseded by merry-go-rounds cannot be discounted. It is probable that there are many other traditions among the secrets of showmanship that are unbroken continuations of the locational practices of antiquity.

City and gameboard

As I have shown above, in former times the grid was a powerful symbol of the structure of the world, and of divine or human dominion over it. The form of the world, the layout of the countryside, the capital city, the holy temple of the gods and the palace of the king were all symbols of order expressed as the grid. The grid not only defined the centre and the perimeter, but also the differing qualities of locations on its surface. The most powerful image of this manifestation is in the *Holy City*. The gridded square pattern which Etruscan augurs used when laying out the ground-plan of a city has parallels all over Europe and Asia. In the *Vastuvidya* (locational geomancy) of India, the square grid is the basic pattern upon which cities and temples are laid out.

Board games are linked inextricably with divination, astrology and sacred geometry, and the designs of traditional gameboards preserve their sacred origins. In some cases, the boards on which the games are played are identical with the canonical plans of temples, sacred enclosures and holy cities. Chess, the best known and most widespread board game in modern times, is of divinatory origin. Some Chess historians have connected it with the ancient Chinese game of *Siang k'i*, whilst others deny the Chinese connection. Whether or not it was a forerunner of Chess, *Siang k'i* has strong connections

Nº.76· MERLIN'S OAK

39. *Merlin's Oak, the sacred tree on which, according to tradition, Carmarthen's prosperity, and even very existence, depends (see p. 137).*

with divination. *Siang k'i* is translated usually as The Astronomical Game or The Figure Game. Here, there is a close affinity between the gameboard and the diviners' boards which gave rise to the magnetic compass used today in *Feng-Shui*, the Chinese art of placement. This game was played with the aid of dice.

The earliest known instructions for the canonical form of cities are in the *Arthasastra* of Kautilya, who was prime minister to the ancient Indian ruler Candragupta Maurya. This gives the grid of nine lines by nine as the canonical form, making the city have a layout of eight by eight square blocks. The legendary capital city of Krishna, Dvaravati, however, was believed to have been laid out with eight streets crossing at right angles. Similarly, the *K'ao-kung Chi*, a classical Chinese text, describes the layout of the royal Chou capital city thus: 'The carpenters demarcated the capital as a square with sides of nine *Li*, each side having three gateways. Within the capital, there were nine meridional and nine latitudinal streets, each of the former being nine chariot-tracks wide.' This description shows us that the capital was a 'chessboard' grid of 64 squares. The administrative centre was the central quarter area of the gird, four by four.

In Vedic India, the eight by eight chequerboard was called *Ashtapada*. The earliest known mention of board games in literature is in the *Brahma-Jala Sutra*, which contains words attributed to the Buddha Gautama. There, he describes the trivial things that occupy the thoughts of the unenlightened, among them playing *Ashtapada* and *Dasapada*. The *Mahabhashya* (second century CE) defines *Ashtapada* as 'a board in which each line has eight squares', and the word *Ashtapada* was used to describe the grid employed in land survey. The French writer Bernouf, in *La Lotus de la Bonne Loi*, an obscure work published in Paris in 1854, cites a passage from a northern Indian Buddhist text where the planet herself is described as 'The Earth on which *Ashtapadas* were fashioned with cords of gold'.

A later use of the grid laid out on the ground is recorded by the Iranian writer Hamza al-Isfahani, who lived in the early part of the tenth century. Writing about the construction of the city of Jundu-Shapur by the Sassanian king Shahpur (240–270 CE): 'The plan of the city was after the fashion of a chessboard: it was intersected by eight times eight streets.' A later Iranian commentator noted that 'the figure was after this fashion, but chess had not been invented at this time'. Another of these *Ashtapada* cities was Nishapur in Khurasan. The later Islamic geographer Mustawfi wrote in 1340: 'In the days of Chosroes ... the old town of Nishapur had been laid out originally on a plan of a chessboard with eight squares to each side.' The city of Jundu-Shapur had a grid of eight lines, whilst that of Khurasan was built according to the prescription of the *Arthasastra* with eight squares. In much more recent times, the Indian city of Bangalore was laid out by Vidyahadar Bhattacharyya, and in 1857, the Burmese city of Mandalay was located and designed according to canonical prescription by five officers of state. Mandalay was one of the last great Holy Cities laid out as a mandala according to canonical principles, which included the sacrifice of 50 people as foundation offerings to be deposited beneath various key places in the grid, including four who formed the basis of the royal throne at the centre.

The traditional layout of the Holy City plan is one which has an even number of lots or blocks intersected by an odd number of streets in each direction. Thus a city laid out, as was Nishapur, as a grid of eight by eight squares, had seven streets running in each direction, or nine if we include those immediately inside the walls. The Roman city of Thamugadi (Timgad), in modern Algeria, the plan of which is illustrated here, was laid out similarly, but with a grid of 12 squares by 12 (144 in all). Although there have been slight alterations to the plan, the effect of such a grid is well illustrated at Thamugadi. A regularly-laid out city with an even number of blocks, like this one, will have a crossroads at the centre, whilst that with an odd number will have a block at its centre. This central point is the *omphalos* of the city, and in board games, which echo the Holy City plan, this central point is called the *navel*. It is actually called *foibeny* ('navel') in the game of *Fanorona*, played in Madagascar, and *pusat*, with the same meaning, in the Malay version of *Alquerque*. On the ancient gameboard found at Ballinderry, Éire, in 1932, the central King's Square forms the navel of an anthropomorphic board.

The divisions on a gameboard, or within the city, reflect other aspects of traditional cosmology. The earliest Indo-European cosmology asserts that at the centre of the Earth, the world mountain, Mount Meru, is surrounded by seven zones of sea and seven of land, increasing in height towards the centre. Outside this is the world ocean with four continents mirroring the four quarters of the heavens. One western manifestation of this layout was Tara, the sacred and political centre of ancient Ireland. Tara had seven ramparts around the holy settlement, in the centre of which was a great central hall where the High King resided. Around these, at the four quarters, were the halls of the provinces. Of course, in addition to symbolizing the parts of Ireland they represented, these halls signified one of the four seasons, the four elements and many other of the fourfold correspondences.

When Christian monks cursed Tara, the old Pagan centre of Ireland, the High King, Domnall, son of Aed, founded a new headquarters at Dún na nGéd, by the River Boyne. Like Tara, it was encompassed by seven large earth ramparts, seven zones of land and seven of water. At the centre, the highest building was the Great Hall. To the north of this was the Assembly Hall of Ulster and to the east, the Hall of Leinster. South of it stood the Hall of Munster and to its west the Banquet Hall of Connacht. The largest building was at the centre, giving the whole ensemble the appearance of the world mountain. This parallels exactly the ancient concentric square cities described in old Indian texts, whose layout included the positional segregation of society. The four castes – priests, soldiers, tradesmen and labourers – lived in the various zones, the highest caste being situated in the middle of the town. The highest caste also had the highest houses, giving the city the form of a mountain. Similarly, this characteristic can be found in the layout of several ancient board games, where the array of pieces reflects some aspect of the ordering of society. For example the central point of the *Tafl* group of games, which includes the Irish game of *Brandubh*, is occupied by the largest piece, the King or Branán. Surrounding him are his warriors. Just like the halls of Tara, they defend the four cardinal directions, and are attacked from the four quarters by the opposition.

This world mountain theme has always captured people's imagination, and has often been used in twentieth century representations of 'cities of the future'. These idealist designs have as their basis those implicit beliefs in the cosmic order

40. *The coat of arms of the city of Amsterdam has at its centre three crosses or saltires which signify justice, being the stylized crossing-points of the sacred grid of jurisdiction.*

held by the ancients which led them to the construction of their traditional Holy Cities. They are expressions of the supposed connection between good social order and rigorous, canonical town-plans, a theory which is out of favour today. One of the most notable of these future cities was envisaged in 1919 by the visionary German architect Bruno Taut. His concept of *die Stadtkrone* (the Crown of the City) arranged the geometric centre of a new city in an identical arrangement to the old Indian and Irish Holy Cities. At the middle of the city, a vast faceted crystalline glass tower was to symbolize human beings' striving towards the divine. Similarly, Hans Kampffmeyer's contemporary project for a new city called *Friedenstadt* was derived from this archetypal concept, which was influential in Germany until the rise of Hitler. Visionary illustrations of these unbuilt projects show the Sun rising behind the towers, the tallest of which is at the centre of the gridded, orientated cities. Clearly, these archetypal sacred layouts, created in accordance with geometrical-cosmic laws, will continue to manifest themselves in ways appropriate to the times.

Just as there are different board games with different numbers of squares, so, on a larger scale, different grids have been adopted for various purposes of state, from tribunals to monasteries. A very important sixteenth century complex of ecclesiastical buildings designed according to one of these sacred grids is the monastery of San Lorenzo, El Escorial. This gridded plan is one which its architects believed to be of great antiquity, reproducing the symbolic design of an earlier sacred enclosure. El Escorial was erected on the instructions of King Philip II of Spain as a thanksgiving to God for Spanish victory in the Battle of San Quentin. On the eve of the battle, the king had sworn a holy vow that, should the forces of Spain be triumphant, he would build a monastery dedicated to St Laurence, on whose day, August 10, the battle was fought in 1557. When the foundations were laid, the orientation was aligned on sunset on St Laurence's day, an astrologically favourable time which was also historically symbolic. The general plan of the building, supposedly recalling the appalling death of Laurence on a gridiron, is a grid. Although the foundation was aligned on the relevant solar orientation, work actually commenced on St George's day, April 23, 1563, and took 21 years to finish.

The building incorporates many aspects of sacred geometry and symbolic design. Because the original architect died shortly after the foundation, the main work was entrusted to Juan de Herrera, who, like Philip II, was an adherent to the ideas of the medieval mystic Ramón Lull. At his previous commission for Valladolid cathedral, Herrera had applied music-derived harmonic dimensions to the building. He continued his use of symbolic geometry at the Escorial. The grid plan of the building, whilst echoing Laurence's death, was actually derived from the square layout ascribed to the Camp of the Israelites. The re-establishment of the ancient divine order was an important goal of Jesuit mystics in Spain at the time, and considerable research was undertaken to determine the precise geometry and structure of the sacred buildings described in the Old Testament. One result of this research was the monumental work entitled *In Ezechielem Explanationes*. Written by Juan Bautista Villalpanda and Jeronimo Prado, both Jesuit priests, the book described and explained the complex structure and symbolism of the Temple of the Jews and its interpretation in the vision of Ezekiel. Although the book was published after the completion of El Escorial, Villalpanda had worked with Herrera on the symbolic design of the building.

In their book, Villalpanda and Prado reconstructed the layout of the Camp of the Israelites according to traditional interpretations. The Camp itself was arranged on a grid of 100 squares (ten by ten), subdivided geometrically to give various orientated correspondences between astronomical features, astrological qualities and the various tribes and divisions of the Israelites. According to the biblical book of *Numbers*, the Camp, which was arranged around the portable temple known as the *Tabernacle*, had one of the 12 tribes of Israel as guardian of each direction. The tribe of Ruben raised its standard in the south; Ephraim, to the west; Dan to the north and Judah to the west. The authors assigned a sign of the zodiac to each tribe. Starting in the south, they are: Ruben, Aquarius; Simeon, Pisces; Gad, Aries; Ephraim, Taurus; Manasseh, Gemini; Benjamin, Sagittarius; Dan, Scorpio; Asser, Libra; Napthali, Virgo; Judah, Leo; Issachar, Cancer; and Zebulon, Capricorn. Each tribe occupied one square of the 100-square grid, situated regularly around the perimeter of the large square. Inside the enclosure of the large square, four more single squares were occupied by the Levites, who administered the structure, equipment and staffing of the Tabernacle, Moses and Aaron. These four squares are arranged at the corners of a square of 16 at the centre of the square of 100. This layout gives a regular distribution of single squares across the grid which has the effect of making four corner squares of 16 squares, each with a single occupied square at its corner. Between these four quarters are a cross, two squares in width, making the quartered square of the Holy City plan, a universal form.

The plan of the Camp of the Israelites drawn up by Villalpanda and Prado has some discrepancies when compared with the account in the book of *Numbers*. In the biblical description, the four standards of Ruben, Ephraim, Dan and Judah are guarding the four quarters, which can be interpreted as being at the centre of each side of an orientated square, in the positions where gates would be. The Spanish account, however, places them at the corners of the square. The biblical account also locates the Camp of Moses and Aaron to the east of the Tabernacle, whilst in Villalpanda and Prado's grid, it lies to the south-east. If the Camp had the design claimed by the Jesuits, then it appears that it was orientated with its corners towards the cardinal directions and the four sides facing the four quarters of the heavens, like some later European mystic squares. This would have the effect of orientating the Tabernacle itself on a north-west to south-east axis, perhaps upon a Midwinter Solstice sunrise alignment.

The Spanish interpretation of the Camp of the Israelites also allocates zodiacal correspondences to the spaces between the occupied squares. Taking the Jesuit cardinal orientation, the south-western space is dedicated to Mars. North of this is the Tabernacle itself, and in the north-western corner, the planet is Venus. The centre of the north side has Mercury, and the north-eastern, the Sun. The middle of the east side, towards which the entrance of the Tabernacle faces, is ruled by the Moon, the south-east has Saturn, and finally, the south is ruled by Jupiter. Whether this version of the Camp of the Israelites is the actual plan they used, handed down to the time of Villalpanda and Prado by Rabbinical or Christian Qabalists, or whether it was derived from non-Jewish occult sources, the plan is certainly within the tradition of the sacred grid. Whatever its origin, as described by the Jesuit researchers the plan is identical with the board used in the game of *Gala*, which can be interpreted similarly (see Chapter 9). One of the several versions of Great Chess, played on a ten by ten chequerboard, may also have some esoteric connections with this tradition.

The parallel between the city, astrological diagrams and board games is expressed in the French, Italian and Arabic languages, where the squares of a gameboard are sometimes known as the equivalent word for *house*. The whole board had architectural connotations in ancient India, being called *kosh-thika* or *koshthagara*, meaning a storehouse or granary. This association is reflected by the name of the central square in Nine Men's Morris, the *pound*.

Sacred number and sacred geometry

Many sacred diagrams have a hidden structure which under-lies seemingly separate patterns. In esoteric thought, such patterns are alternative unfoldings of a basic geometrical theme, linking the more complex forms together in a symbolic and structural unity. There are several major patterns which fall into this category, one being the quartered square of the Holy City plan. Another, related, array is the pattern of dots or points with one in the centre and the other eight forming a cross around it. The numbers eight and nine are closely related in sacred layout, myth and astronomy. In her work *Eight and Nine; The Sacred Numbers of Sun and Moon in the Pagan North* (1982), Prudence Jones wrote: 'In the Nordic universe, there are nine

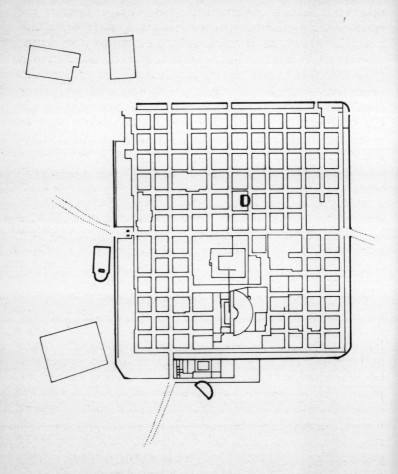

41. *The gridded Roman city known now as Thamugadi, in Algeria. It was laid out in the second century of the present era as a grid of 12 by 12 (144) squares (see p. 146).*

worlds, four in the horizontal plane, four on the vertical, and Midgard, our own world, in the middle of them all. Here we have eight outliers and one central focus, perhaps the magical unifying number.' This 'one surrounded by eight' pattern is almost universal, having a basic geometrical structure in square geometry, and a universal symbolism. Here, eight is seen as the number of being, enfolded by nine. Nine represents the 'lunar' method of reckoning, which starts from the single unit, and expands the number by repetition. Eight is the corresponding 'solar' number, which starts again from the unit but which subdivides it regularly by repeated halving. Astronomically, the number nine occurs in conjunction with eight in the 99 Moons or lunar months which make up eight full solar years. In the old day reckoning of the North, nine nights were necessary to complete the period of eight full days, the old Pagan week. Nine is thus the sacred number of completion, as in the space between the Eight Ifins of the Ogham alphabet and the magic grid of the European north. In pre-Christian Europe, the number eight was very important, recurring in saga and myth, often with connotations of fixity, or a stay at a central point. Northern myth tells of the trickster-god Loki, who lived in the centre of the Earth for eight winters, the hero Siegfried, who was compelled to serve eight years with King Gibich, and the Swan-Maidens who lived with Wayland the Smith and his brothers for eight winters. In these instances, the ninth comes as a change: deliverance from their plight.

Eight is a solar number of time measurement, both of the day and of the year. In traditional measure, it is the natural division of length, weight and volume by successive halvings. It survives in the eight furlongs in the mile, the sixteen ounces in the pound, and eight pints in the gallon. It is the difference between the board defined as lines on which the pieces are places, and the lines of a board where the pieces are on the squares formed by the lines. Many eightfolds are produced by nine operations. Frey, the Norse God of Fertility, had a magic ring which, after eight full days (nine nights), magically produced a further ring. Here, we have the motif of infinite extension which relates to the mysteries of the rune ING -

The nine dot pattern: armature of the absolute

There is a symbolic arrangement of points known as the *Nine Dot Pattern* which underlies many sacred diagrams and the arrangement of playing-pieces in the *Tafl* group of games. These include the shield-knot, a sigil used in the magical protection of buildings; the *fylfot*, another sacred sigil symbolizing the cycles of the seasons; the arrangement of defending pieces in the board game of *Tablut*; and as the central design of the classical labyrinth. The *fylfot* pattern is best known from the so-called *Ilkley Swastika*, an ancient symbol carved on a rock on Ilkley Moor, Yorkshire. A similar Bronze Age inscribed *fylfot* exists on a stone at Tossene in Sweden, and in a medieval church *graffito* at Sutton in Bedfordshire. It is known also from an ancient sword-hilt found in Denmark. An ancient puzzle, recorded by the nineteenth century antiquary J. Romilly Allen, refers to the form:

> Four rich men and four poor men have their houses situated symmetrically at the corners of two squares, one within the other, the houses being in two straight lines at right angles to each other. The houses of the rich men are outside; in the centre is a pond of spring water, and the houses of the poor men between the houses of the rich men and the water supply. The rich men desire to build a wall, which, although giving them free access to the water, shall exclude the poorer neighbours. How is it to be done?

The form of the hypothetical wall is, of course, the *fylfot* pattern. It is interesting that the ancient Chinese tradition of the well-field layout is echoed in this English puzzle.

This fylfot design is related geometrically to the ancient Chinese sigil known as *Yin* and *Yang*. The interpenetration of these two polarities around the central unity is plain. In ancient Europe, the sign signified the wholeness of the year, with the four arms representing the changing four seasons. An astronomical interpretation sees it as the four seasonal positions of the constellation of *The Plough* in relation to God's Nail, the Pole Star or cosmic axial centre. The pattern is inherent in the board game of Ludo, otherwise known as *Ucker*. Although in its present form it dates only from 1896, it is derived from the ancient Indian game of *Pachisi* (see Chapter 8).

Labyrinths and magic squares

Many race games, such as the group containing *Ashtapada* and *Saturankam*, follow paths comparable with those of traditional labyrinths. Unlike the puzzle mazes in which one can get lost, these labyrinths are unicursal, with a single path to the centre from the outside. There are five different broad classes of unicursal labyrinth, of which the Classical labyrinth is one of the most elegant. A design pregnant with extensive symbolism, its layout is related directly to the grid pattern. When making full-sized Classical labyrinths, all that is needed to draw the labyrinth on the ground is a rope with 16 knots defining 15 units of equal length, and five wooden pegs. Four of the pegs mark the corners of a square measuring eight by eight units (64 squares), that of the Magic Square of Mercury and the *Ashtapada* Chequerboard, whilst the fifth fixes the cord to the ground. During the drawing of the labyrinth, the cord bends around these pegs to create the curves of the appropriate sectors. The first peg is inserted in the ground on one side of the square, so that it is three units from one corner, and five from the other. The cord is attached to this peg, and the first part of the labyrinth composed of semicircles centred on this peg is formed by marking out along the lines of knots numbers 2, 4, 6, 8, 10, 12, 14 and 16 from the fixing-point. Once this is done, the knotted cord remains attached to the original peg, and the cord is taken round the corner pegs, which become the centre of new radii. Finally, the end of the cord is brought to the opposite side of the grid. The space left between the end when brought round clockwise and counterclockwise, which is diametrically opposite the fixing-point, becomes the labyrinth entrance. The rest of the labyrinth, inside the square itself, is marked out by a specific division of the grid which echoes Indian *Yantra* designs and the Holy City plan. The small French pavement labyrinths at Mirepoix and Toulouse are laid out on nine square tiles, showing that the later and more sophisticated Christian labyrinth design is still related to the sacred grid. The central points of the unorthodox Christian pavement labyrinths at St Omer, France and Guent, Belgium, likewise have nine square tiles. For further details of the

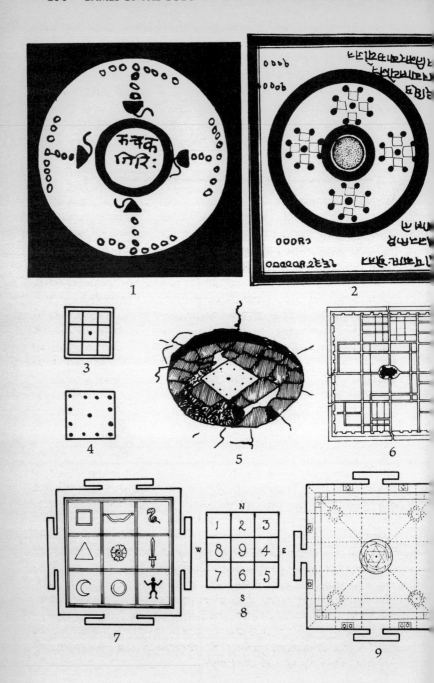

1

2

3

4

5

6

7

8

N

1	2	3
8	9	4
7	6	5

W   E

S

9

significance of labyrinth design see my book *Earth Harmony* (1987).

The use of the cord to lay out a form resembling a labyrinth is recorded in *Færyinga Saga* in the tale of Thrond where his magical lattice work had nine circles were drawn out from it in all directions. The numerology of the cords used in various canonical measurements is related to that of the chains used in African geomantic divination and also the Witches' Ladder and Witches' Cord (see Chapter 3).

Magic squares

Magic squares are directly related to the sacred grid, being the numerical mystery which underlies the physical form. In the western tradition, there are several standard squares which are assigned to various planetary powers. In a magic square, the numbers of the smaller squares which compose the larger are arranged in such a manner that taking any row, the sum of the numbers will be the same. The simplest magic square is the square of nine, ascribed to Saturn, where each line adds up to 15 and the total of all the numbers added together is 45. This is the square of the Pagan magicians of northern Europe.

$$
\begin{array}{ccc}
4 & 9 & 2 \\
3 & 5 & 7 \\
8 & 1 & 6
\end{array}
$$

42. *The cosmic centre and the grid.* 1. *The* Rucaca Continent *of Hindu cosmology.* 2. *The* Nandisvara *diagram, showing satellite components around the centre, as in the* Tafl *group of board games.* 3 *and* 4. *The nine-square grid with the central point compared with the 13-dot pattern used on the foundation-plates of Hindu temples.* 5. *Foundation-pit beneath a Bengali temple.* 6. *The original ground-plan of the Burmese city of Mandalay, geomantically laid out in 1857.* 7. *Hindu* Yantra *of the astrological planets and the Moon's nodes, with the Sun at the centre.* 8. *Layout of a priest's house, Malabar, India. (The areas of the nine-square grid each have specific uses: 1 – for studying the* Vedas*; 2 – for storing wealth; 3 – grain; 4 – for performing ceremonies for the dead; 5 – kitchen; 6 – shrine of the household god; 7 – place for making offerings; 8 – reception of guests; 9 – courtyard).* 9. Yantra *underlying a Hindu temple*

The four by four grid is assigned to Jupiter, each rank or file of numbers adding up to 34. The sum of all the numbers is 136.

4	14	15	1
9	7	6	12
5	11	10	8
16	2	3	13

The grid of 25 squares (five by five) belongs to Mars, each line being 65, totalling 325.

11	24	7	20	3
4	12	25	8	16
17	5	13	21	9
10	18	1	14	22
23	6	19	2	15

The six by six grid of 36 squares is that of the Sun. Each line adds up to 111, and the total to 666. This number is the infamous *Number of the Beast* of the *Revelation of St John the Divine.*

6	32	3	34	35	1
7	11	27	28	8	30
19	14	16	15	23	24
18	20	22	21	17	13
25	29	10	9	26	12
36	5	33	4	2	31

The fifth grid is that of Venus, measuring seven by seven. Each rank or file is 175, total 1225.

22	47	16	41	19	35	4
5	23	48	17	42	11	29
30	6	24	49	18	36	12
13	31	7	25	43	19	37
38	14	32	1	26	44	20
21	39	8	33	2	27	45
46	15	40	9	34	3	28

The sixth grid is allocated to Mercury, being the familiar *Ashtapada* or chequerboard grid. The added sums are 260 a line and a total of 2080 for all the numbers.

```
 8  58  59   5   4  62  63   1
49  15  14  52  53  11  10  56
41  23  22  44  48  19  18  45
32  34  35  29  25  38  39  28
40  26  27  37  36  30  31  33
17  47  46  20  21  43  42  24
 9  55  54  12  13  51  50  16
64   2   3  61  60   6   7  57
```

The final table is that of the Moon, being nine by nine. The added numbers are 369, with a total of 3321. This square is especially important, because it is the first square which is a square of a square (3 x 3 x 3 x 3). It is the basis of the game of *Tawlbort*, and the *Paramasiyaka* grid of Hindu *Vastuvidya*.

```
37  78  29  70  21  62  13  54   5
 6  38  79  30  71  22  63  14  46
47   7  39  80  31  72  23  55  15
16  48   8  40  81  32  64  24  56
57  17  49   9  41  73  33  65  25
26  58  18  50   1  42  74  34  66
67  27  59  10  51   2  43  75  35
36  68  19  60  11  52   3  44  76
77  28  69  20  61  12  53   4  45
```

As in all things, these magic squares have a series of correspondences to which they refer: a number, deity, week-day, tree and quality. Below are the central and northern European correspondences:

Number	Magic Square	Day Name	Deity (Classical)	Deity (Northern)	Tree	Character
1	36	Sunday	Apollo	Sól	Birch	Good
5	81	Monday	Selene/Luna	Mani	Willow	Bad
2	25	Tuesday	Mars	Tiw/Tyr	Holly	Good
6	64	Wednesday	Mercury	Woden	Ash	Good
3	16	Thursday	Jupiter	Thor	Oak	Bad
7	49	Friday	Venus	Frigg	Apple	Bad
4	9	Saturday	Saturn	Norns	Alder	Neutral

Eliphas Lévi assigned each of these seven magic squares to one of (his version of) the ancient Seven Wonders of the World, as follows:

Saturn	Solomon's Temple in Jerusalem
Jupiter	The Image of Zeus at Olympia
Mars	The Hanging Gardens of Babylon
The Sun	The Colossus of Rhodes
Venus	The Tomb of Mausolus
Mercury	The Pyramids
The Moon	The Temple of Diana at Ephesus

Lévi believed that the structure of these great constructions was based upon the geometry and numbers inherent on these magic squares. It is an area of research which has not yet been fully explored. The various grids upon which board games are played can be understood with reference to these numbers, and the games themselves can be investigated with regard to their corresponding qualities.

7

SYMBOLIC BOARD GAMES

There are three possible means of demarcation of the spaces or *points* upon which the playing-pieces must be placed in a board game. If the pieces are pegs or stones, they can be inserted in holes made for the purpose in the ground or the board. These holes may be joined by lines showing permitted moves. The best-known of the *Merels* group of games, *Nine Men's Morris*, is primarily of the peg-hole and line variety. Because of the design of the *Merels* board, it is not possible to play the game on a chequered board or a grid. If the game is played using stones, beans or the more familiar crafted pieces, these are placed at the junctions of lines. *Merels*, described below, is unusual in that it cannot be played on a gridded board. *Chess, Draughts, Tafl, Fox and Geese* and other allied games can. Here, there are two options. Pieces can be placed upon the intersection of lines, or in the cells between the lines. These cells may be distinguished only by the dividing lines themselves, or may be coloured in rows or alternately, as in the familiar chequerboard. The board composed only of a grid of lines appears to be the earlier form. Traditional Indian Chesscloths have a grid of eight by eight lines upon which the men are placed, making the board a grid of seven by seven squares. This relationship of square to line is important, for it determines whether there will be a central point on which a playing-piece can stand, which, symbolically, is the major distinction in board games.

Merels

There are two 'families' of board games which encapsulate
these cosmological principles better than any others. They are
the group of games known as *Merels* – Nine Men's Morris and
its variants – which have a non-orientated structure, and *Tafl*,
which has a centralized structure. Both have boards which
reflect the ancient sacred view of the structure of the world,
and modes of play which have symbolic meaning which can be
recovered by comparison with myth, legend and parallel folk
traditions. The design of the Nine Men's Morris board is very
ancient, and perhaps pre-dates the game itself. It exists in
prehistoric rock-scribings in a cave at Malesherbes near
Fontainebleau, France, and another can be found at War-
scheueck in Austria. Another notable ancient *Merels* board
carving is at Hazar Sum in Afghanistan. The Afghan carving
is accompanied by a stylized rendering of a horned beast. A
board dating from the Bronze Age inscribed on a flat stone,
discovered at the burial site Cr Bri Chualann, County
Wicklow, Éire, may be one of the oldest games yet found, as
the others are without doubt patterns used for something
other than play. Boards or patterns for various versions of the
game are known from around 1400 BCE in ancient Egypt.
Those in Egypt are carved on the roofing-slabs of the temple at
Kurna, whilst the remains of a board were found at Troy. It is
also one of the most widespread, being known in Europe,
north and central Africa, Madagascar, the Middle East and the
Indian subcontinent, and, as games introduced by settlers, in
the Americas and Australasia.

The name *Merels* applies to board games where pieces are
first entered on the board, one at a time by alternate players,
then, once all are entered, used to produce alignments by
subsequent movements. The name *Merels* comes from the Low
Latin *merellus*, meaning a token, counter, or coin. In this group,
of games, all of the pieces have the same power of movement,
being distinguished only by colour.

The simplest of the *Merels* group is not usually thought of as
a board game, being the familiar Noughts and Crosses. This
game, which is known also as Tic Tac Toe, Tit Tat Toe, Kit Cat
Cannio (Suffolk dialect), *Tripp Trapp Trull* (Swedish) and *Tik Tak*

Tol (Norwegian), is usually drawn on paper, but there are magnetic 'travelling sets' available. The object of the game is to make a line of three noughts or crosses or, in northern Sweden, the figures 1 or 2. Whatever the figures, in Sweden, a winning line of three is known as a *mill*. When someone wins at the game there, the traditional call is '*Tripp Trapp Trull, min kvarn är full.*' In Swedish, *qvarn* means mill. It is a word cognate with the English *quern*, a hand mill. In all of the more complex versions of *Merels*, this word is used to describe an alignment of pieces belonging to the same player. In this simple game, the line of three is not always called a mill. An old English rhyme goes:

Tit tat toe,
Here I go,
Three jolly butcher boys,
All in a row.

Unlike true *Merels* games, Noughts and Crosses is just a game of entry which allows no movement once a piece has been entered. This makes the game ideal to play on paper, but because no movement is permitted, it is not a very satisfying game to play. Many a drawn game ensues because it is impossible for the person who starts the game to lose except by error.

A more advanced version of Noughts and Crosses is Nine Holes, relict 'boards' of which may be recognized cut into the fabric of ancient buildings, including the cloisters at Westminster Abbey. The utmost simplicity of Nine Holes makes it probable that many surviving boards have gone unrecognized as to their use. It is unlikely that for such a basic game, despite its former popularity, any custom-made boards existed before the modern era. Often, nine holes were made in the ground, as shown here in the illustration of a seventeenth century Dutch wall-tile, formerly in the possession of A.R. Goddard, an expert on *Merels* at the beginning of this century. In former times, playing Nine Holes was a serious matter, played for money, with side bets placed on the predicted outcome of games. Outdoor games could accommodate a larger number of spectators and punters than an indoor match, and could be more readily played in out-of-the-way places in countries where gambling was forbidden. Playing Nine Holes some-

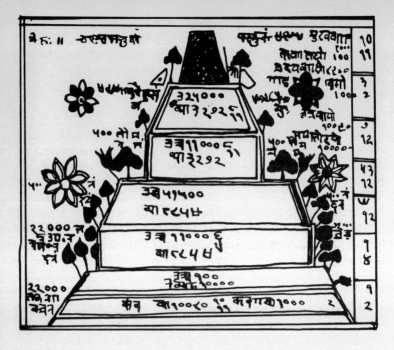

43. *The Indian cosmic holy mountain known as Meru has various levels, each with specific dimensions. From an original manuscript illustrated in W. Kirfel's* Kosmographie der Inder *(1920)* (see p. 147).

times brought the players trouble, for the pastime was frowned upon by many. In 1699, for example, an ecclesiastical court in the Isle of Man punished two people for 'making nine holes with their knives after evening prayer'.

In this game, which can be played on the intersections of a simple quartered square, or just in nine orthogonally-arranged holes, each player has three pieces in hand. These are entered alternately, one at a time, with the aim of creating a line of three, known as a mill. When all are entered, the players move pieces alternately, leaping the pieces into any unoccupied space until a mill is created, when the miller is the winner. Nine Holes can also be played with each contestant having four pieces, each piece having the power of movement only to the next unoccupied space. This appears to be a late variant of the game. Traditionally, drawn games were scored to Old Nick or Old Tom.

Although rarely played today, once Nine Holes was suffi-
ciently widespread to draw the attention of literary men. In his
*Hesperides, or the Works, both Humane and Divine, of Robert Herrick,
Esquire*, (1648), Herrick wrote:

> Raspe plays at nine-holes and 'tis known he gets
> Many a tester by his game and bets.

In his *Polyolbion*, Michael Drayton wrote disapprovingly: 'The
unhappy wags which let their cattle stray; at Nine Holes on the
heath while they together play.' Elsewhere, in his *Muses*, he
wrote: 'Down go our hooks and scrips, and we got to nine
holes.'

In his great work on games, published in 1694, Thomas
Hyde mentions the popularity of Nine Holes in the Nether-
lands, where it was known as *Driesticken* (Three Sticks). It was
also played in German-speaking countries, where it was called
Kleine Mühlenspiel (the Little Mill Game). The next version of
Merels in an ascending scale of board-size and complexity, is
Three Men's Morris. It is played on a square board like Nine
Holes, but with diagonals along which the pieces can move. It
was played in China 2500 years ago at the time of Confucius,
where it was called *Luk Tsut K'i*, and is popular today in Ghana,
where it is called *Achi*. This game is also known as Three Peg,
Three Pin, or Three Penny, and in Cumbria as Cop Crown. In
Spain, it is called *Alquerque de Tres* or *Castro*, and in Catalonia it is
known as *Marro*. The word *Merels* from which the *Morris* in
Nine Men's Morris is derived, has a connection with 'hopping',
which is part of the game of Nine Holes, for the French name
for Hopscotch is *Merelle*. The origin of the dancing known as
Morris may well be part of this tradition.

As in Nine Holes, each player has three sticks, stones or
merels, entered in the same way as in Nine Holes, but here, the
pieces are moved alternately one step at a time along any of the
lines into a vacant place, without leaping. When a mill is
formed, the game is won and lost. Boards for this game have
been found in the roof slabs of the Kurna temple, at the
Roman military fort at Corbridge, Northumberland, and in
several English cathedral cloisters.

Five Men's Morris and Six Men's Morris, otherwise known
as *Smaller Merels*, is an expanded variant of Three Men's Morris,
playing on a pattern which has one small square inside a larger

square, connected to it by lines which run from the centre of each side of the inner square to the corresponding points on the outer square. The players each have five or six pieces, which, when they are all entered, are moved alternately, one step along any line to a vacant place. Leaping, as in Nine Holes, is not permitted. When a mill is made, the person with the mill can remove an opponent's piece from the board. This continues until one player has only two pieces left, when they are the loser.

Although this game is sometimes also known as Five or Six Penny Madell, there is another game to which the name Six Penny Madell properly belongs. This is played on a different board diagram entirely: three concentric triangles, linked together by lines at the apices. There are two variants of this board, one having lines linking the middle of each side, as in the conventional square *Merels* boards. Each player has six pieces, entry and play being according to the same set of rules as other *Merels*. The design of the board is very close to the old protective sigil known as the *Valknut*, one of the emblems of the law of continuity within the universe, especially associated with Odin.

Of the *Merels* family of games, the *Larger Merels*, best known as Nine Men's Morris, is the most popular and the most widespread. Boards date back as far as the Bronze Age, and the game is played today in most countries of the world. A game so widespread is to be expected to have many different names, yet almost all are based on the local word for mill. An alternative English name for the game is The Shepherd's Mill. In Germany, the game is called *Mühle, Mühlespiel, Mühlebrettspiel, Mühlen* or *Mülchen*, which in some parts of the United States has given rise to the derivative form *Mule*. Sometimes, to distinguish it from the *Smaller Merels* it is called *Doppelmühle* (Double Mill). In Flemish and Dutch, it is called *Molenspel* or *Negensticken* (Nine Sticks). Scandinavian names include *Møllespil* (Denmark), *Kvarn* or *Dubbel-Kvarn* (Sweden) and *Mylna* or *Mylla* (Iceland). The latter name is also used in Switzerland, along with the German *Mühle*, the French *Jeu de Moulin*, and the Italian *Molina* and *Mulinello*. Catalan Nine Men's Morris players call it *Marro*. In the Czech language, it is *Mlyn*; in Russian *Melnitsa* or *Melnchny*; Hungarian, *Malomjatek* and *Malmosdi*.

In Ireland, the game was known traditionally as *Cashlan*

Gherra (Short Castle), whilst in Cumbria, it was Short Crown, to distinguish it from Cop Crown. In England, there are almost as many variants as dialects. In Wiltshire, it is called *Madel, Marl, Medal* or *Ninepenny Marl* and in Dorset, *Marells*. In the Forest of Dean, the name is *Marrel, Maulty* and *Mutty*. In Cheshire, the game is *Miracles*, a name used as well as *Miraele* in Oxfordshire. *Marlin, Marriage* and *Ninepins* occur in many places, whilst the terms *Merryal, Merrylegs* and *Meg Merrylegs* appear to be restricted to Lincolnshire. The Northamptonshire name of *Merryholes* reminds us that *Merels* is just as readily played with sticks stuck in holes as with pieces on a board.

The board on which Nine Men's Morris is played is an expansion of the *Smaller Merels* board, being composed of three concentric squares linked by a line at the middle of each side. As in the other *Merels* games, each player has an equal number of pieces – nine – and enters them alternately. Each time a player makes a mill, and this is possible before all of the pieces are entered on the board, any opposing piece can be removed, excepting one which forms part of an existing mill. Losing a piece during entry almost certainly means losing the game.

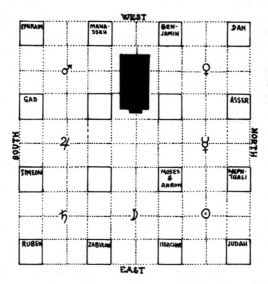

44. *The Camp of the Israelites, according to Villalpanda and Prado in the sixteenth century. This pattern is identical with the northern European board game known as* Gala *(see p. 149).*

When one player has only two pieces left, the game is lost. There can be no draws, as immobilization also spells defeat.

The game of Nine Men's Morris is a subtle one, not as simple as the uninitiated might think at first glance. A most lethal position in the game is when a *Double Mill* or *Running Jenny* is formed, that is a five-piece arrangement where the movement of one piece from a mill automatically creates another mill. To form such a configuration is to win the game, as all of the opponents' pieces are doomed. The alternative *Double Mill* names for Nine Men's Morris used in German and Swedish refer to this capability which does not exist in the *Smaller Merels* games. In Icelandic, there are special technical terms to describe the various forms of *Double Mill* – *Svikamylna*, *Rennihestur* and *Krossmylna*. In German, the *Double Mill* is known as *Zwickmühle,* and in the Danish tongue is called *Rendemølle*.

This is the standard game of Nine Men's Morris, but variants exist, especially in the United States, which give a player who has only three pieces left the right to jump to any unoccupied point on the board, as in Nine Holes. Unfortunately, this late addition destroys the strategic character which is the essence of the game. Sometimes other variants of *Merels*, developed in Europe after 1400, are encountered. These are varieties played on boards to which diagonals have been added, and further pieces, making them Eleven or Twelve Men's Morris. In these versions, the corner lines cannot be used for making mills. A version played using three dice, the throws of which control the entry of pieces onto the board, is described in the *Alfonso Manuscript*. Throws of 6, 5, 4; 6, 3, 3; 3, 5, 2; or 2, 4, 1 allow an existing mill to be broken, and an opposing piece introduced onto the board.

The standard version of Nine Men's Morris is the most mature game of the *Merels* family, being large enough to provide for interesting play, without the destruction of its strategic character by added corner lines or leaping pieces. By whatever name it was known locally, the game of Nine Men's Morris was very common in former times in the countryside. The simplicity and versatility of the game was its great strength in a poor and uneducated rural society. A contributor to William Hone's *The Everyday Book*, July 1826 tells of the shepherds of Salisbury Plain who played Ninepenny Marl on boards chalked on any appropriate surface – a table top, the crown of a hat, the side of a pair of bellows, etc. Another contributor to the journal recalled the popularity of the game in Norfolk, where it was played using beans or coloured stones as pieces. The writer relates an anecdote about a great *Merels* player called Mayes who lived at North Walsham in the county. The gamester was such an addict of Nine Men's Morris that his associates laid a wager that they could prevent him from attending church on Sunday by distracting him with some games. Accosting him on his way to church, one of them drew a *Larger Merels* board in the roadside dust and started to play with him. The games went on so long that not only did he miss Sunday service at the church, but his dinner, too, and received a severe scolding from his wife when he finally arrived home!

The makeshift nature of *Merels* play meant that anything suitable could be and was used for both board and playing pieces. In 1860, John F. Wise wrote of black and white beans being used as pieces in the game played in Warwickshire, and there are records of stones, coins and sticks in use. Unlike Chess, the transient nature of most *Merels* 'boards' reduces the chances of finding ancient *Merels* sets almost to zero. Because of this, the former immense popularity of the game is largely unrecognized. Among surviving ancient *Merels* boards are two cut in the grand flight of steps of the shrine at Mihintale, Sri Lanka (9 – 21 CE). A fragment of a Nine Men's Morris board was found in the Godstad Viking ship burial, dating from around 900. A fragment of a board, incised on stone, exists in the Kölnische Stadtmuseum in Cologne, Germany. In England, the cloisters of several post-Conquest cathedrals and abbeys, including Canterbury, Gloucester, Norwich, Salisbury and Westminster, where, like Nine Holes, the game was a pastime for the monks. Boards were cut into the choir-stalls of the churches at Soham, Suffolk, and Ludlow, Shropshire. A notable *Larger Merels* board is scratched into a windowsill in the medieval church at Finchingfield, Essex. This has one of the central scotches (scratches) continued across the middle of the central square, though whether this is a playing variation of the game or a careless delineation of the board is unknown. Others exist in churches at Hargrave, Northamptonshire; Ickford, Buckinghamshire; Kirkby Underdale, Yorkshire; Sparsholt, Berkshire, and in the Lady Chapel at Wixford,

Warwickshire. Outside the ecclesiastical sphere, *Merels* boards have been found at the castles of Castle Acre, Dover, Hemsley, Norwich and Scarborough. John F. Wise commented: 'The Nine Men's Morris board, instead of being on the earth, is now

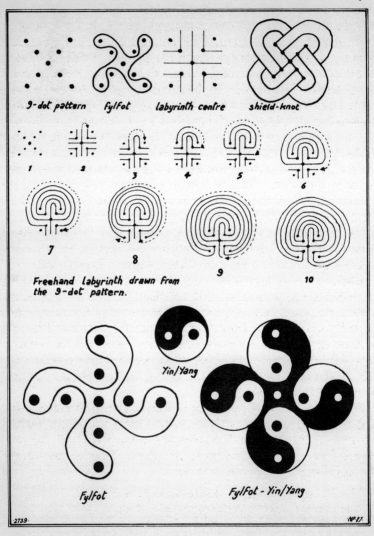

45. *The nine-dot pattern and its derivatives. Analysed as four* Yang *and* Yin *sigils, the* fylfot *signifies the unity of opposites in all four directions, balancing the central point.*

more frequently cut on the corn bins of stables at the Warwickshire farmhouses.' A notable example existed carved on the lid of a corn chest at a farmhouse near Halford in Warwickshire, a place where an outdoor *Merels* pitch also existed. As a protective sigil, the pattern of the *Larger Merels* board is carved on tombstones at Dryburgh Abbey, Worksop, and Arbory, Isle of Man. The chancel arch at Singleton, Sussex, also has a stone in which the pattern is incised. This, like the patterns incised on the steps of the temple in Sri Lanka, is probably the use of the board design again as magical protection. Today, Nine Men's Morris is a popular pastime, but it went through a bad patch between the 1930s and the 1960s, when it almost died out in Britain. In *The Watney Book of Pub Games*, published in 1966, Timothy Finn noted the importance of the Stratford-upon-Avon area in the continuation of the game into modern times. He mentions that at that time, the game was still being played at the Bell Inn at Shottery, the Alveston Manor Hotel and the Black Swan Inn (known locally as *The Dirty Duck*) in Stratford itself. A space for playing Nine Men's Morris on a large scale was marked out in the gardens of the Memorial Theatre at Stratford-upon-Avon. In Sussex, another place where Nine Men's Morris survived as a pub game before its present revival, the board used had holes into which sticks were put. One player had sticks with a short side branch, whilst the other had just straight sticks. Today, various modern boards are available, ranging from travelling sets with magnetic pieces or pegs to boards with depressions in which coloured marbles are placed, and finely-crafted wooden boards with custom-made *merels*.

Nine Men's Morris boards, or rather, pitches, were often cut out of doors in the turf of the leys, or in the grass at the end of ploughed fields. William Shakespeare, in his play *A Midsummer Night's Dream* (*c.* 1593), refers to the game. Titania, bewailing the appallingly wet summer, says:

> The fold stands empty in the drowned field,
> And crows are fatted with the murrion flock;
> The Nine Men's Morris is fill'd up with mud,
> And the quaint mazes in the wanton green
> For lack of tread are indistinguishable.

This is the outdoor *Merels* pitch, like the turf mazes of the next line, common in Shakespeare's day. Often, this reference is wrongly interpreted as an indication that both turf mazes and *Merels* pitches were becoming disused in Shakespeare's day. Fittingly, it was in Warwickshire, Shakespeare country, that examples of outdoor Nine Men's Morris pitches existed in use until the earlier part of this century at Halford and Whitchurch. Had they been on the way out in the bard's time, they would not have lasted. Although the practice of making them has now lapsed, *Merels* pitches cut in the turf are part of the tradition of delineating sacred figures on the ground, like the *Ashtapada* grid of ancient Indian geomancy, magic figures to promote the growth of crops, and the great chalk-cut hill figures of horses and giants in southern England.

John Clare, the 'Peasant Poet' of Northamptonshire, mentions the game in his 1835 *Rural Muses* in a sonnet entitled *The Shepherd Boy*:

Pleased in his loneliness he often lies
Telling glad stories to his dog, or e'en
His very shadow, that the loss supplies
Of living company. Full oft he'd lean
By pebbled brooks, and dream with happy eyes
Upon the fairy pictures spread below;
Thinking the shadowed prospects real skies
And happy heavens, where his kindred go.
Oft we may track his haunts where he hath been
To spend the leisure which his toils bestow,
By nine-peg-morris nicked upon the green,
Or figures cut upon the trees to show
Where he a prisoner from a shower hath been.

Symbolism of the Nine Men's Morris board

The design of the Nine Men's Morris board is an ancient sigil which probably pre-dates its use as a gameboard by many years. In her works on the *Glass Mountain and the Merels Game*, the German archaeologist Margarete Reimschneider studied the connections between the *Merels* board and the symbolism of the divinatory grid in Babylonian and Hittite religions and showed the connection between this design and the three levels of the ancient step-pyramid design. In ancient Mesopo-

46. *The* fylfot *pattern and the classical labyrinth are related geometrically. These are found together deep in the abandoned stone mines at Chaldon in Surrey, where they appear to have been used in some sort of magical rituals. Inscriptions found with other examples date them to around 1600 (see p. 154).*

tamia, this stepped form was the basis of the ziggurat, a representation of the cosmic holy mountain. The lowest or outermost level was symbolized by the metal brass or bronze, the middle silver and the uppermost gold. The three grades of winner at the modern Olympic Games are based on this ancient tripartite division of the holy mountain. Seen as a flattened version of the holy mountain, the lines joining the three squares of the *Larger Merels* board on which Nine Men's Morris is played are the stairways which link the levels together.

Geometrically, the *Larger Merels* board is based upon a grid measuring six squares by six (seven lines by seven). *Merels* is unlike other games, for the distance between points is not significant, pieces being placed on intersections and corners only. Numerically, the design is composed of 16 lines, and encloses nine areas. The outer enclosed area is 20 units square; the middle is 12, and the centre four. There are 24 points on the board, and 18 of these are in use when all of the pieces are entered. These numbers have many connections with the calendar and traditional divination systems.

When a mill is formed, it can only exist in one of the four quarters of the board. Each of these quarters can be seen as having nine points, three shared with each adjacent quarter. It is probable that each quarter symbolized one of the Moon's phases, as did each of the four faces of the holy mountain step-pyramid. The use of the word mill to describe a line of three *Merels* seems to be connected also with the cosmological symbolism of the early horizontal water mills used in northern Europe. These mills were composed of three functional elements arranged in a line, linked by the vertical axle-tree. The lowest part was the under-house, which contained the paddles driven by the fast-flowing mill stream. The paddle arrangement was connected directly to the axle-tree, which passed through the floor of the mill building and through the middle of the lower millstone without contact. Above, the upper millstone was connected to the axle-tree, and rotated with the paddles below to grind the wheat or barley. Symbolically, the axle-tree was seen as linking the underworld, traversing the middle world, and causing the upper world, the millstone which symbolized the starry heavens, to rotate. Just as the correct arrangement of these elements allowed the miller to grind the grain, so the mill in *Merels* allowed the player to grind the opposition.

Merels, Nine Men's Morris in particular, has further mill symbolism. In Yorkshire and some other counties, the central area of the *Merels* board is known as the *pound* or *bushel*. Sometimes a similarly named circle is drawn inside this inner square. Apart from being a measure of weight and capacity, *pound* has the meaning of a place of enclosure, which is sometimes applied to the water in a mill pond. Also, the apparatus used in crushing apples in cider-making were known as *pounds* in some parts of the country. The old usage of *bushel* has the meaning of the metal lining of the central bearing of a cart axle or any other rotating mechanical device, such as a water-mill axle-tree. Nowadays, the word has been shortened to *bush*. Such symbolism, rare in games invented now, pervades the games of *Merels* and *Tafl*. When we play them, we link in to the whole mode of thought which underlies this cosmic symboligy, whether we are conscious of the fact or not.

Tafl

The *Tafl* group of games comprises several versions of the basic game played on a series of gameboards of ascending size, using an increasing number of pieces. The common feature of the *Tafl* group is the odd number of squares or spaces on the boards, giving a central square upon which the king-piece is set at the beginning of the game. The smallest known board (indeed, the smallest playable board) is a seven by seven grid (49 squares or positions), and the largest to have been used measured 19 by 19 (361). Between these two extremes, boards of 9 by 9 (81), 11 by 11 (121) and 13 by 13 (169) are known to have existed. The basic rules of the game are preserved in those of the Scandinavian game of *Tablut*, once played in England as Tawlbort. *Tablut* is a *Tafl* game played in Lappland, whose rules were noted down by the celebrated Swedish scientist and antiquary, Linnaeus, when he visited the country in 1732. This game, played on an 81 (nine by nine) square board, is typical of all the *Tafl* group. In Lappland, where the nomadic way of life meant that everything had to be portable, it was played on a 'board' consisting of a cloth onto which the squares had been embroidered. The British version of the game, Tawlbort, was doubtless played on conventional wooden, metal or walrus ivory boards.

In *Tablut*/Tawlbort, the central square, known in Lappland as the *konakis*, the navel of the board, was occupied by the king piece. In Linnaeus's time, the Lapps called this the Swedish king, and around him, in orthogonal alignment, forming a cross with the king at the centre, were his eight defenders, the Swedish soldiers. The opposing side, known as the Muscovites, had 16 'soldiers', arranged in fours at the centre of each side of the board. Three on each side occupied the centre three squares, whilst the fourth occupied the remaining space in line with the king and his defenders. The embriodered pattern on the cloth 'board' emphasized the starting-places of both Swedish and Muscovite forces.

47. *The small Christian labyrinths at Toulouse and Mirepoix, France, are made from nine tiles, reproducing the nine-square grid. This is the example from Toulouse (see p. 155).*

The playing pieces were of distinctive abstract design, being carved from wood or bone. The Swedish king was the largest piece, having a truncated conical base topped by three circular tiers, one above the other, terminating in a low point. Swedish soldiers again had the conical base, but in their case, it supported a short column topped by a conical point. Finally, the Muscovite soldiers had a circular base above which was an asymmetrical upper part, terminating in a cleft apex something like the top of the conventional Chess bishop. Of course, when the game is played today, there are many different possible designs for Swedes and Muscovites.

In *Tablut*, all the pieces move only orthogonally to any vacant square: there is no diagonal movement or leaping over other pieces. Pieces are captured if they are 'bracketed' by two opposing pieces, making a straight line of three, with the captured piece between the other two. When a piece is captured, it is removed from the board. The Swedish king, however, is captured only if it is bracketed on all four sides by Muscovites, the only exception being if the king stands on a square next to the *konakis* or King's Square, when only three opposing pieces need surround him. The *konakis* is reserved for the king alone, and no other pieces are allowed on it.

The game is won and lost when the king is surrounded by the Muscovites (a Muscovite victory), or when the king reaches the edge of the board (a Swedish victory). If an unblocked way for the king to reach the edge of the board is found during a 'Swedish' move, then the 'Swedish' player must warn the opponent with the word *Raichi*, a sort of equivalent to *Check* in Chess. It two clear routes exist, then the 'Swedish' player says *Tuichi*, the equivalent of *Checkmate*, for the king must reach the edge of the board in his next move.

In medieval European literature, there are many literary references to the various versions of the game of *Tafl*. Some are in Norse sagas, whilst the Celtic literature of Ireland and Wales furnishes further information on the local variants of the game. A convenient way of classifying these is with regard to the number of squares on the board and the number of pieces used. The simplest is undoubtedly the ancient Irish game known variously as *Brandub, Brandubh, Brandul, Brannaib*, or *Buanfach*. It was also known as *Cennchain Conchobar* (Conchabar's Fairhead). In Iceland, the lexicographer Jón Ólafsson of Grunnavik (died 1799) recorded the name *Kotungatafl* (The Crofters' Game) for the same game. Whatever its name, it was played on a board measuring seven squares by seven (49).

A marvellous survival of a *Brandubh* gameboard was discovered during the excavation of a *crannog* (artificial island) in a bog at Ballinderry, near Moate, County Westmeath, Éire in October 1932. Apart from its intrinsic interest as an intact surviving ancient gameboard, its design is an overt expression of three related geomantic traditions. Firstly, the gameboard has a handle carved like a human head, making the board itself the equivalent of the body. The board is drilled with holes to take pegged game-pieces, similar in concept to a modern travelling chess or draughts set. The central point upon which the king stood is marked out with circles, indicating the navel of the figure whose body is the board. This central navel or *omphalos* upon which the king stands, was traditionally the centre of the world, and so the symbolism of the Indo-European myth of the body of the slain ancestral giant as the foundation of the world exists in this gameboard.

In *Brandubh*, the king, known as the *Branán* or *Brenin* was protected by only four pieces known as knights, and opposed, as in all games of *Tafl*, by twice the number of attackers. In Iceland, the defenders were called *riddurum*, and the attacking pieces were known as *pedjunum* (pawns), which is Chess terminology, but of course the 'knights' defending the king did not have the power of movement of the Chess knight, but rather, as with their opponents, that of the Chess rook.

The game of *Fidchell* or *Fidcheall*, traditionally invented by the god Lugh, is probably another version of *Brandubh*. Cormac's *Glossary*, written around the year 900, states, not very helpfully, 'Firstly, the Fidchell is four-cornered, its squares are right-angled and black and white men are on it, and moreover it is different people that in turn win the game'. This does not give any indication of the number of squares, or the number of playing-pieces. There is some possibility that the remark that different people in turn win the game refers to some sort of rigged alternate winners, in the manner of the Malagasy game of *Fanorona* mentioned in Chapter 9. *The Book of Rights*, also has a reference to *Fidchell*: 'It was a board of silver and pure gold,

48. *The pattern of the* **Larger Merels** *board is very ancient. Top left: Prehistoric rock-scribing from Hazar Sum, Afghanistan. Top right: Prehistoric scribing from Warshaueck, Austria. Bottom: Ancient stone* **Merels** *board from Cologne, Germany.*

and every angle was illuminated with precious stones, and [there was] a man-bag of woven brass wire.'

The ancient British or Welsh version of *Fidchell* is mentioned in *The Red Book of Hergest*, where it is called *Gwyddbwll*. The legendary *Gwddbwll of Gwendolen* was another richly-worked set, the board being of gold and the men of silver. Its magical qualities were such that when set up, the pieces would play by themselves, a supernatural version of modern computer chess!

The British version of the 81-square game (*Tablut*) was called *Dawlbwrd, Tawlbort* or *Tawlbwrdd*, which is translated as *throw-board*. This game was identical with *Tablut*, having 16 pieces on one side attacking a *Brenin* and eight pieces on the other side. It is mentioned in Arthurian legend in *Y Seint Graal*, and also in the laws promulgated by the Welsh king Howel Dda (914–943). In Howel's laws, a *Tawlbwrdd* board was given to a judge on taking office. This act is a direct connection between the ritually laid out place of judgement and the board, which is its microcosmic reflection. The use of a square enclosure laid out as a grid on the ground as a place of jurisdiction was formerly a practice in the common law of northern Europe. It survived in Germany until the eighteenth century in the illegal summary courts of Westphalia, known as the *Vehmgericht*.

The corpus of laws in *The Dimetian Code* have an important reference to *Tawlbwrdd*: the compensation value of various classes of board:

> The king's *Tawlbwrdd* is six score pence in value; a *Tawlbwrdd* of the bone of a sea animal is three score pence in value; a *Tawlbwrdd* of any other bone is thirty pence in value; a *Tawlbwrdd* of hart's antler is twenty four pence; a *Tawlbwrdd* of a bullock's horn, twelve pence; a *Tawlbwrdd* of wood, four legal pence.

This prescription tells us that in tenth century Wales, the game was popular with all classes of society, ranging from richly-worked examples in precious metals to the simple wooden boards of the peasantry.

A description of a later version of *Tawlbwrdd* is preserved in one of the *Peniarth Manuscripts*, in the National Library of Wales, written by Robert ap Ifan in August 1587. This version was played on a board of 121 squares (11 by 11), which was made with alternate dark and light rows. Like all the other *Tafl* games, this one was played:

with a *Brenin* in the centre and twelve men in the places next to him, and twenty four lie in wait to capture him. These are placed, six in the centre of every end of the board, and six central places. Two players move the pieces, and if one belonging to the king comes between the attackers, he is dead, and thrown out of the play; and if one of the attackers comes between two of the king's men the same. If the king himself comes between two of the attackers and you say 'Watch your king!' before he moves into that place, and he is unable to escape, you catch him. If the other says '*Gwrrheill*' and goes between the two, there is no harm. If the king can go ... along the line, that side wins the game.

Reaching the 'line' – the edge of the board – gives the king dominion over the whole area. He has travelled successfully from the navel at its centre to its outer limits. This concept can be found in the writings of the Welsh Bard Taliesin in his celebrated work *The Spoils of Annwn*: 'Praise to the Lord, Supreme Ruler of the High Region, who has extended his dominion to the shore of the world.'

Although our record in Wales of the 121-square version of *Tawlbwrdd* is later than the 81-square examples, there does not appear to have been any consistent enlargement or diminution in board size over the years. A larger version of *Tafl* was discovered among the grave-goods in the great ship burial at Gokstad in Norway. It was a fragment of a double-sided board with Nine Men's Morris on one side and a 13 by 13 *Tafl* on the other. This may have been the now-lost game of *Ólafs Kongs Tafl* (King Ólaf's *Tafl*), for it is believed that this may have been the burial of King Ólaf I, Ólaf Elf of Geirstad.

The largest known *Tafl* board is the enormous *Hnefatafl* board, which as 361 places. A fragment of a *Hnefatafl* board of this size was excavated at Vimose in Denmark. Unlike the other versions of *Tafl*, *Hnefatafl* was played on a grid of lines, and not, so far as is known, on a board consisting of squares. The layout of the pieces on the board is recorded in an English manuscript dating from the time of King Æthelstan (925–940), when, in a vain attempt to give the game an overtly Christian meaning, monks renamed it *Alea Evangelii*. There are also references to *Hnefatafl* in several Norse sagas, and it was played widely in England and Scandinavia before the introduction of Chess, which eventually superseded it. The *Fornaldar Saga*, written in about 1256, records *Hnefatafl* being played in England. Recounting the wars of earlier centuries, the Saga tells us that warriors named Hvitserkr and Sugurð were playing at *Hnefatafl* when a messenger from King Ælla arrived. This dates the play of *Hnefatafl* in England to around 856 CE.

Norse literature records many versions of *Iafl: Færingstafl, Foeritafl, Freystafl, Ólafs Kongs Tafl, Tanntafl* and *Worptaflspel*. The *Rigsthula* (pre-1220) tells of children learning to swim and play at *Tafl*. Rig, alias the Norse god Heimdall, was the legendary organizer of society, and may symbolize the arranger of the playing-pieces. The Orkney ruler, Earl Rognvaldr (1135–58) boasted among his many accomplishments: 'I am strong at Tafl-play.' The *Króka-Refs Saga*, dating from the fourteenth century, but a re-write of an earlier version, states that from Greenland a man named Gunnar sent three gifts to King Harald of Norway, including a *Tanntafl*. This was a double-sided board on which *Hnefatafl* and *Skaktafl* (Chess) could be played. The board found in the Gokstad ship burial is such a *Tanntafl*, but for Nine Men's Morris instead of Chess. The word *tann* means tooth or tusk, referring to the morse (walrus) ivory favoured by Norse board-makers. Morse ivory was a readily-available durable material, and many playing-pieces, such as the Lewis Chessmen now in the British Museum, were carved from it. The walrus also had a symbolic meaning, signifying death, echoing the fatalistic aspects of board games. The play of *Tafl* was the downfall of at least one monarch. In the summer of 1250, the Danish king Eric IV *Plogpenning*, an unpopular man known as *Ploughpenny* for his taxation of the peasants' ploughs, was on his way to aid the beleagured town of Rendsburg on the Eider. He visited his brother, Abel, in Schleswig, and, whilst engrossed in a game of *Worptafelspel* (literally, *Throw-board-play, Hnefatafl*) with a knight named Henrick Kerkwerden, he was assassinated by his brother.

In *Hnefatafl*, the king who stood at the centre of the board at the beginning of a game was known as the *Hnefi*. This word appears to be cognate with the word *navel* (old English, *nafela*; Old Teutonic, *nabalon*), and the now-obsolete English word *nave*. A nave was the central part of the block of a cartwheel through which the end of the axle was inserted and from which the spokes radiated. In all its meanings, it has connotations of centrality. It is probable that the central point or

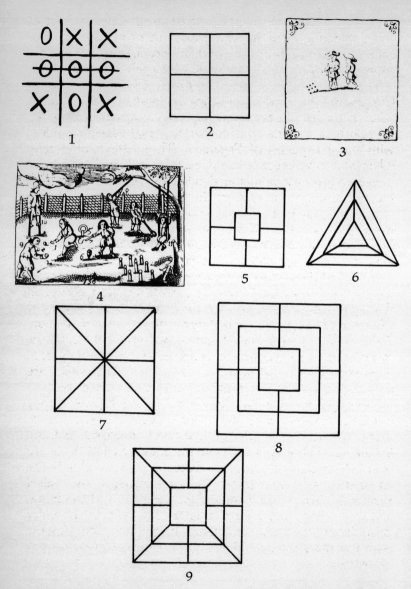

49. The **Merels** *family of games, and the ninefold: 1. Noughts and Crosses; 2. Nine Holes; 3. Seventeenth-century Dutch tile showing Nine Holes; 4. Boys' games, 1672, showing nine pins with the central 'king pin' larger than the others; 5. Five Men's Morris; 6. Six Penny Madell; 7. Three Men's Morris; 8. Nine Men's Morris; 9. Eleven or Twelve Men's Morris.*

square in *Hnefatafl* was called the navel, paralleling the usage of this geomantic term for the central point on other board games in other parts of the world. In *Hnefatfl*, the pieces radiate from the *Hnefi's* central position like the spokes from a wheel.

The attempt by a tenth century Christian cleric to Christianize the symbolic meaning of *Hnefatafl* by re-naming it *Alea Evangelii* had the fortunate happenstance of preserving for us aspects of a game which otherwise might have been lost with the extirpation of Paganism. There, the numerology inherent in the original board game, which had traditional Indo-European cosmological significance, was transferred to Judæo-Christian numerology. In Ælfric's *Vocabulary*, written around the year 1000, *Hnefatafl* was referred to by its Christian name of *Alea*, and the *Aleae* or pieces as *tafelstanes* (table stones). In this terminology, the *Hnefi* was called the *Pirgus* or *Cynigstan* (King Stone), which started at the centre – the throne square.

Unlike *Merels*, where the disposition of the game-pieces depends on the skill of the players, and is different each time, the layout of *Tafl* is more like the familiar board games of Chess and Draughts, which start at the same fixed position. *Tafl* is unlike these games, because in Chess and Draughts, opposing sides have equal forces and combat each other from opposite sides of the board. In *Tafl*, the king's forces are defending the centre, whilst the attacking forces are attempting to gain dominion over the centre, which, however, they cannot touch. In *Merels*, the centre is not in the game at all, being the *pound* into which captured pieces are impounded, and in Chess and Draughts, the centre is merely part of the board over which combat proceeds. One exception to this is the enigmatic game known as *Gala*, erroneously also called Farmers' Chess, which comes from Germany and Denmark, and is detailed in the next chapter. *Tafl* reflects the older cosmology of the middle kingdom, with the king occupying the central *omphalos* and defending it against the external forces of destruction.

Game-piece names

Although in English Chess, Draughts and *Merels* pieces are known as *men*, there was formerly much more variation in terminology. In most languages, the Draughts pieces are female, being called *dames* or their equivalent. The old Scottish term for a chequerboard or Draughts board is *Dambrod* (Dame Board), showing that this usage formerly existed in Britain. The game of Draughts is called *Dams* in Scottish, *Damespiel* in German, *Damm* in Icelandic and Dutch, *Dammen* in French, *Damspel* in Swedish, and *Damen Jokoa* in Basque. In the Norse *Hervarar Saga ok Heiðreks*, there is recalled a contest between King Heiðrek and an old man who is Odin in disguise. The contest takes the form of cryptic questions and answers, an ancient method of teaching which is now relegated to children's riddles. One of these is: 'Who are the maids that fight weaponless around their lord, the brown ever sheltering and the fair ever attacking him?' The answer, of course, are the pieces in *Tafl*. The question of the masculinity or femininity of pieces is vexed. In the symbolic system of Pythagoras, odd numbers were deemed male and even ones female. When applied to *Tafl*, the king is single and male, and there are even numbers of all of the other pieces, making them female. This works, too, for Draughts, where the modern English version has 12 pieces, and the Continental or 'Polish' version has 20. The game of *Alquerque* is unusual because there the white pieces are considered male and the black female. As in Chess, white always starts the game. In old Irish versions of the game of *Tafl*, however, the pieces are called *fiana*, soldiers, which appears to have been the most common interpretation.

In the *Tablut* game of the eighteenth century, the defence of the Swedes against the Muscovites expresses the political concerns of the day. The earlier terminology of the pieces, found across Europe and in Britain, referred to the playing pieces as *Hunns*, reflecting the interests of an earlier age. The attack upon Europe by the Hun-Yü, a ferocious Turkic warrior-tribe, around the year 375 was enshrined in later European tale-telling as *The Battle of the Goths and the Huns*. It is clear that when they referred to the playing-pieces of *Tafl* as *Hunns*, they were referring to *Tafl* as a battle between Goths at the centre, and attacking, external, Huns. However, as with any game which has undergone many changes during its development, unimportant names are often changed around. In *The Greenland Lay of Atli* it is remarked that the *Hnefi* (king) is often beaten when the Hunns are taken, referring to the pieces on the king's side. In *Hornklofi's Raven Song* is another allusion to *Tafl*: *'They are well cared for, the warriors who move the Hunns in Harald's Court'*. Whatever the names given to the pieces, their disposition and movements reflect the eternal struggles of the world, as revelant today as the day they were first devised.

8

CHESS AND DRAUGHTS

For many years, there have been traditions that Chess has a far greater symbolic significance than a mere pastime might at first appear to have. Among other things, it has been connected with mental training, military strategy, complex mathematics, divination, astronomy and astrology. Over the years, various theories and opinions have been ventured on the origin and meaning of Chess. In his monumental work *Science and Civilization in China*, Joseph Needham states that a quasi-astrological technique evolved in China between the first and sixth centuries CE for determining the state of balance or imbalance between the complementary qualities of *Yin* and *Yang*. Needham believes that this divinatory technique was adopted by military diviners, perhaps forming the basis of the board game known as *Chaturanga*.

However, the name of this game is not Chinese, but comes from the Sanskrit, meaning 'quadripartite'. This term was used to describe the Indian army which had four elements, reflecting the fourfold division of the world and its microcosm, society. Before the invasion of India by the army of Alexander the Great in 326 BCE, the Indian army was composed of four different branches: elephants, cavalry, chariots and infantry. In addition to the four branches of troops, there were the king (the *rajah*), and his counsellor, (the *mantri*). The troops consisted of elephants (*gaja*), horses (*asva*), chariots (*ratha*), and pawns (*pedati*). The failure of chariot warfare against the Greek armies of Alexander in 326 BCE led the Indians to abandon that form of warfare shortly afterwards. As *Chaturanga* games had these divisions, it would date the game to before Alexander's incursion, several centuries before the Chinese astrological board divination.

Some Chess historians have connected the game with the ancient Chinese pastime of *Siang k'i*. The name of this game is translated usually as The Astronomical Game or The Figure Game. Whether or not it was a forerunner of Chess, *Siang k'i* has strong connections with divination, for there is a close affinity between the layout of the gameboard and ancient Chinese diviners' boards which were the forerunners of the *luopan*, the magnetic compass used today in *Feng-Shui*, the Chinese art of placement. Unlike Chess, this game was played with the aid of dice.

The board on which *Chaturanga* was played was that of *Ashtapada*, the eight by eight (64 squares) grid of a version of race game which, like modern Ludo, was played with dice. Early references to the game may therefore refer to any game played on the *Ashtapada* board, either the actual game, or *Chaturanga*. Ancient references to board games were often made by commentators who had little or no knowledge of the actual mode of play of the games. This is a problem researchers of old games often encounter, and can be seen in many medieval representations of Chess, where it is rare to find a board depicted which has the correct eight by eight chequers.

Ashtapada is one of a group of race games played on a square board, whose movements have some connection with the layout of traditional unicursal labyrinths. These games include *Thayyam*, played on a five by five (25 squares) board; *Ashta-Kaste*, seven by seven (49); *Ashtapada*, eight by eight (64); and *Saturankam*, nine by nine (81). These grids all have mystical connections with magic squares, being randomized by the use of dice. The cosmologist C.P.S. Menon believed that the chequered playing board came from the custom of representing the year-cycle and its subdivisions in a square format. This format survived in European horoscopes until the eighteenth century, and is still employed in laying out the figures in divinatory geomancy. The children's game of Fortune Telling, played today in Britain, involves a paper square folded on the same pattern. Allied symbolism exists in the square cosmographic mosaic pavements of medieval Europe, such as those at Xanten in Germany and at Canterbury Cathedral and Westminster Abbey in England. These are overt symbols of the structure of the world, with the four directions, elements, and humours laid out in corresponding geometrical patterns and coloured stones. Menon argued that the Chess board originated as a symbolic planisphere upon which the motion of the seven planets of traditional astronomy were represented by corresponding pieces located in appropriate correspondences. He speculated that the Knight's move in chess may have originated in the movement of heavenly bodies in their orbits 'round the corner' of the square planisphere. The similar jumping moves of the *fil*, forerunner of the Chess bishop, and other pieces in unorthodox Chess games, would have the same origin and meaning.

According to an old Indian legend, which recurs in Persian and Arabian literature, the game of Chess, or at least its forerunner, *Chaturanga*, was invented by one man, Sissa, a Brahman at the court of King Balhait. The king ordered the sage to devise a game which would display the usefulness of personal judgement, anticipation and knowledge, as opposed to fatalism which was implicit in games of chance using dice. Sissa used the board of the old game *Ashtapada*, and on it, he placed pieces representing the four branches of the Indian army, led by the king and his counsellor. Sissa chose battle as the prototype for the game because war displayed all of the qualities that Balhait had specified.

The king applauded Sissa for his wisdom in creating a game which expressed all of the principles of justice, and instructed that examples of *Chaturanga* should be placed in every temple as an ideal training in the art of warfare. Balhait asked Sissa to

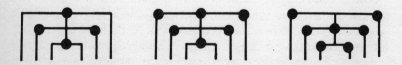

50. *The three fatal positions in* Merels, *where the opponent cannot win: There do not appear to be English descriptions for the positions, other than a* Running Jenny, *but in Icelandic, there are specific terms for all three (left to right):* Svikamylna, Krossmylna *and* Rennihestur.

name his reward. As a priest, Sissa replied that the usefulness
of his invention was reward enough, but when pressed by the
king, said: 'Give me a reward of grains of corn on the
chequerboard. On the first square, give me a single grain. On
the next, two, on the third, four, and on the fourth double that,
and so on until the last square of the board.' The king thought
this little enough, and tried to change the Brahman's mind, but
he insisted on the grain.

Balhait ordered his servants to bring grain, but before long,
the truth dawned that all the grain in India would not suffice,
for the enormous total of 18,446,744,073,709,551,615 grains
would be required to fulfil the payment. The medieval Arab
sage Al-Beruni calculated that this total would amount to 2305
mountains, more than in all the world, and more recent
calculations claim it is enough corn to cover the whole surface
of the Earth to a depth of nine inches. The king is reported to
have wondered whether to admire the invention of *Chaturanga*
more than Sissa's mathematical ingenuity in requesting the
corn as payment. The precise meaning of this story is unclear,
for the number $2^{64}-1$ may have had some cosmological
meaning in ancient Hindu tradition. However, it demonstrates
the ancient Indian expertise with numbers, and a recognition
of the myriad combinations of moves possible in the game. It
is feasible that a single person, using the sacred grid and
religious ritual as a base, created *Chaturanga* in the Punjab at
some time near the end of sixth century, but his or her name
is uncertain. According to Islamic mythology, the game of
Chess was invented by Qaflan, a philosopher who devised the
game to symbolize human beings' relationship with the
environment and destiny.

In his book *Mandragorias seu Historia Shahiludii*, published in
1694, Thomas Hyde, Professor of Arabic at Oxford University, wrote a history of Chess, which he called *Mandragorias*, or
Mandrake Play. Professor Hyde claimed that Chess was
invented in India by Nassir Dahir in about 500 CE, and was
played first in Persia at the court of Chosroes the Great, in the
mid sixth century. He believed that the game reached China at
about the same time. According to modern Chess scholarship,
in China around the year 800, *Chaturanga* became transformed
into its modern form of Chinese Chess. Through Korea, it
reached Japan, and there it became *Shogi*. Fa Xian, a Chinese

Buddhist pilgrim who wrote a detailed account of his stay in India at the beginning of the fifth century does not mention the game, and Chess commentators have taken this to signify that the game was then unknown, or at least, uncommon. Travelling westward, *Chaturanga* reached Persia in about the year 600, and the first known reference to Chess is in a Persian romance called *Karnamak-i-Artakshatr-i-Papakan*, written around the year 600. The hero of the story is noted for his abilities in 'ball-play, horsemanship, *Chatrang*, hunting and other accomplishments'. After the Arab conquest of Persia (638–651), the game now altered into *Shatranj* was carried to the farthest reaches of the Islamic Empire. Through the Moors in Spain in the eighth century, and the Islamic conquerors of Sicily, it was transmitted to Christian Europe. *Shatranj* reached Russia in the ninth century by way of the Caspian–Volga trade route, and from there northward into Scandinavia via Viking trade-routes through the Baltic.

The version of the game which was transmitted to Europe from the Arabs was *Shatranj*, a game played in Islamic countries for about 1000 years. The array of pieces in *Shatranj* is similar to that of modern Chess, except that there is a *firzan* (counsellor) in place of the queen and a *fil* in place of the modern bishop. Other differences from modern Chess are that pawns are allowed only one move at a time, and can be promoted only to a *firzan*. In *Shatranj*, a player could win by checkmate, stalemate or bare king (king without any other men of same colour on board). Only checkmate, where the king is *en prise* and cannot move to safety, is a winning move in modern Chess. The array of the pieces in *Shatranj* was thus: rook, knight, *fil*, king, *firzan*, *fil*, knight, rook, with eight pawns in the second rank. The *Shatranj fil* did not move diagonally like the modern Chess bishop. Like the knight, it was a leaper, but jumping the coordinates 2,2. In the medieval European version of the game, this piece was known as the *aufin*, a name derived from the Persian *pil*, itself a literal translation of the original Sanskrit name *gaja*, an elephant. The *fils* were much weaker than modern Chess bishops, as they could neither guard not attack one another. The *firzan*, *fers* or *firz* (from the Persian *farzin*, counsellor) was also quite a weak piece. It was moved one square diagonally in any direction, and, like a modern bishop, could thus move only on one colour, restricted to 32

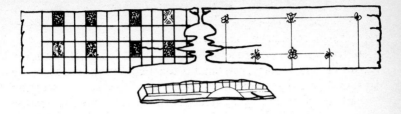

51. *Northern European board game fragments. At the top is the piece found in the Gokstad ship burial, Norway, with* Tafl *on one side and* Merels *on the other, and below is the fragment of* Hnefatafl *board from Vimose, Fünen, Denmark. The Vimose board is older, dating from around 400 CE, whilst the Gokstad board is about 500 years younger.*

squares of the board.

By the year 1000, *Shatranj* was well known in Europe, and the *Einsedeln Manuscript*, written a century later, records the use of *Shatranj* rules in Europe at that time. There is a mention of King Canute playing the game in the year 1029 against the Jarl Ulfr, and, as with other things, once a monarch adopted something, it became fashionable among his subjects. The considerable communication between distant countries at this period facilitated the rapid progress of the game. One great Jewish Chess master, Abraham ben Meir Ibn Ezra (*c.* 1092–*c.* 1167), born in Tudela, Spain, worked as poet, philosopher and mathematician in England, France, Italy, Spain and Egypt. The author of several Hebrew books on Chess, Ibn Ezra wrote one of the first poems on Chess in the language – *The Song of Chess*. The game described there has the same rules as those of *Shatranj* except that the *fers* had the power of leaping on its first move. Around 1475, in Southern Europe, the game altered into its modern form. The *fers* was replaced by the queen, and the *aufin* by the bishop. On reaching the opponent's first rank, a pawn could become a queen rather than a *fers*.

The *Alfonso Manuscript* is a key source of information about ancient board games. Completed in 1283 by order of Alfonso X the Wise (1221–84) King of Castile and Léon 1251–84, the monumental work is divided into seven parts. The first is devoted to Chess and contains 103 problems of Arabic and European origin. The Chess in the *Alfonso Manuscript* has an advance on *Shatranj* in allowing the *firzan* a first leap and the pawn's first two-square move of modern Chess. The fourth part contains 14 *fairy* problems, where unorthodox numbers of pieces, often with aberrant moves, are set up to create a philosophical problem. There are also various forms of Great Chess, played on the 100-square board, and Must-Capture Chess, where failure to capture leads to the offending piece being *huffed* as in modern English Draughts. The *Alfonso Manuscript* is a remarkable document, for it records many versions of games which otherwise would be lost. There is a version of Four-Handed Chess, and a game called *Los Escaques*, an astronomical game played on circular board. In addition to these unorthodox games, there are also the conventional games of *Alquerque*, Nine Men's Morris etc.

Unorthodox versions of chess

Great Chess is rarely encountered today, yet it is a very complex and interesting expansion of the standard game. It is played on a board of 100 squares, and obviously requires more pieces and thought than does orthodox Chess played on a board with 64 squares. Great Chess is sometimes known as Tamerlane's Chess, because Tamerlane the Great was supposed to have been a great enthusiast for it. The array in Great Chess is different from orthodox Chess. There are additional pieces known as camels, and two pieces known as giraffes which move one square diagonally and then forwards as far as unoccupied squares will allow. The game ends in checkmate or stalemate as in the standard version.

Another version of unorthodox Chess formerly more popular than today is Four-Handed Chess. This is played by four players, usually as teams of two, This game is believed to be a very early form of Chess, being related to the fourfold layout of *Chaturanga*. Around the year 1030, al-Beruni wrote about an Indian form of the game (from corner, left to right, *r*, *n*, *fil*, *k*, with pawns in front), played with aid of dice. An eighteenth century version played in Russia was played on a special board which consisted of a 68-square board with four by four extensions at each of the corners. These extensions were bastions or citadels available only to the appropriate player, linking this form of Chess with games like *Asalto*, and the board with some labyrinth designs. Another extended-board version of Four-Handed Chess was devised by George Hope Verney (1842–96). In his book *Chess Eccentricities* (1885), he described a game using the standard eight by eight board with additions of eight by three to all sides (192 squares). The game was played using two sets of Chessmen. The club he formed to play the game survived until World War II.

Zatrikon or Round Chess is known from the tenth century at the latest from Islamic and Byzantine manuscripts. Also known as Byzantine Chess, the game was popular in Constantinople for many years. It is only vaguely related to the Chess we know today, but it bears that name because it has pieces similar to conventional Chess. The array of pieces is as follows: the first rank has four 4 pawns; the second, a rook, knight, *fil* and king; the third, a rook, knight, *fil* and *firzan*; and the fourth, four pawns. The array on the opponent's side is a mirror image of the other. In *Zatrikon*, unlike *Shatranj*, pawns are not promoted, a *firzan* can capture a *firzan*, and a *fil* can capture a *fil*. *Zatrikon's* circular board allows moves impossible in Chess on a square board, for there is a central fourfold division known as the *citadels*. At the start of a game, the king and *firzan* are on the perimeter, and if a player can move a king into this citadel, he or she, cannot lose. This has a parallel with the later north German and Danish board game known as *Gala*, whose central four squares have a special affinity with the kings.

Draughts

The origin of Draughts or Checkers is obscure, but it appears that it is a game created from the amalgamation of elements from three other games popular in medieval Europe: Chess, Backgammon and *Alquerque*. It is believed to have originated in the South of France around 1100, when it was called *Fierges*. This game used the Chess board, onto which the pieces of Backgammon were placed and played with according to the rules of *Alquerque* (see page 212). The pieces of the new game were called *Ferses*, after the piece in *Shatranj* and medieval European Chess. The game is mentioned in the *Chronique* of Philip Mouskat (1243), where promotion to *King of Fierges* is reported. In this game, there was no compulsory capture, as in

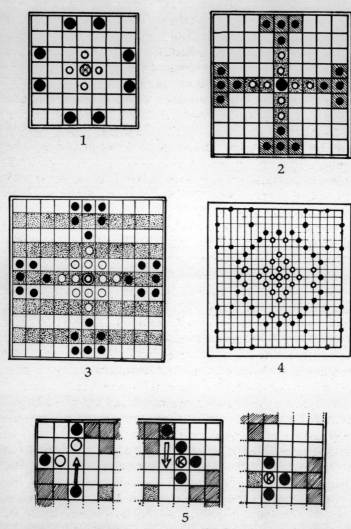

52. Tafl: 1. Brandubh, *as played on the Ballinderry game board, seven by seven (49);* 2. Tablut, from Lappland, *nine by nine (81), the* Paramasayika grid; 3. Tawlbwrdd, *after Robert ap Ifan, 1587, 11 by 11 (121);* 4. Hnefatafl, *played on a board of grid lines 19 by 19 (361);* 5. *Modes of capture in Tafl. Left: Capture of two white pieces at once by bracketing. Centre: Capture of king by surrounding. Right: Capture of king against the* konakis *by three opponents, when the king is not permitted to enter the* konakis.

later versions. When compulsory capture was introduced in about 1535, with its attendant *huffing*, or removing a piece which failed to make a capture, the old game became known as *Jeu Plaisant*, as opposed to the huffing game *Jeu Forcé*. By this time, the pieces had been renamed after the queen in Chess, *Jeu de Dames*, and it is called versions of this in most European languages. There are several varieties of Draughts or Checkers, named after the countries where they are played or are supposed to have originated. Obviously the best known in English-speaking countries is Standard Draughts, known alternatively as English Draughts. This is played on the common chequerboard of 64 alternately coloured squares, with the black square at the player's left. Each player has 12 pieces, which are placed on the black squares only nearest to the player. Black moves first.

In Standard Draughts, pieces move forwards only, to the next vacant black square on the next rank. If there is a vacant space beyond an opponent's piece, then that piece must be captured by leaping into that space, and the captured piece removed from the board. It is compulsory to capture, and failure to do so results in that piece being *huffed*. English Draughts is thus *Jeu Forcé*. When there is a choice of pieces to be captured, any choice is allowed. When a piece reaches the opponent's back rank, it is promoted to king, by the opponent placing another piece on top of it. The king may move either forwards or backwards, and capture in any direction, but it cannot capture in the same move that it has become a king.

Another important variety of the game is Spanish Draughts, which is played on the standard chequerboard, but orientated with a black square at the right-hand side of the first rank instead of on the left as in English Draughts. The rules are similar, but when there are several pieces *en prise*, the player must capture the largest number. A king has a greater power of movement than in the standard game; it can be moved along as many vacant squares in a diagonal as the player wishes. It can capture any opposing piece on the diagonal, so long as there are one or more unoccupied squares beyond the piece to be captured. If there are pieces *en prise* on another diagonal crossing the unoccupied squares where the king would land, it must turn and capture these, continuing captures as far as possible.

A version known as Spanish Pool in the United States and Minor Polish Draughts or German Draughts in England is also played on the standard board. In this variant, whilst pieces move forwards only, they are allowed to capture backwards, and kings have the same powers as in Spanish Draughts. In Russian Draughts (*Shaski*), when an ordinary piece reaches the opponent's first rank, it is crowned king. If further pieces are *en prise*, it may then continue on its way as a king of Spanish Draughts type. Italian Draughts have a further variant of standard rules. As in Spanish Draughts, it is compulsory to capture the largest number of pieces at a move. A king can only be captured by another king, and if there is a choice of capture between an ordinary piece and a king, then the king must capture. Turkish Draughts is another variety which uses the 64-square board. Each player has 16 pieces, which are arranged on the second and third ranks of their own side of the board. Pieces move one square at a time in any direction other than backwards, and capture by a short leap as in Standard Draughts. Kings are created in the usual way, but in Turkish Draughts, the king can only move orthogonally and not diagonally. Kings can capture in a similar way as in Spanish Draughts.

Continental Draughts or Polish Draughts, both misleading names, describe the variant of the game played on a board measuring ten by ten squares (100). It arose in Paris in the eighteenth century, being played in the cafés which until the nineteenth century were known for their Chess and Draughts players of world-beating quality. The first book on Polish draughts was published in Paris in 1727 by a writer using the *nom-de-plume* Quercetaine. Polish Draughts is so-called because it is supposed to have been invented by a Polish count in Paris. It is the only popular game played on a 100-square board, though Great Chess and *Gala* also use a board of the same dimensions. Polish Draughts is a version of Spanish Pool played on a larger board, but with the same rules. It is probable that the inventor expanded the Spanish variety of the game onto a Great Chess board. In Polish Draughts, each player has 20 pieces. When a piece reaches the opponent's back rank, but there are still pieces *en prise*, then it cannot be crowned as a queen (with the same powers of movement and capture as the king of Spanish Draughts), but continues to capture as many

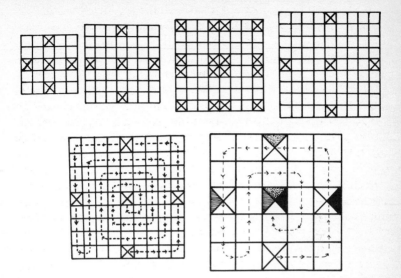

53. *A family of race games played in India since antiquity gave us the board on which Chess is played. Top row (left to right):* Thayyam *(five by five, 25 squares);* Ashta-Kashte *(seven by seven, 49);* Ashtapada *(eight by eight, 64, the Chess board);* Saturankam *(nine by nine, 81, the* Paramasayika *grid). Below left: The path followed by the playing pieces in* Saturankam. *Each player has four pieces, as in the modern Ludo. Right:* Thayyam's *board reproduces the canonical colours of the four directions. South, top, yellow; west, right, black; north, bottom, white; and east, left, red. The playing-pieces, four of each colour, are related to these direction-colours (see p. 187).*

as possible. The largest number possible must be captured at one move.

Diagonal Draughts is little played today, but it is a simple variation on the game of Standard Draughts. Twelve pieces per side are arranged across the corner of the board to the right-hand of each player, but apart from this, the rules are

identical with Standard Draughts. Another odd variant is
Pyramid Draughts, where only ten pieces are used on each
side, arranged in ranks of four, three, two and one. No capture
is permitted, the object of the game being to occupy the
opponent's first rank with one's own pieces. Pyramid
Draughts appears to be allied to the games of *Halma*, Chinese
Checkers, and more distantly to *Asalto*, where the object is to
occupy the opponent's 'fortress' or starting positions. *Halma* is
played on a grid of 16 by 16 (256) squares, with 19 pieces for
each player. Pieces can move one square at a time in any
direction, and leap over opponent pieces without capture. Like
Chinese Checkers, which is played on a hexagonal board, and
can accommodate up to six players, *Halma* can be played by
four players, when they attempt to occupy the opposite corner
of the board. In the four-handed version, each player has 13
pieces. Unfortunately, as with many games, there is a confusion in terminology, for I have in my possession an early
twentieth century German travelling game called *Schwedisches
Steckhalma*, but this is a version of English Solitaire, and not a
true *Halma*! Such are the problems of board game
nomenclature.

The Knight's and other 'Tours'

The Knight's Tour is the name given to the array of
continuous moves that a Chess knight can make so that each
of the squares on the standard Chess board is visited in the
tour. Because of its interesting topological qualities, the
Knight's Tour has always attracted the attention of mathematicians and mystics. There are millions of variations possible
in the Knight's Tour, so many that the precise number has
never been calculated, and enthusiasts have tended to explore
tours which have some unusual geometrical or numerical
qualities. In art and architecture, the patterns formed by
Knights' Tours are ornamental in themselves, having a deeper
significance which is not apparent to uninitiated viewers. In
the early part of this century, the American theosophical
architect Claude Bragdon made use of them as architectural
ornament, and wrote on them in his book *Projective Ornament*.
Bragdon used one of Euler's closed tours as a binding on

another of his books, *The Beautiful Necessity.*

On a standard Chess board, there are two types of Knight's Tour possible: the open tour, in which the knight does not arrive back on the square where it started, and the closed tour, where it does. It is impossible to produce a closed tour with fourfold symmetry on the Chess board, but twofold symmetries are possible. If each of the squares is numbered with regard to each move by the knight, then it is possible to approach a magic square which is also a Knight's Tour. A 'semimagic' square was first published by William Beverly in *The London, Edinburgh and Dublin Philosophical Magazine and Journal of Science,* August 1848. Each rank and file add up to 260. Unfortunately, this is not a true magic square of Mercury, for the two diagonals do not add up. The fully magic Knight's Tour is, however, theoretically possible. Because of the relative popularity of orthodox Chess, tours using other leaper pieces, such as the camel and giraffe of Great Chess have not been fully investigated. Fully magic tours are only possible on boards with square sides which are multiples of four, and therefore Great Chess, with its ten by ten square board, would not support such a tour.

Cheskers

There is a hybrid game of Chess and Draughts, which was invented just after the end of World War II by Solomon W. Golomb. Called Cheskers, a portmanteau word combining Chess and Checkers, it uses the standard eight by eight chequerboard. Pieces are placed on the black squares only, as in Draughts, and the first rank of each side has (from left to right) pieces with the power of movement of a bishop, two knights, and a piece Golomb dubbed the *cook*, doubtless a pun on Knights' Tours! The cook has the power of movement of the camel, a piece used in a Persian version of Great Chess known as Tamerlane's Chess. The camel and the cook move three squares forwards and one square at right angles. In Cheskers, each player has a further eight *men*, arranged as in the starting-point for Draughts.

In Golomb's game, the men and kings capture by the short leap, as in English Draughts. The bishop, cook and knights

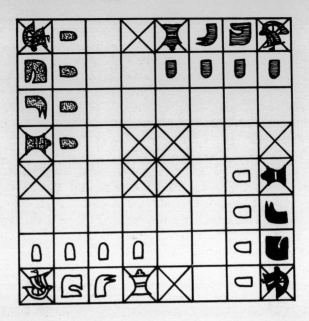

54. *An early version of* Chaturanga, *played on the* Ashtapada *board, after* Raghunandana (see p. 187).

capture as in Chess, by occupying the opponent piece's place. Capture is compulsory for the Draughtsmen, unless the 'Chess' pieces can also make a capture, when that alternative is permitted. When a man reaches the opponent's first rank, it is promoted to king, bishop or cook, according to the player's wishes. Victory comes some way through the game, when all of one player's kings are lost.

Mental powers and board games

To be able to play any but the most basic games effectively, one must have an aptitude for thinking about and understanding the way that the game develops. Because each board game is a formalized system of structure, both in terms of the board and the moves that the various pieces make upon it, the playing of such games cultivates in its players the ability to grasp its underlying patterns. From early times, it has been believed that a familiarity with these patterns has a much wider application in the world off the board. There are many examples from ancient literature and from various different board games. In the Norse *Frithjof's Saga*, Hilding is sent to obtain some advice on military procedure and the conduct of war, and finds his comrade Frithjof playing *Hnefatafl* with Björn. When addressed, Frithjof gives no direct answer, but says: 'A bare place on your board which you cannot cover, and I shall best your pieces there.' Björn then replies: 'A double game, and two ways of meeting your play', to which Frithjof retorts: 'Your game is to attack the Hnefi and the double game is sure to be.' Here, skill at *Tafl*-play is seen as applicable in the field of military combat. It is not surprising, then, that we find such skills commemorated in lists of accomplishments of warriors. Earl Rognvaldr of Orkney (1135–58) boasted: 'I am strong at *Tafl*-play.'

Because Chess mastery is held in greater regard than mastery of other board games, it is often thought by non-players of Chess that some special qualities are required to be a Chess Master. As in any field of expertise, this is true, but the precise nature of these qualities are seemingly more elusive than would at first appear. They concern not just the mind, but the whole person's interaction with the environment, physical and spiritual. Pietro Carrera (1573–1647), priest and author from Militello, Sicily, wrote on Chess in *Il Gioco degli Scacchi* (1617) in which he dealt with various aspects of the game including blindfold play and mental preparation for the game. This involved methods which now would be seen as mental preparation, and others of a more magical bent. The player must abstain for some days from meat to clear his brain and also to let blood, he should take both purgatives and emetics to drive the humours from his body, and he must be sure to confess his sins and receive spiritual absolution just before sitting down to play in order to counteract the demonic influence of magic spells.

A more modern analysis comes from the Dutch professor of psychology, Adriaan de Groot, who wrote a book entitled *Thought and Choice in Chess* (1978), which collated the results of his experiments to determine the nature of Chess Masters' thought processes. Surprisingly, he found that there was no difference between the processes of thought of Masters and others not so skilled at the game. De Groot found that Chess Masters actually considered fewer choices, contrary to earlier theories that Masters considered a wider range of moves than lesser players. De Groot believed that strong players consider strong moves only, whilst weak players consider all moves, including the consequences of moves that a Master would never make. The Master recognizes valid patterns which have worked in the past, and integrates them with the patterns perceived on the board. It is not the mechanical memorization of the supposed 50,000 patterns suggested by some analysts, but a deeper recognition of forms of configuration and their development. It is an understanding of a deeper structure, a right-brain recognition akin to the perception of the meaning of symbols. The notable success of Jewish players through the years has been attributed by some writers to the similarity of the structure of the *Talmud's* symbolically discursive methods to the spatial ability required to play Chess.

The better Chess players visualize the play as whole configurations of pieces, having 'dynamic perceptual ability' as de Groot puts it. Chess or other board game mastery requires a high capability of non-verbal spatial consciousness. Experiments on the memory capabilities of good Chess players looking at positions from real games showed that relative locations are recognized. When mistakes are made by good players, often whole arrangements of pieces are remembered correctly, but misplaced by perhaps a square. Masters retain a greater awareness of position, and can remember greater amounts of game information than weaker players. The best of them can remember many simultaneous positions, as in simultaneous games. But when random arrangements of Chessmen were tested, then the Masters' memory served them no better or worse than anyone else. Their pattern recognition is within the framework of the internal structure of the game. This is important, for the development of Chess skills may have relevance in other fields, and other games may develop appropriate parallel skills. Skill in *Tafl*-play was certainly considered to be a fit training for the warrior in ancient northern Europe.

This belief appears to be at the basis of the current strength of Soviet Chess. Two of the founding fathers of modern party communism, Karl Marx and Lenin, were both avid Chess

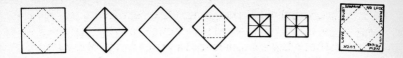

55. *The sequence of folds required to make the children's game of* Fortune Telling *reproduces the patterns used since time immemorial for horoscopes and sacred grids (see p. 187).*

players. According to Wilhelm Liebknecht, the leading German revolutionary communist who was assassinated in 1919, 'When Marx got into a difficult position, he would get angry, and when he lost a game, he would fly into a rage.' Likewise, his follower, Lenin, became angry and depressed when he lost at Chess, though later this unlikeable trait was altered by official Soviet historians as unfitting for the model upon which Soviet Man was based. Because Marx and Lenin had been interested in the game, and it was claimed by some that its mind-training qualities had aided their political acumen, Chess became a power to be reckoned with after the Russian revolution.

Despite Lenin's interest in Chess, it was not he but N.V. Krylenko who was responsible for the great Soviet domination of the game which continues to this day. In 1924, after Lenin's death, Krylenko founded a nationwide Chess organization based on the Trade Union and Physical Culture Soviets. In 1936, the Soviet Communist Party organ *Pravda* published a front-page commentary on Chess Grandmaster Botvinnik's tie with Capablanca at Nottingham. This was rightly seen as a triumph for Soviet Chess, but, serving propaganda, *Pravda* used the occasion to praise Lenin's Chess playing in the glowing tones of hero-worship:

> Lenin's main interest in Chess lay in the relentless struggle, in making the best move, and in finding a solution to a difficult, sometimes almost hopeless, situation. The fact of winning or losing meant less to him. He enjoyed his opponent's strong rather than his weak moves and he preferred to play strong adversaries.

Occasionally, other countries have encouraged Chess as a means of mental improvement. Some years ago, Luis Herrara Campins, President of Venezuela, ordered that Chess become part of the syllabus of schools in Caracas, the capital. Campins's intention was that Chess should aid the 'democratization of intelligence', an attempt to raise the average academic performance of all atudents. As a means of eliciting 'creative powers' and intelligence in the 'masses' in 'a bold and revolutionary initiative', the Venezuelan project taught Chess to children from the age of six. After a period of some months, tests indicated that 'the methodical teaching of Chess helps to elevate the IQ', because it 'develops a new method of thinking' from a new form of self-motivating abstract exercise.

Blindfold play

A seemingly astonishing feat – Chess played without sight of the board, otherwise called *blindfold chess* – has been part of the repertoire of Masters, and was especially popular before 1940. It is not part of Soviet Chess, however, as it was banned in the USSR in 1930 as being stressful and dangerous to mental health. Its provenance is much earlier than the twentieth century, however, for it pre-dates modern Chess altogether. The great Arab *Shatranj* player Sa'id bin Jubair (665–714) is supposed to have been the first person to turn his back on the board when playing. After him, most *Shatranj* Masters were capable of blindfold play. The earliest known display of blindfold play in Europe took place in Florence in 1266, when in an exhibition match a Saracen named Buzecca played three games simultaneously, one over-the-board and two blindfold. As an exhibition of his prowess, the Italian priest Giovanni Girolamo Saccheri (1667–1733) played three games unseen and then recalled all the moves afterwards.

Although these masters astonished their contemporaries, a widespread knowledge of the possibility of blindfold games was not apparent until the exploits of the great Chess Master François André Philidor (1726–95), who was also a good self-publicist. He played blindfold publicly against two opponents in Paris in 1744 and afterwards at Berlin in 1750. Philidor arranged the matches so well that it was believed widely but wrongly that he had originated such play. He did not disillusion his adoring public. Another well publicized blindfold match was conducted by Harry Nelson Pillsbury (1872–1906), who played 21 opponents during the Hanover Chess Tournament of 1902, won 3 drew 22 lost 7.

Blindfold play has been applied also to other board games, most notably Draughts. Robert Stewart, born in Scotland in 1873, was one of the greatest Draughts players of all time. He played for an astonishing 21 years without ever losing a match (1901–22), and was a Master at blindfold play. He made 15 simultaneous demonstrations of blindfold play, and never lost, playing up to 25 games at a time. At Cowdenbeath in 1904, he defeated all 14 players, and at Peebles in 1905, defeated 12 and drew with three of his 15 opponents.

The American Draughts and Chess Master Newell W. Banks played 20 games blindfold simultaneously at Bethlehem, Pennsylvania, in 1933. The result was 17 wins and three draws for Banks. When he was 60 years of age, Banks played six games simultaneously blindfold, four hours a day, on 45 consecutive days. By the end of the marathon, he had won 1131, drawn 54 and lost just two, and never seen a board. As one part of this feat, he played 62 games in four hours, winning all but one, which he drew.

Another of Banks's remarkable feats was a match in which he played 25 Chess and 81 Draughts matches simultaneously. Six of the Draughts matches were played blindfold. At the end of the session, he had won 22 games of Chess, stalemated two and lost one, while on the Draughts side, he had won 65, drawn ten and lost none of the seen boards, and won four and drawn two of the blindfold matches. Other great blindfold Draughts Masters included Samuel Gonotsky, active in the 1920s, and Robert D. Yates (1857–1885).

Living board games

Living games are played with human beings for pieces, moving on a giant board. Although Living Chess is the best known form, the playing of games with living pieces probably predates that game. It is possible to play living games with any board game, but it is probable that the practice began with relatively simple race games. The Moghul Emperors of India had the courtyards of their palaces laid out as *Pachisi* boards,

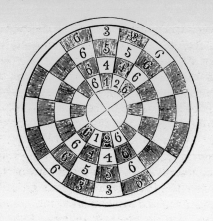

56. Layout of the Zatrikon *board. Figures represent playing pieces: 1. King; 2. Fevée or* Firzan *(forerunner of queen); 3. Rook; 4. Knight; 5. Aufin (forerunner of bishop); 6. Pawns (see p. 193).*

upon which slave girls dressed in either red, yellow, black or green acted as game-pieces. The remains of courtyard pave- ments on which *Living Pachisi* was played still exist at Agra, Allahabad and Fatehpur Sikri. The slaves moved around the board on the instructions of the players, who threw the dice when seated at the central point, known as the *char koni*, or throne. This central *char koni* reflects the *konakis* or King's square at the centre of the *Tablut* board and the Königstuhl at the middle of the Mystic Plot of the *Vehmic* courts of Westphalia. All of these are part of the same ancient Indo-European locational tradition. The allegory of leaders manipu- lating their subjects like 'pawns' may come from this ancient Indian practice.

Living Chess has been known in Europe from at least the fifteenth century. It was usually performed as a rehearsed exhibition game for spectators, or just as a solved chess problem. Although it has rarely been played on a regular basis, in 1891 a *Club of Living Chess* was formed at Dublin to perform games to raise money for charity. In 1892, one of its members, Dr Ephraim McDowell Cosgrave, wrote *Chess With Living Pieces*. The club no longer exists. Subsequently, games have been played only occasionally, usually at festivals. A game was played during the Festival of Britain in London in 1951 between International Grandmasters Rossolimo and Broadbent.

Living 'pieces' used with other games are even less common. On June 24, 1897, Queen Victoria's Diamond Jubilee, a game of Nine Men's Morris was played at Saffron Walden, Essex, as part of Lord Winchelsea's Pageant performed by his own Order of Chivalry. The living *Merels* were girls against boys. The 'board' or pitch was a square with sides of 45 feet drawn with lime-white on the grass. The 'pieces' were attired suitably in appropriate costumes. The boys were dressed in black with red sashes and caps, whilst the girls wore white, with green sashes and headbands. Although the actual moves in the game are not recorded, the lady controlling the girls was victorious. The author was involved in a similar game against Jeff Saward at the *Faery Fayre* at Lyng, Norfolk, on July 25th, 1981. The sides were not segregated sexually, red and green ribbons held in the hands of the 'pieces' being used to distinguish the sides. The author was victorious in this game, which, like the Saffron Walden game, was played seriously, and not as a rehearsed spectacle. The moves of the Lyng game are unrecorded, too.

OTHER SYMBOLIC BOARD GAMES AND GAME-PIECES

Fox and Geese and its allies

A game which is neither *Merels* nor the classic *Tafl*, but which was popular in former times in northern Europe is Fox and Geese, once also known as Fox and Hounds. This is known in other languages by similar Fox and Geese names: in German, it is the same, *Der Fuchs und die Gänse; Fuchs-und-Hühnerspiel* (Fox and Hens Game) and *Fuchs im Hühnerhof* (Fox-in-the-Chicken-yard). In Sweden, it is the Fox Game, *Räfspel*, and in Iceland, Fox-Chess, *Refskák*. Another Norse name is *Hala Tafl*, the Tail Board, and it has also been called *Hnettafl* and *Hnottafl*. Although it is not a centre-versus-the-periphery *Tafl* game, it was called a *Tafl* because the game begins with the pieces on the board at prescribed positions. Geometrically, the board is derived from a grid of six by six, the same grid which underlies the *Larger Merels* board. The Fox and Geese board is completely different, however, being cross-shaped, composed of five large squares each quartered to make 20 small squares. Variants have been found with as few as 33 or as many as 65 holes or points, and a more modern variant has 72. This cross-gridded pattern is very close to the sacred grid found on Hittite bronze standards, emblems of the gods.

The earliest known version of Fox and Geese had 13 small pieces – the geese – playing against one larger one – the fox. A goose is moved first. All of the pieces can move only on space at a time along a line to any adjacent vacant point. Only the geese can be captured, when the fox leaps over one into a vacant space beyond it. If there are others in suitable sequential positions, then the fox can leap these too, as in Draughts. The game ends when the geese hem in the fox, immobilizing it, or when the fox has captured so many geese that they can no longer surround it. A later version of the game increases the number of geese to 15 or even 18. There, as an alteration to the earlier rules, movement of the geese is restricted, being forwards or sideways, but not backwards. There, no diagonal moves are permitted. Another, even newer, version of the game apeared in the magazine *Christian Woman* in July 1985. In this version, the geese can only move forwards but the fox can move forwards, backwards, sideways or diagonally. In addition to this, a new winning position was introduced, where the back three spaces of the board (where the geese start), marked with asterisks, become the 'goal' of the fox. In this variant, if the fox reaches these spaces, then the player manipulating the geese is the loser. This winning position is an inversion of the winning position in *Asalto*, which itself is a post-medieval game derived from Fox and Geese. It shows that even the oldest games are always in a state of evolution, and unless 'standard rules' are recognized by an authority, as in Chess or Draughts, many variant and even new versions will be played.

Asalto can be played on the Fox and Geese board, but usually one of the arms of the cross is marked out as a fort or bastion. This is defended by two pieces (equivalent to the fox), which are assulted by 22 opposing pieces. The object is similar to Fox and Geese, except that in *Asalto*, the attackers must immobilize the two defenders, or occupy the entire fort. The final expansion (so far) of Fox and Geese dates from the middle of the last century, when the game of Officers and Sepoys was marketed as a topical reference to the 'Indian Mutiny'. This has an expanded version of the Fox and Geese board with 72 points on a cross-shaped grid to which two extra points have been added, making a besieged fort of 17 points. In this game, three officers have to ward off 50 sepoys. The attribution of the game to the 'Indian Mutiny' may well be appropriate, as it appears that the board variation is taken from the group of similar southern Asian games known as Cows and Leopards.

The original version of Fox and Geese is believed to have a Norse origin, being known from the thirteenth century, though from its board design it could easily be derived from the group of games which originated in the ancient Egyptian board game of *Zamma*, played on a sacred grid. Its mode of play,

57. Medieval European Draughts players (see p. 1951).

however, where two unequal forces are in combat, is typical of games traditionally popular in northern Europe. It was played in Norse countries at an early date, for it is mentioned in the *Grettis Saga* and the *Vilmundar Saga*. Like Nine Holes and *Merels*, the game was a welcome pastime for bored monks in medieval monasteries. A carved Fox and Geese board exists on some stone seats at Gloucester Cathedral, dating from before the fifteenth century. Although it later became the game of rustics, in the fifteenth century, Fox and Geese was played at the court of the Kings of England. During the Wars of the Roses, in the reign of King Edward IV (1461-1483), it was recorded in the accounts of the Royal Household that 'Two foxes and twenty-six hounds of silver overgilt' had been purchased to form 'two sets of merelles'.

During the next century, the game waned in popularity, perhaps aided by the Reformation's disapproval of games. By the seventeenth century, Fox and Geese was considered fit only for rustics and imbeciles. In *A Fine Companion*, (1633), Shackley Marmion wrote, disparagingly: 'Let him sit in the ship and play fox and geese with the foreman.' The low intellectual status ascribed to Fox and Geese players can also be seen from Lovelace's verses in *Giochimo* (1656): 'Men that could only fool at fox and geese are new-made politicians by thy book.' The repudiation of Fox and Geese, formerly a Royal pastime, by the urban sophisticates of the seventeenth century, did not kill off the game however, for there still exist finely-made sets of the eighteenth century, the possession of the wealthy and educated. As the popularity of Fox and Geese waned, the board found a new lease of life in the games of *Asalto* and Solitaire.

As with many games' nomenclature, Solitaire is subject to confusion, for the American name for the English one-handed card game of Patience is Solitaire. This game has no connection with the board game of the same name. Little is known of the origin of the board game called Solitaire, but it is said to have been devised in France by an aristocrat imprisoned in solitary confinement. When this happened is not known, but it was mentioned by the German mathematician Leibnitz in 1716, and as the tale is often associated with the French Revolution of 1789, it may well be entirely apocryphal. One German name for it – *Schwedisches Steckhalma* – may indicate a Scandinavian origin, perhaps during the Thirty Year's War. Whatever its origin, Solitaire is obviously a one-handed derivation of Fox and Geese, for it is played on the same board, but with more pieces. The central space or point – the *navel* or the board – is empty at the beginning, the game begins by one piece leaping over another into this space. The piece which has been leapt over is removed. This continues, with any piece being allowed to leap over any other into an adjacent vacant space, until only one piece is left. Various elegant problems exist, where certain numbers of pieces or patterns must be left. Like many of the systems of divination and games, the intricacies of Solitaire have been of great interest to mathematicians, and as a game it remains popular today.

Pentagram

Pente Grammai, otherwise known as *Pentalpha* or *Pentagram*, is known to have been played in ancient Egypt and Greece. The board on which it is played is the ancient mystic sigil known as the pentagram – the five-pointed equilateral star. Like the *Merels* board design, this is primarily a sign of magical invocation and protection which served also to satisfy the needs of game-players. A reference to the game comes from a preserved fragment of a lost work by Sophocles, and a pentagram is among the board games carved on the roofing-slabs of the Kurna temple. The game, which may still be played in Crete, is played by entering nine pebbles or pieces into the board one at a time, making three moves in a straight line at each entry until all nine are entered. This is similar to Solitaire, and very difficult to work out for those who do not know the way to do it. Once a piece is entered, it remains where it is.

The game is known from Sikkim and Assam as *Lam Turki*, in parts of India as *Kawwa Dand*, and elsewhere as *Kaooa*. In *Kaooa*, the game is played with one tiger and seven kaooas as a version of Fox and Geese. The kaooas attempt to hem in the tiger, whilst the tiger captures the kaooas by a short leap into a vacant space. Like the *Larger Merels* board, the pentagram is *par excellence* a magic symbol of protection and invocation.

Alquerque

Somewhat similar in appearance to the old Fox and Geese boards where diagonal movement was permitted is the game of *Alquerque*, which was popular in the medieval period. It appears to have originated in ancient Egypt in a game whose ancient name is unknown, but which is known now as *Zamma*, of which a board survives among the roof-slab scribings at Kurna (*c.* 1400 BCE). The modern version of this game, which is played in north Africa, varies slightly from the ancient one in that the board is modified by reducing the number of ranks and files, whilst permitting pieces to remain on diagonal lines. The board is a nine by nine grid (81 points), on which 40 black pieces, described as men, conflict with 40 white pieces, described as women. When played in the Sahara, the men are represented by short sticks, whilst the women are pieces of camel dung. Black starts, and pieces move forward one space at a time. Capture is by leaping over the opponent's piece in any direction, even backwards, and it is compulsory, refusal to capture being punished by the offending piece being *huffed*. When a piece reaches the opponent's back row, it is promoted to a *mullah*, which is the equivalent of a king in draughts, and

58. Many closed Knight's Tours of the Chess board make intricate and pleasing patterns. This one, discovered by the mathematician Euler, was a favourite of Claude Bragdon (see p. 198).

moves like the king in Continental (Polish) Draughts, along any marked line as far as that line is unoccupied. It can capture by either a short leap, or at a distance by a long leap, but it cannot leap over a piece a second time. The game is won when all of one player's pieces are captured.

By reduction of the size of the board, *Zamma* became the Spanish/Arab game of *El-Qirkat* or *Alquerque*. *Alquerque* uses a square board consisting of a five by five grid of lines, with alternate points connected by diagonals. Mentioned in an Arab book *Kitab al-Aghani* (tenth century), *Alquerque* is detailed in the famous *Book of Games* of King Alfonso X of Castile (1251–1282). Like *Zamma*, *Alquerque* is played rather like Checkers or Draughts, and may be their forerunner, as both use 12 pieces per side. The game, or a close variant of it, was played in medieval England. Boards of *Alquerque* exist carved in the cloisters at Norwich Cathedral and in St Mary's Church at Cavendish, Suffolk, on the chancel tomb of Sir George Colt, who died in 1520. In its ecclesiastical context, the pattern of the gameboard may have a magically protective function. Although it may have been widespread in the past, *Alquerque's* English name is now lost or unrecognized, and the game is no longer known in Britain. The Victoria and Albert Museum in London has an *Alquerque* board on a game-box once in the possession of the Swiss Wappenwyll family, and the game was popular formerly in France and Italy. In Italy, the game is known as *Merelle*, and in Sicily as *Marella* or *Riga*. Unlike *Zamma*, there are no kings or mullahs created from pieces which reach the opponent's base line.

Fanorona

The game of *Fanorona* from Madagascar is an important link between the use of divination boards and games played purely for pleasure or gain. *Fanorona* is believed to have been derived from a board game of greater antiquity, probably from *Zamma*, perhaps by way of *Alquerque*. It is played on a board scribed with a grid of nine by five lines, with alternate points connected by diagonals. This arrangement gives a board with 45 points upon which playing-pieces can be arranged. In *Fanorona*, there are 44 pieces, 22 black and 22 white, Qabalistic numbers representing the 22 positive, upperworld, beneficent powers in combat with the 22 negative, underworld, malevolent powers. These pieces are placed on the board so as to leave the central point unoccupied at the beginning of a game. This central point is seen as the centre or *omphalos* of the world, known as *foibeny*, the navel. This attribution has parallels in northern European board games, overtly expressed in the Ballinderry game board found in Ireland, which is effectively a human body upon which the game is played out.

The game commences when imbalance is created by one of the white pieces moving on to the *foibeny*, replacing emptiness and neutrality with one of the polarized forces, challenging its opposite into action. Where the move ends on a point in contact with an opposing piece, this piece is taken. Capture of opposing pieces can be an approach, or, if already in contact, as at the start of a game, by withdrawal from contact. Not only single pieces, but lines of opposing pieces in contact in the direction of approach or withdrawal are captured. Capture is compulsory. On subsequent moves, each move must involve a change in direction from the former capturing move, and if a player's move attacks the opponent in two batches simultaneously, only the pieces in one direction may be removed. When one player has lost all the pieces, the game is over. The divinatory aspect of *Fanorona*, which depended in part on the disposition of the remaining pieces at the end of the game, from whose patterns were read the sought prognosis, was closely related to *Sikidy*, the local variant of divinatory geomancy.

This divinatory aspect of *Fanorona* is even more apparent

from the second game of a series. Known as a *vela* game, the losing player starts play, and the previous winner has to lose his pieces deliberately until 17 have been captured. Until 17 are gone, the erstwhile winner is not allowed to capture any opponent pieces, and the opponent captures only one at a time. After 17 have gone, then play resumes its normal course, but obviously the former loser is now victorious. The third game is standard, the fourth *vela*, and so on.

As a game of combat, *Fanorona* is clearly an unsatisfying game, for it takes no account of superior skill, as would Nine Men's Morris or Chess, for it wipes out any advantage, and levels the score. But *Fanorona* cannot be seen in terms of a game of skill, for it has a symbolic and divinatory function. It represents the essential unity of the combating forces of the world, and guarantees that the loser now will later win. As a form of meditation for two people, it could not be better. In Madagascar, the Royal House employed ritual professionals who played *Fanorona* on important days of state when important decisions were to be taken, or the outcome of events involving combat were required to be known. The days of state themselves were chosen according to the art of astrological and numerilogical calendar correspondences, and interpretation of the games carried out with regard to their qualities. Almost the last act of the former monarchy of Madgascar was a ritual game of *Fanorona*. On September 30, 1895, the French army was on the verge of defeating the Malagasy, who had attempted to regain independence from France. Beseiged in the capital, Antananarivo, Queen Ranavalona III ordered the ritual professionals to play a game of *Fanorona* to determine the outcome of the war. Many of the older attendants of the queen, and those who had retained their traditional Pagan beliefs through the Christianization of the country a few years earlier, were vitally concerned with the outcome of this *Fanorona* game. To them, the game was as relevant to the future of their nation as the combat raging outside the city, or, rather, it was magically identical with the battle. In both game and battle, the Kingdom of Madagascar was the loser.

59. *The Indian board game of* Pachisi, *played anticlockwise around the central* char koni, *is the original of the popular game of Ludo (illustration 60). Both are closely related to the* Thayyam *group of games (illustration 53), and have 16 playing-pieces, the same number as the geomantic sigils, the shields of the Thracian legions, the squares of the Mystic Plot and the Scandinavian runes, all of which symbolize the cycle of completion.*

Surakarta

The Indonesian game of *Surakarta* is named after the town of the same name on the River Solo in central Java. The game is played on a square grid measuring six by six lines. All of the grid lines except those at the corners are connected to the others by lines which arc around the corners, creating a version of the *shield-knot* design. *Surakarta* is played with 12 pieces on either side. In Indonesia, these are represented by stones for one side and shells for the other. Pieces move orthogonally for as many squares as are vacant, and capture of other pieces is by replacement. Capture, however, is possible only after a piece has traversed one of the curved sections.

Despite its limited distribution today, *Surakarta* has a board and a mode of play which relates it to protective designs which are found throughout Asia and as far away as northern Europe. Grids or patterns with corners like *Surakarta* are close relatives to the medieval European cosmographic mosaics found in many cathedrals, which symbolize the four elements and the *Quintessence* at the centre. The *Surakarta* plan also relates to a variant of the labyrinth design found in England and France. The turf maze on the common at Saffron Walden, Essex, is the sole surviving ancient English turf labyrinth with this design, though an outsize copy of it was made in the early 1980s at Milton Keynes. Another major example formerly existed at Sneinton, Nottingham. It was destroyed in 1797 by enclosure and ploughing of the common on which it was situated. This maze was the subject of a famous nineteenth-century engraving, frequently reproduced, which shows penitential monks traversing it on their knees.

Gala and Courier

Gala and *Courier* are two games played formerly in limited areas of Germany, whose structure and modes of play are very important to our understanding of the symbolic aspects of board games, yet which are rarely played today except by board game enthusiasts. Although games such as *Tafl* and Fox and Geese faded in popularity because of the relatively undemanding qualities of the games, this accusation cannot be levelled at *Gala*. The game of *Gala* is one of the most sophisticated of all board games, equalling if not surpassing Chess in the complexity and subtlety of its possibilities. *Gala*, otherwise known as Farmers' Chess, is a game about which relatively little is known. It was restricted to a very small area of Schleswig-Holstein, once Denmark but now part of the Federal Republic of Germany.

Gala is played on a board of ten by ten (100) squares, which

60. Ludo, an English game derived from Pachisi, *and patented in 1897, but now a popular and out-of-copyright game played in many lands.*

is subdivided by *deflection lines* in the form of a cross two squares wide. This divides the board into four corner squares measuring four squares by four, and the inner cross. The four central squares of the cross are of importance in certain circumstances as will become apparent. *Gala* is played by two players, each of whom have 20 pieces, white and black, black starting play. The pieces begin in fixed positions at the corners of the four quarters of the board.

As in Chess, there are several types of piece in each side, each with specific powers of movement which are further modified by their position on the board. Each player has two kings, which start at the corner squares corresponding to the players. These are larger than the other pieces, all of which are of identical size and distinguished by coloured paint. *Gala* kings, which have gold tops, have the same move as the Chess king: one square at a time in any direction, except when on any of the four squares at the centre of the board, when a king may leap to any other unoccupied square on the board except the 40 occupied at the beginning of the game. Apart from this, there is no leaping or castling. Each side has eight minor pieces which are the rough equivalents of Chess pawns, moving one square at a time, but apart from this, have far more flexibility than do the Chessmen. They are identified only by their basic colour, black or white. These minor pieces move diagonally one square at a time until they reach a deflection line, then they can move one square at a time in any direction. If they are moved back across the deflection line on to either of their side's minor pieces' starting lines, however, and they are moved again, they must then go diagonally to the deflection line, as before. In addition to the eight minor pieces, each player has five orthogonal pieces, whose movement is that of the rook in Chess. These are identified by green tops. Two of these orthogonal pieces guard the king on the right of the board, standing on the two squares adjacent to the corner, whilst three stand on the left-hand side of the board, with only the central one adjacent to the king. Orthogonal pieces move in a straight line, but on crossing a deflection line, they move on one square diagonally. Subsequent moves within the central cross are in straight lines, unless another deflection line is traversed.

The fourth type of *Gala* piece is the diagonal piece, of which there are also five a side, arranged on the board as a mirror image of the orthogonal pieces. These have red tops, and move diagonally from their starting places, and diagonally within the four quarters of the board outside the deflection lines. When they have crossed the deflection line, these pieces move orthogonally within the cross, until they cross another deflection line, when they move diagonally again. When crossing the deflection line, these pieces cannot make an acute angle, that is, effectively double back on their route.

These complex conditions based upon place on the board can make pieces on the opposite side of the board under attack. Minor pieces are not allowed to capture when crossing the deflection lines, but all other pieces, including the kings, can. The diagonal pieces are not allowed to capture a opponent's piece standing on an adjacent square on the other side of a deflection line. The object of the game is the capture of the opponent's kings. When a move threatens a king, the player must call *Gala!*, the equivalent of *Check!* As in Chess, if the threatened piece can be moved, it must be moved. If it cannot, it is captured at the next move. When one player has lost both kings, the game is over.

Although it has been called Farmers' Chess, this is probably a name given to it by non-players who called any board game Chess (as in Iceland, where Fox and Geese was called *Refskák*, Fox Chess). Unlike any version of Chess or its forerunners, *Gala* has no leaping pieces. Whilst it resembles superficially the four-handed version of *Chaturanga* (described in the previous chapter), that game had leaping pieces and no deflection lines. The arrangement of *Chaturanga*, too, had the fourfold asymmetry of the ancient Indian mystical good luck sign, the swastika. This pattern does not occur in *Gala*. *Gala* appears to be a game which had origins separate from Chess, perhaps in early medieval European magic, and it is probably significant that in their influential book on sacred layout, *In Ezechielem Explanationes*, Villalpanda and Prado claimed the same layout for the Camp of the Israelites.

Gala has the most geomantically significant design of any version of side-to-side board games. It reproduces the four-square pattern which underlies ancient Indian earth harmony and the Etruscan discipline. In its cross, with different rules than the rest of the board, it echoes the tradition of the Four Royal Roads of Britain, roads upon which the everyday rules of conduct were different from the rest of the country. *Gala* brings in the dual concepts of a side-to-side conflict, whilst

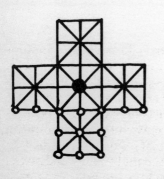

61. *The board and starting position of Fox and Geese.*

retaining the fourfold symmetry of the square board. The central four squares are the *omphalos* of the *Gala* board, which, like the central *konakis* in Tablut, have a special connection with the king, but in a different way. Because the *Gala* board has an even number of squares, there cannot be a single central point as in *Tafl*.

Courier is a German game dating from at the latest the end of twelfth century, played in village of Ströbeck until early nineteenth century. It appears to have died out completely now, though the rules and mode of play is known. *Courier* was played on a chequerboard measuring eight by twelve squares (96). Players faced long side of the board, with a light-coloured square to right. The white side is composed of rook, knight, *alfil, courier, mann,* king, *fers, schleich, courier, alfil,* knight, and rook. The array of black is a mirror image of this. On the second rank stand 12 pawns per side. *Courier* has three pieces not encountered elsewhere: the *schleich* moves one square laterally in four directions; the *mann* one square in any direction, and the *courier* like the bishop in Chess. The king can neither leap nor castle. The standard opening gambit was to move the pawns in front of the rooks and *fers* to the fourth rank, then to leap the *fers* to a square immediately behind a pawn. Because the game is no longer played, most of its nuances are lost to us. At least one illustration of the game of *Courier* is known, the painting wrongly titled *The Chess Game* by Lucas van Leyden (1494–1533).

Dablot

The Lappish game of *Dablot Prejjesne* from Frostviken is another unusual northern European board game in the mould of *Gala* and *Courier*. *Dablot Prejjesne* is a side-to-side board game which is played on a board very similar to that of *Alquerque*, except that the *Dablot* board has diagonals linking every point. The board is a grid measuring six squares by five, with the pieces moving along the lines between the 72 points. Each player has 28 minor pieces, known on one side as tenant farmers, and on the other as lappish warriors. In addition to the minor pieces, each side has two more important pieces, the landlord and land-lord's son, on the side of the tenant farmers, and the Lappish prince and Lapp king as their opponents. All of the pieces have the same power of movement along any line to the nearest unoccupied point. Capture is by leaping over the opponent, but only when on the next point, not by long approach. A series of leaps, as in Draughts, is allowed when possible, but capture is not compulsory. The minor pieces cannot capture the opposing king or landlord. The landlord's son and Lappish prince can capture the other, or minor pieces, but not the king or landlord, whilst the major pieces can capture any other. The game is won and lost when all of one player's pieces are captured or immobilized. If a single piece, other than the king and landlord, is left on each side, then single combat takes place, with the pieces moving towards one another until the person with the next move captures the other to become winner.

As a game of combat, *Dablot* is similar in concept to the *Tafl* group of games, where a settled population is attacked by marauding nomadic forces. *Tafl* sees this as the king at the centre of the world, assailed by the 'four corners of the world'. *Dablot* gives the settled tenant farmers the same status as the marauding nomadic Lappish warriors.

The decline of old board games

Many of the old board games survived in the more remote parts of Europe, in some cases until the late nineteenth century, when collectors of folklore and rural tradition recorded them before they were lost forever. In Britain, *Tafl* survived longest in Wales, far from the capital and court, and in Europe, the last outpost of the game before its present-day revival was remote Lappland. Fox and Geese was a common game in Iceland in the eighteenth century, when already in England it was despised by intellectuals, or had transmogrified into Solitaire. Like *Tafl*, it survived with great popularity in places more isolated from the sophisticated society of the great cities. Fox and Geese was played in the country villages of Lincolnshire and Shropshire until World War II. Local board games, even the intricate and interesting ones like *Gala* and *Courier*, seem to have lapsed once the close-knit societies of villages were disrupted by the Industrial Revolution. Several other related games, the design of whose boards are known to

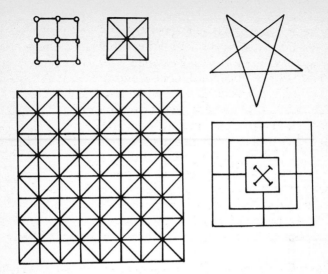

62. Game boards/magical sigils carved by stonemasons on the roofing-slabs of the temple at Kurna, Egypt, before their erection. They include Nine Holes, Three Men's Morris, Pentagram, Zamma and Nine Men's Morris.

us, are completely lost. Nine Men's Morris seems to have been more tenacious than any of the foregoing games, and has maintained its popularity until the present.

Ancient game-pieces

In former times, as pastimes board games had fewer competitors, and were played everywhere by all ranks of society. Most games, however, were played with stones or beans on makeshift 'boards' drawn in the dust of the ground, chalked on tables, or scratched into stone pavements and benches. Ancient game-pieces are usually difficult to identify. Perhaps the oldest and the largest are the so-called *Folkton Drums*, artefacts made of carved chalk dating from the 'beaker' period (*c.* 1800–1500 BCE). They measure about five inches across, and could have been used for outdoor play of *Merels* or a similar game. However, the identification of the Folkton Drums as game-pieces is only conjectural, and they are classified as 'ritual objects'. Many other excavated items are certainly usable as playing-pieces. If they are not recognizable artefacts like Chess pieces, they are usually small counters which might have been used as calculation-pieces on an exchequer board or as tokens in gambling. Many of these items have been found over the years and can be seen in museums. They are usually bone discs with no distinguishing marks. Such pieces could have been used in games such as *Merels* or *Ludus Latrunculorum*, an old Roman board game similar to Draughts but with orthogonal movements.

In Britain, post-Roman burials have proved fertile ground for the discovery of game-pieces. Forty bone 'counters' with inscribed circles on them have been excavated at Sarre in Kent; 63 from a cemetery at Faversham; 46 from Keythorpe; 56 from Shudy Hill in Essex, and others from Cold Eaton in Derbyshire and Loveden Hill in Lincolnshire. Urn No. 11 at Loveden Hill contained 17 counters: four had three holes each, and one similar was unpierced. Eight had two holes; four of a different kind had two holes and one had no holes. At Castle Acre, Norfolk, Urn No. 48 contained three quartz pebbles and three bone pieces, perhaps for playing Nine Holes or Three Men's Morris. The items from Keythorpe and Sarre were found in association with bone dice. A *Merels* board was discovered recently at Castle Acre, and Norfolk was a stronghold of *Merels*-playing until the present century.

A Saxon cemetery at Lackford, Suffolk, excavated by T.C. Lethbridge in 1951, contained a burial with 24 counters. They were made of ivory, probably of the kind from the tusks of the walrus, known as Morse. Although badly burnt, they were analysed. It was found that 11 of them had been black and 13 white. The fifth century Saxon cemetery as Caistor-By-Norwich in Norfolk yielded several important game-pieces, most notably those from grave No. N59, where a cremation urn contained 33 paling-pieces and about 39 *astragali* from sheep and other ungulates. The game-pieces comprised 22 white ones of bone, and 11 dark ones of stone, probably shale. The *astragali* were almost all identical, except for one, from a roe deer, which bore a runic inscription (see Chapter 2).

Excavated ancient game pieces range from readily available objects to richly-carved artefacts. Pieces of horse teeth have been found in graves at Taplow, Berkshire, and Faversham, Kent. Two black and two white pieces were discovered in a grave at Illington in Norfolk, and many finds have been made in Europe, most notably at Maagard, Denmark and Guden-dorf, Hemmoor and Wehden in Germany. Many variant forms are known. In the Mote Hill at Warrington, Lancashire, some pieces of jet, probably from a *Hnefatafl* set, were discovered in the nineteenth century. A very fine bone *Tafl* piece was found at Woodperry in Oxfordshire, having a furrowed top reminiscent of the later bishop in Chess. A turned, helmet-shaped game-piece of dark horn was recovered from the Gokstad ship burial along with a fragment of game board. More elaborate pieces have been found at Bawdsey, where a tenth-century piece of carved jet is decorated with the English version of Borre-style ornament. A piece described as a Chess rook of Morse ivory, found at Bildeston, Suffolk, and dating from the twelfth century, is on view in the British Museum. It is very unusual, as it is composed of two standing beasts in combat.

The best known ancient playing-pieces are the so-called Lewis Chessmen. These date from the twelfth century, and were discovered on the Isle of Lewis in the last century as a large hoard containing many pieces. They are richly carved walrus ivory pieces, some of which are recognizable as *Shatranj* men, and others which appear to be *Hunns* of the *Tafl* game. Many of the pieces have elaborate carving on them, some of them runic in origin, including the *Gar* rune. The connection of teeth (either morse or horse) and board games is indicated in the Norse name *Tanntafl* which is referred to in *Króka-Refs Saga* as a board with *Hnefatafl* on one side and Chess on the other. Literally, this means *tooth-board*, showing the common association of teeth with playing pieces. This may be echoed in Greek mythology, where dragons' teeth are sown in the ground only to spring up as ranks of fighting men.

When one encounters old game-pieces in museums, they are often wrongly described. In the British Museum, for example, the *firzans* of the Lewis Chessmen are described as queens, even though the queen was not invented until the fifteenth century. Because of the vitality of games, and their refusal to become static, similar confusion has existed for millennia. In the old Indian game of *Chaturanga*, for example, the piece which became the Chess rook was a chariot, known by its Sanskrit name, *ratha*. After the Islamic conquest of north

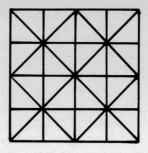

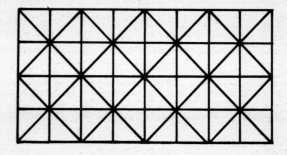

63. Above: Alquerque; *Below:* Fanorona.

India, the Arabic and Persian word *rukh*, also meaning a chariot, was applied to this piece, but the inhabitants of Bengal confused the word with the Sanskrit term *roca*, meaning a boat. Bengali craftsmen carved the piece as a boat. When the game reached Europe, the word sounded the same as the Italian word for a tower, *rocco*, and the European craftsmen obliged by creating the modern Chess rook, which some call a castle.

When new discoveries of ancient playing-pieces are made, it is to be hoped that investigators will take more notice of the nature and meaning of these enigmatic figures than they have before. Because of their relatively small size, game-pieces and even boards can survive in unlikely places, and their rediscovery can add new dimensions to our knowledge. In 1983, at Gloucester, Ian Stewart made the remarkable archeological find of an intact medieval Tables (Backgammon) set consisting of a whole board and the 30 playing-pieces. These pieces, carved from red deer bone and antler, depict zodiacal signs, Labours of the Seasons, archers, riders, lovers, people eating and drinking, birds, centaurs and even an elephant. They were found on a medieval rubbish dump, perhaps discarded during an ecclesiastical purge against games. The designs on the playing-pieces reinforce the ancient belief that the game of Tables, now known as Backgammon, symbolized the movements of the planets through the zodiac, affecting the lives of people below on Earth. They are similar also to the roundels inlaid on the floor in several European cathedrals including Canterbury, where the Signs of the Zodiac and the Labours of the Seasons surround the cosmological *Opus Alexandrinum* pavement. The similarity is so great that one might speculate that the cathedral pavements are permanent records of the ceremonial board games played in pre-Christian temples during important or dangerous astrological events. Discoveries like the Gloucester find may reveal yet more information on this important, yet little researched, connection.

10

GAMES, MAGIC AND ORTHODOXY

The spiritual view of reality has been held as the orthodox world-view for the greater part of human history. Its interpretation, however, has been subject to the relationships and struggles within human society. There are several sacred views of the world, and the attitude to divination is conditioned by them. In societies with a fragmented, pluralistic, view of the world, such as our own, divination is tolerated, for there is no totalitarian authority, human or divine, which it might challenge. The centralized, hierarchical view which goes along with the Holy City and Divine Kingship, however, is the opposite of this. Through sacred rites, administered by exclusive priesthoods, the monarchs of old carried out the will of the gods on Earth, or so they believed. According to this general principle, those who disregarded the hierarchy's rites were doomed to fail and, ultimately to perish. Those who observed the rites according to the prescribed form, succeeded and prospered. In such a centralized arrangement, all human relations to transcendental powers are expressed and, in some measure, determined by, these sacred rites. Divination by the priesthood is part of this ritual system, but divination by individuals is not only a breach of privilege, but a breakdown of the cosmic social order. Individual attempts to surpass the rites by direct access to the gods or by personal relationships with transcendental powers were considered not only impious, but a transgression of the cosmic social order, and were punished with appropriate severity.

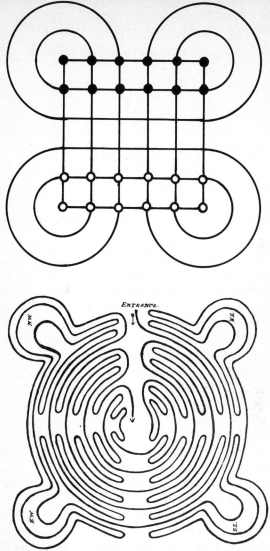

MAZE ON SAFFRON WALDEN COMMON. *From a drawing by Mr. Joseph Clarke, in the Saffron Walden Museum.*

64. *Above: Board of the Indonesian game* Surakarta, *whose unique mode of play, where pieces must traverse the curved portions before capture, is unknown elsewhere. These curves drawn out from a square grid are similar to the description in a Norse saga of a grid drawn by a magician to call up spirits.*
Below: Saffron Walden maze

Games and religious law

Divination, and its spin-off, game-playing, came into this area of direct access which was held to be usurping the privilege of priesthoods, and many religious systems have concerned themselves with its suppression. The bypassing of authority by ordinary people has always been considered a threat by those in command, who have always attempted to stop it. Equally, it has been perennially impossible to prevent. The priests of ancient Israel attempted to reserve spiritual or supernatural powers to themselves, as evidenced by the biblical prohibition: 'There shall not be found among you anyone who practises divination, or a medium or a necromancer. For whoever does these things is an abomination to the Lord' (*Deuteronomy* 18.11). Whilst the people were prohibited from the practice of magic, kings like Solomon were adepts of the highest order. This scriptural restriction was taken later by Christian prelates as their model for banning astrology, palmistry and other forms of divination. These prohibitions were usually extended further to include dice and board games, a tacit recognition that such games were more than mere diversions, having supernatural connotations.

As early as the sixth century before the Common Era, Gautama, the Buddha, had spoken against board games. In the *Brahma-Jala Sutra*, which is reputed to be the actual words of the Buddha, he describes the trifles which occupy the thoughts of the unenlightened, among them the playing of *Ashtapada* and *Dasapada*. However, because they were considered to be a trifling waste of time, rather than trespassing upon priestly territory, board games were not proscribed in the manner of many religions, and many historians of Chess have noted the intimate connection between the spread of the game and Buddhism in the Far East.

European prohibitions began with the Pagan Roman emperors. In ancient Rome, various emperors issued occasional edicts against gambling. Such pastimes were not banned completely, however, being restricted to the festival of Saturnalia. This midwinter festival, the forerunner of Christmas, was a time when various licentious revels were permissible, and that included gaming. Later, when the Christian religion became official, the clergy waged an active campaign to stamp out divination and games. In England, the *Penitential* of Archbishop Ecgbert (736–66 CE) threatened those who 'exercise divinations and soothsayings or keep vigils at any spring or other creature, except at the church of God'. But nearly three centuries later, in his *Laws* (1020), King Canute ordered 'we earnestly forbid any heathenship: that is a man reverence heathen gods, the sun and the moon, fire or flood, wells or stones, or trees of the wood ... sacrifice or divining.'

Often, these miscellaneous arts were categorized in compendia of prohibitions, the publication of which continued until the seventeenth century. Hugh of St Victor (1096–1141) wrote of the various sorts of 'mancy' frowned upon by the church:

Mantike, that is aeromancy, geomancy, hydromancy, necromancy, and pyromancy. The 'mancies' of the four elements, plus that of departed spirits, which might be associated with the fifth element, the *Quintessence*, and the alchemical arts.

Mathematica, including *Auspicina Horæ*, the observation of planetary hours; *Aruspicina Hara*, another name for Hepatoscopy, the

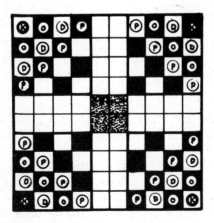

65. *The* Gala *board, ten by ten (100 squares). K: king; O: orthogonal; D: diagonal; P: pawn. The shaded squares at the centre are the four squares from which a beleaguered king may leap to safety.*

examination of livers and entrails of sacrificed animals; Augury; and Horoscopia, that is astrology.

Sortilegia, the casting of lots, divination by dice, books etc.

Maleficia, ill-doing by incantations, conjuring with demons, elementals and other non-incarnated spirits.

Præstigia, that is the creation of illusions, including those arts which are now wrongly called 'conjuring' or 'magic' – legerdemain and prestidigitation.

This appears to be a traditional classification, perhaps drawn from Islamic sources, for the *Compendium* of the Moslem scholar Husayn 'Ali Wa'iz al-Kashifi similarly classified the 'occult sciences' known as *Khafiyyah* into five categories. These are *Limiya*, magic; *Kimiya*, alchemy/chemistry; *Himiya*, the conjuration of the souls of the departed, and discarnate spirits; *Simiya*, the obtainment of visions; and *Rimiya*, legerdemain and juggling.

The repeated attempts by kings and prelates to ban divination, dice play and games in general constitute a chronicle of continued failure. Often, the attempt was concentrated on stopping the clergy from gaming. A letter written by Cardinal Petrus Damiani, bishop of Ostia, to pope-elect Alexander II in 1061 condemned 'the madness of dice or chess', as one of the 'disgraceful frivolities' forbidden to clergymen. In France, the king later canonized as St Louis forbade dice play and even the manufacture of dice was a criminal offence. In Iceland, laws copied from Norwegian regulations promulgated at Nidaros (Trondheim) around 1235, condemned dice-players to second-degree outlawry. An edict of King Magnus Hakonsson (reigned 1263–1280) confirmed the law. In 1241, the municipality of Strasbourg passed a bye-law restricting dice play in a manner of the modern English licensing hours for public houses: anyone found at play in house or tavern after the third stroke of the *wachteglocke* (curfew bell) would be arrested and punished. In 1404, the French *Synod of Langres* was still trying to stop clergymen from gambling. By 1420, in addition to dice and board games, cards were being added to the repertoire of the gamester, and in that year at Bologna,

Italy, a bonfire of cards and dice was made in the market-place by clergymen. The incineration of games by John Capistran was commemorated by a print issued at Nürnberg in 1452, which shows dice, cards and Backgammon being consigned to the flames.

In places where the game ban was not total, the more humane Roman tradition was continued. There it was customary for the ban to be lifted for the duration of the 12 days of Christmas. Writing on Christmas Eve, 1494, Margery Paston recounts that she sent her eldest son to Lady Morley 'to have knowledge what sports were used in her house in Christmas next following...and she said that there were no disguisings, nor harping, nor luting, nor singing, nor loud sports, but playing at the tables, and chess and cards.' In 1495 an edict issued by King Henry VII of England banned card-playing to servants and apprentices except at Christmastide. Some years later, King Henry VIII banned all card-playing except at Christmas time. In Scandinavia, the game of *Gnav*, a gambling game using cards or blocks of wood, was exclusively a Yuletide pastime, gambling being illegal at other times.

In Russia, the church authorities fought a losing battle against games, especially Chess. Originally, only clergy were prohibited, but then the ban was extended to all members of society. One early edict reads: 'No clergy nor layman shall play at *Xerniyu* (Hazard – a dice game), chess or tables.' In a chapter entitled *'On Evil Living'* in a work by the Proto-Hierarch Sylvester (*c*. 1550), the churchman threatened: 'But the man who does not live according to God and the Christian life...who is a drunkard, or practises witchcraft and divination...or plays chess...' shall dwell in hell. Finally, in 1561, Czar Ivan IV made *Tablei* (Backgammon) illegal under the civil code. Perhaps the revulsion against Czarist and ecclesiastical game prohibitions is partially behind the Soviet predilection for Chess today.

In the middle of the sixteenth century, the Catholic church, under pressure from Protestant reformation, began to prohibit books on occult subjects. The *Index* of Pope Paul IV issued in 1559, for example, prohibited aeromancy, certain branches of astrology, augury, chiromancy, geomancy, haruspicy, hydromancy, onomancy, physiognomy, pyromancy, necromancy, nigromancy, the notary art and sortilege. Gamesters were

small fry compared with the occultists and scientists being persecuted by the Inquisition.

Since then, most Christian priests have made a distinction between games played for pleasure, which are approved, and games played for money, which are not. Of course, Puritanism frowned upon all forms of entertainment, and games were in the forefront of their blanket prohibitions. 'The playe of Cards is an Invention of the Devill,' wrote one Puritan tractarian, 'which He found out that He might the Easier bring in Ydolatrie amongst Men.' In the American colonies founded by Puritan zealots, laws were soon enacted against all forms of game. In 1624, the Virginia Assembly ordered: 'Mynisters shall not give themselves to excesse in drinking or yette spend their time idelie by day or night, playing at dice, cards or any unlawful game.' In 1656, a law was passed at the Plymouth Colony of the 'Pilgrim Fathers' creating a penalty for card-playing for upper-class adults at 40 shillings. Children, servants and slaves were to be 'corrected att the discretion of their Parents or Masters and for the Second Offence to be Publickly whipt.' In this period, it was usual for students at universities, classified along with servants, slaves and apprentices, to be prohibited from all forms of games, including football and its more dangerous variant, *Camping*. In countries where authoritarian religious zeal is strong, the phenomenon still occurs. As recently as 1979, the Ayatollah Khomeini prohibited the playing of Chess in Iran because he believed it to be against his interpretation of Islamic law. It is very sad that the inhabitants of the country which produced modern Chess are at the present time prohibited by law from playing it.

66. *Game pieces: Top row: Bone 'counters' of the early (pre-Christian) Anglo-Saxon era, from Pagan cremation burials; runic astragalus from Caistor-by-Norwich, Norfolk, translated as* Raihan. *Second row (left to right):* Merel *from grave at Taplow, Berkshire;* Merel *of horse tooth from Faversham, Kent;* Tafl-*piece, bone, from Warrington, Lancashire; carved* Tafl-*piece from Warrington; Folkton 'Drum'. Third row: Tafl-piece from Woodperry, Oxon; eleventh-century* Shatranj *or Chess-piece from France; king from the 'Lewis Chessmen', morse ivory. Bottom row: Astrological chessmen designed by Max Esser, Germany, 1932; knight (comet), king (Sun) and pawn (Moon's phase) (see p. 223).*

(272)

CXXXIV.

Ludus Aleæ.

Dice-Play.

(273)

We play with Dice.   *Tesseris (talis)* 1.
either they that throw   ludimus,
the most take up all ;   vel *Plistobolindem* ;
or we throw them tho-   vel immittimus illas
row a casting Box 2.   per *Fritillum* 2.
upon a Board 3.   in *Tabellam* 3.
marked with Figures;   numeris notatam,
and this is   idque est
Dice-players game   *Ludus Sortilegii*
at casting Lots.   *Aleatorum.*
   Men play by   *Sorte & Arte*
Luck and Skill   luditur
at Tables   *Calculis*
in a pair of Tables, 4.   in *alveo aleatorio,* 4.
and at Cards. 5.   & *Chartis Lusoriis,* 5.
   We play at Chesse   *Abaculis*
on a Chesse-board, 6.   ludimus in *Abaco,* 6.
where only art   ubi sola ars
beareth the sway.   regnat.
   The most   Ingeniosissimus
ingenious Game,   ludus est,
is the game at Chesse, 7.   *l. Latrunculorum,* 7.
wherein as it were   quo veluti
two Armies fight   duo exercitûs
together in Battel.   prælio confligunt.

(304)

CXLIX.

Gods Providence.   *Providentia Dei.*

Mens States,   *Humanæ Sortes,*
are not to be attributed   non tribuendæ sunt
to Fortune,   *Fortunæ;*
or Chance,   aut *Casui,*
or the Influence of the   aut *Siderum Influxui,*
Stars (Comets 1.   (*Cometa* 1. quidem
indeed are wont to   solent nihil boni
portend no good)   portendere)
but to the provident   sed provido
Eye of God 2.   *Dei Oculo* 2.
and to his   & ejusdem
Governing Hand : 3   *Manui rectrici,* 3.
                even

(305)

even our sights,   etiam nostra *Prudentia*
or oversights,   vel *Imprudentia,*
or even our Faults.   vel etiam *Noxa.*
   God   *Deus*
hath his Ministers   habet *Ministros* suos
and Angels, 4.   & *Angelos,* 4.
who accompany   qui *Homini,* 5.
a Man 5.   à nativitate ejus,
from his Birth,   se associant,
as Guardians,   ut *Custodes* ,contra
against wicked Spirits   *Malignos Spiritus,*
or the Devil, 6.   seu *Diabolum,* 6.
who every minute   qui minutatim
layeth wait for him,   ei insidias struit,
to tempt   ad tentandum
and vex him.   vel vexandum.
   Woe be to the mad   *Væ* dementibus
wizzards and witches,   *Magis & Lamiis*
who give themselves   qui *Cacodæmoni*
to the Devil (being   se dedunt,
enclosed in a Circle, 7.   (inclusi *Circulo,* 7.
calling upon him   eum advocantes
with Charms)   incantamentis)
they dally with him,   cum eo colludunt,
and fall from God !   & à Deo deficiunt !
for they shall receive   nam cum illo
their reward with him.   mercedem accipient.

         X   *Judi-*

67. *A seventeenth-century view of games and magic can be seen from these pages taken from Johan Amos Commenius's work* Orbis Sensualium Pictus, *the English/Latin version of which was published at London in 1672. The text of the first spread reads:*
Dice-Play. We play with Dice 1. either they that throw the most take up all; or we throw them thorow [through] a casting-Box 2. upon a Board 3. marked

Games and magic

Part of the reason for prohibiting games was that a sub-theme of their play was the magic spells which people used to ensure victory. The great expert on Chess and other board games, Daniel Willard Fiske, wrote of the occult spells known as *Kotruvers* connected with games:

> There still exist in Icelandic old magical formulas to enable one to win at *Kotra* (Backgammon), just as there are others applicable to chess. One of them runs thus: 'If thou wishest to win at Backgammon, take a raven's heart, dry it in a spot on which the sun does not shine, crush it, then rub it on the dice.

That these spells were of Pagan origin can be seen from the use of the raven, which was the oracular bird of Odin and the hero-god Bran of ancient Britain. As Pagan magic, *Kotruvers* were forbidden by the Church authorities, who believed in their effectiveness as much as did their users.

The prohibition did not stop their use. The Icelandic folklorist Bishop Jón Árnason recorded this one: 'The Backgammon player should cry "Olave, Olave, Harold, Harold,

with figures; and this is Dice-players game at casting lots. Men play by Luck and Skill at Tables [Backgammon] in a pair of Tables, 4. and at Cards. 5. We play at Chesse on a Chesse-board, 6. where only art beareth the sway. The most ingenious Game, is the game at Chess, 7. wherein as it were two Armies fight together in Battel.

Further on in the book, fortune and chance are dismissed. For God's Providence, Commenius writes:

Mens States are not to be attributed to Fortune, or Chance, or the Influence of the Stars (Comets 1. indeed are wont to portend no good) but to the prevident Eye of God 2. and to his Governing Hand: 3. even our sights or oversights or even our Faults. God hath his Ministers and Angels, 4. who accompany a Man 5. from his Birth as Guardians, against wicked spirits of the Devil, 6. who every minute layeth wait for him, to tempt and vex him. Woe be to the mad wizzards and witches, who give themselves to the Devil (being enclosed in a Circle, 7 calling upon him with Charms) they dally with him, and fall from God! for they shall receive their reward with him.

As can be seen, the message conveyed by separate pages in the same book was as inconsistent as the theological arguments being advanced.

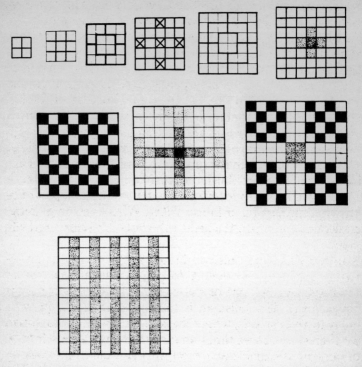

68. Illustration to Appendix 3.

Erik, Erik".' This regal formula or other spells could also be written in runic and placed beneath the board, or between the knees or elsewhere on the competitor while playing. Árnson also gave the following magical operation: 'In order to win at *Kotra*, take the tongue of a wagtail and dry it in the sun; crush and mix it afterwards with communion wine, and apply it to the points of the dice, then you are sure of the game.' Interestingly, this spell must be more recent than the first, for it involves classical 'Black Magic', i.e. inverted Christianity, wrongly using the Christian sacrament of the consecrated communion wine as a power-source rather than independent principles. *Kotruvers* are mentioned in various Icelandic edicts, such as the *Jónsbok Code* of laws. At least one person is known to have been executed for using *Kotruvers*. In 1681, Árni Pétursson was burnt alive in the presence of the Icelandic *Althing*

(Parliament) for having practised 'witchcraft'. He had confessed that he had used *Kotruvers* in playing Backgammon.

As might be expected mainstream western occultism has several magical techniques for winning at gambling. One is especially interesting because it involves a portable version of the *Geomantic Act* where a serpent's head is pegged to the ground in a foundation rite. On the first Thursday of the full Moon, at Jupiter's planetary hour, the words *'Non licet ponare in egarbona quia pretium sanguinis'* are written on virgin parchment. The head of a viper is then severed and placed in the middle of the writing, after which the four corners of the parchment are folded over the head to finish the talisman. This folding over of a square parchment to form a talisman remains in popular use in the children's game of *Fortune Telling*. When used in gaming, the talisman must be attached to the left arm with a red silk ribbon.

Another gambling talisman involves the use of the crossroads as a place of power. A formula is written on virgin parchment, but in place of the snake's head, a silver coin is wrapped in it. The talisman is taken before midnight on a Sunday to a crossroads, where the coin is buried. The magician must then stamp three times on the ground with the left foot, pronouncing the magic words on the parchment and making the sign of the cross between each word, nine in all. The magician then departs without looking back. On the next day, the magician returns to dig up the coin, which is then carried to the gaming-table as a lucky charm. The *Grimoires* which recommend these techniques often remind the magical gambler to donate ten per cent of the winnings to the poor as an offering, with the threat that if the precept is ignored, the magician will lose!

APPENDIX 1

Moves of orthodox and unorthodox pieces in Chess and related board games:

Amazon
: Combines the powers of the Chess *bishop*, *knight* and *rook*; sometimes used in orthodox Chess in place of the *queen*.

Asva
: The horse in *Chaturanga*, equivalent to the Chess *knight*.

Aufin
: Otherwise *alfin* or *alfil*, medieval European version of *fil*.

Bishop
: Introduced into European (modern) Chess at the end of the fifteenth century: moves on diagonals of the colour it starts on, replaced *alfil*.

Branán
: Central *king*-piece of *Tafl* group of games, moves orthogonally in any direction. The only piece allowed to occupy the central square of the board. Also called *brenin*.

Camel
: Leaper that jumps 3,1. (✓10) in Great Chess.

Cook
: Leaper that jumps 3,1 in Cheskers.

Courier
: From the game of same name, moves like orthodox Chess *bishop*.

Dabbaba
: In unorthodox Chess, moves one square in any direction, but also in some versions has the power of leaping 2,0. (✓4).

Dame
: Alternative northern European name for a *Draughtsman*.

Draughtsman
: Playing piece in Draughts or Dames, with the power of forward diagonal movement and capture by leaping.

Empress	Has the powers of *rook* and *knight* combined. Sometimes called a *dabbaba*.
Fers	Medieval piece took over from *Firzan*, alternative name *fevée*; finally supplanted by *queen*: moved one square diagonally in any direction, 2,0 ($\checkmark$4) or 2,2 ($\checkmark$8) leap on first move. *Fers* created by promotion had this power. When Draughts introduced to England, pieces called *ferses*.
Fil	Leaps 2,2, name derived from the Persian *pil*. (= *aufin*).
Firzan	One square diagonally in any direction (from Persian *farzin*, a consellor).
Gaja	The elephant in *Chaturanga*, equivalent to the *fil*.
Giraffe	In Great Chess, a leaper with the power of moving 4,1. ($\checkmark$17). In some versions of Great Chess, the *giraffe* has the power of moving one place diagonally, then orthogonally as far as possible.
Hunn	Piece in *Tafl* other than *king* or *bránan*.
King (Chess)	Most important piece in Chess, moves diagonally or laterally to any adjacent square not attacked by opposing side, has one special leap move, castling, derived from thirteenth century permission to leap once in game.
King (Draughts)	Promoted *Draughtsman* which has reached the opponent's first rank. In English Draughts it has the power of movement one point diagonally in any direction: in Polish Draughts, it can travel any distance along a vacant diagonal.
King (Tafl)	Also known as *brenin* or *bránan*. Moves orthogonally along a rank or file as far as it is unoccupied. The *Tafl king* is the only piece permitted to occupy the *konakis*, or king's point at the centre of the board.
Knight	Leaper, moves 1,3. Unchanged since earliest times.
Lion	In Great Chess, it moves any distance along ranks, files and diagonals to capture any piece

	on a square any distance beyond an intervening piece of any colour. Cannot be moved unless it jumps.
Man	Generic name for playing piece, as in Chessman, Draughtsman, etc.
Mann	Moves one square in any direction, used in *Courier*, equivalent to the *dabbaba*.
Mantri	In *Chaturanga*, equivalent to the *fers* of *Shatranj*.
Merel	Any playing-piece in the family of games of the same name.
Mullah	Promoted piece in *Zamma*, equivalent to a *king* in Polish Draughts.
Pawn	Moves only forwards on file (from French *poun*, translation of Arabic *baidaq*, infantry soldier).
Princess	In Great Chess, has the powers of *bishop* and *knight* combined: Known as a *wazir* in eighteenth century Persia.
Ratha	The chariot in *Chaturanga*, became the *rook* in Chess.
Rook	Line-piece, moves along ranks and files. Formerly the most powerful piece on the board, requiring the call *Check-Rook* when attacking it.
Schleich	In *Courier*, it moves like a *wazir*, one square laterally in four directions.
Taeflor	Alternative name for pieces in *Hnefatafl*.
Talia	Has the power of the Chess *bishop* but must leap over the nearest diagonal square possible: intermediate between *fil* and *bishop*.
Taeflor	Alternative name for pieces in *Hnefatafl*.
Wazir	Moves one square laterally in four directions.

APPENDIX 2

Glossary of board game and divinatory terms.

Capture	The removal of an opponent's piece from the board.
Char Koni	Literally *throne*, the central point in *Pachisi*.
Check	In Chess, a warning that the opponent's king is *en prise*.
Checkmate	In Chess, the announcement that the game is won and lost.
En prise	A piece which is open to capture at the next move of the opponent.
Fanorona	Malagasy game played on grid of five by nine.
File	A straight line of points or squares running at right angles to the players, also known as a *column*.
Foibeny	Central point of *Fanorona*.
Huff	The removal of an opponent's piece for failing to capture in Draughts.
Konakis	The King's Square in the Lappish *Tafl* game of *Tablut*.
Leap	A jump, usually over an opponent's piece(s).
Merels	A group of related games including Nine Men's Morris, where the object of the game is to make a *mill*, or line of three pieces.
Point	Place on a board where a piece can stand, usually applied to the intersection of lines on a board.
Raichi	In *Tablut*, the equivalent of the Chess term *Check*.

Raml	*Sand*, Arabic name for divinatory geomancy.
Rank	A row of points or squares running across the board at right angles to the players and to the *files*.
Rookie	A beginner at Chess, given the advantage of a rook over a more experienced opponent.
Tablut	Lappish version of *Tafl*, played on nine by nine board.
Tawlbort	English version of *Tablut*.
Tuichi	In *Tablut*, the equivalent of the Chess term *Checkmate*.

APPENDIX 3

Basic square grids used in traditional board games.

Grid dimensions	No. of points	Magic Square	Games using the grid
3 × 3	9	Saturn	Nine Holes, Noughts and Crosses.
4 × 4	16	Jupiter	Five Men's Morris.
5 × 5	25	Mars	Sadurangam, Thayyam.
6 × 6	36	Sun	Nine Men's Morris.
7 × 7	49	Venus	Brandubh, Ashta-Kashte.
8 × 8	64	Mercury	Ashtapada, Chaturanga, Shatranj, Chess, Draughts.
9 × 9	81	Moon	Tablut, Saturankam.
10 × 10	100		Great Chess, Gala, Polish Draughts.
11 × 11	121		Tawlbwrdd (16th century).
13 × 13	169		ólafs Kongs Tafl.
16 × 16	256		Halma.
19 × 19	361		Hnefatafl, Go.